What Readers Are Saying About *Test-Drive ASP.NET MVC*

Test-Drive ASP.NET MVC is a fantastic introduction to the way ASP.NET MVC applications were meant to be developed—in a test-first fashion. Jonathan gently introduces the reader to both ASP.NET MVC 2 and TDD, with just the right dash of ReSharper tips and tricks thrown in for good measure. Highly recommended for those new to ASP.NET MVC or TDD!

► **James Kovacs**
   President, JamesKovacs.com Consulting and Microsoft MVP, ASP/ASP.NET

Test-Drive ASP.NET MVC is a great introduction to a whole raft of techniques for building applications that leverage the ASP.NET MVC framework. The book explores aspects of producing web-based applications in the context of MVC, making sure to point out a good set of tools that you can choose to augment your application development process.

► **Jean-Paul Boodhoo**
   Founder, Nothin' but .NET Developer Bootcamp

ASP.NET MVC represents a great leap forward for .NET developers looking to produce more deterministic (bug-free) applications. In an eerie parallel that's almost certainly intentional, Jonathan's book represents a great leap forward for .NET developers looking to produce ASP.NET MVC code quickly, cleanly, and correctly. Highly recommended.

► **Ted Neward**
   Principal, Neward & Associates

Every developer should understand what MVC is all about. Jonathan's friendly, clear writing style, the practical examples, and the helpful best-practice guidance combine to make this book a must-read for every ASP.NET developer.

► **Jeff Cohen**
   Purple Workshops

Test-Drive ASP.NET MVC

Test-Drive ASP.NET MVC

Jonathan McCracken

The Pragmatic Bookshelf
Raleigh, North Carolina   Dallas, Texas

Pragmatic Bookshelf

Our Pragmatic courses, workshops, and other products can help you and your team create better software and have more fun. For more information, as well as the latest Pragmatic titles, please visit us at http://www.pragprog.com.

The team that produced this book includes:

Editor:	Susannah Davidson Pfalzer
Indexing:	Seth Maislin
Copy edit:	Kim Wimpsett
Layout:	Steve Peter
Production:	Janet Furlow
Customer support:	Ellie Callahan
International:	Juliet Benda

ISBN-10: 1-934356-53-0
ISBN-13: 978-1-934356-53-1
Printed on acid-free paper.
P1.0 printing, June 2010
Version: 2010-6-11

Contents

Acknowledgments

Just like a movie, a book couldn't happen without the support of many others who don't appear on the front cover.

I'd like to thank my publishers, Dave and Andy, who not only provided the opportunity for me to write this book but who also have published and written some of my favorite technical books. They also assigned me a talented and dedicated editor, Susannah Pfalzer. She's been my guide throughout this journey, and without her encouragement and constructive feedback, the text would not be where it is today. Thanks, Susannah!

Thanks to Clinton Begin and Mike Mason for providing role models of how a developer at heart can turn into an author. I'd like to thank the crew of ThoughtWorks University XII—Sumeet Moghe, Krishnan Nair, Deepthi Chandramouli, Michael Aguilar, Deepali Pawar, and Rixt Wiersma—who all helped me get started on writing this book. Also, thanks to all the men and women at ThoughtWorks Canada who provide me with the opportunity every day to work alongside such passionate software professionals.

I also had some in-depth reviewers who helped shape the code and tutorials of this book. These included David Cameron, my long-time friend who also taught me how do debug Pascal back in the sixth grade and worked through the code in this book line by line; Scott Muc, a developer whose tenacity helped give more form to Part III of the book; John Finlay, a programmer who reviewed this book while simultaneously explaining to me why the Hadron Collider will not cause Earth to be sucked into a massive black hole; Radu Muresan, the Romanian who taught me English grammar; and Jennifer Smith, a fellow ThoughtWorker whose detailed comments gave me a ton of ideas for improvement.

Several other reviewers also gave their feedback at different parts of this project. I'd like to thank Puneet Goyal, Ted Neward, Siva Pinnaka, Paul Reimer, Ravi Kumar Pasumarthy, Xingrui Pei, Jeff Cohen, Joe Poon, Ellen Flookes, and Sharan Karanth.

A huge thanks go to my family for supporting me through this endeavor. To my wife, Niki Rickhi, who cheered me on at every step. Niki, you are the most amazing person I know. To my dad, Jock McCracken, who himself became an author a few years ago and has always supported me in following my own dreams. I'd also like to say a special thanks to DK Sing, for all your guidance and wisdom.

My final thanks is to you, the reader, who I hope enjoys the book as much as I enjoyed writing it. May it help you along your adventures in ASP.NET MVC, TDD, and beyond.

Jonathan McCracken, April 2010
jon@nexicon.ca

If at first the idea is not absurd, then there is no hope for it.
▶ Albert Einstein

Preface

It's testable. It's lightweight. It's open source. It's . . . Microsoft? Yes, ASP.NET MVC is an open source web application framework created by Microsoft to cater to the needs of agile software developers. Since its official release in early 2009, it has been downloaded by almost 1 million developers, and it is rapidly being adopted by many organizations because of its efficient development model. Simply put, it's C# on the Web done right.

With this book's test-driven approach to ASP.NET MVC, you'll gain the cutting-edge skills to build your next web application and become a more agile developer in the process.

What Makes ASP.NET MVC Special?

Microsoft offers two web presentation frameworks: ASP.NET Web Forms and ASP.NET MVC. ASP.NET itself is the common set of libraries and features that both ASP.NET Web Forms and ASP.NET MVC work on top of. This supports customers' existing needs with the older ASP.NET Web Forms and their future needs with ASP.NET MVC. Although ASP.NET MVC shares many of the same underpinnings of ASP.NET, it overcomes its brother's weaknesses. ASP.NET MVC was designed using the latest innovations and lessons learned on how to build web applications. This adds up to big productivity improvements for your teams.

Here's what ASP.NET MVC offers that ASP.NET Web Forms doesn't.

Full Control Over Markup

If you've ever developed an ASP.NET Web Forms website, you'll know what a struggle it is to build a site for anything other than Internet Explorer. This is partly because ASP.NET Web Forms was designed for intranet applications where a single browser could be more easily mandated. For most companies, supporting only one browser isn't an option anymore. Many companies are focusing on enabling their partners and customers to perform their work through web applications, so they need to support multiple browsers.

The Achilles' heel of ASP.NET Web Forms is its bloated HTML. It generates complex markup through a string of embedded web and user controls. ASP.NET MVC comes to the rescue with a much simpler solution. Its default view engine, which is confusingly named the *Web Forms view engine*, gives you full control over your markup. No more strange **id** tags with **$** and underscores in them. This pays off when dealing with client-side scripting such as JavaScript. You'll find out more about the Web Forms view engine in Chapter 7, *Composing Views with Ajax and Partials*, on page 139.

Testability

A web application framework that has out-of-the-box testing saves you a lot of time. Most developers building ASP.NET Web Forms applications had to use their own design patterns, such as Model-View-Presenter (MVP), to accomplish this. For developers who don't know much about unit testing, it's less obvious how to approach testing. ASP.NET MVC solves this with a clear way to test your code. I'll be focusing on this point heavily throughout the book to walk you through how to write a well-tested ASP.NET MVC application.

Convention Over Configuration

Following convention saves time. ASP.NET MVC's timesaving conventions keep you out of configuration files, and some conventions give you added benefits, such as search engine optimization. For example, in ASP.NET MVC, URLs to your site become more readable by engines. Instead of http://yourblog.com/Blog/Entry.aspx?id=108 in ASP.NET Web Forms, ASP.NET MVC can do much better, such as http://yourblog.com/Blog/Entry/108/MVC-Makes-Search-Engines-Happy. You can achieve the same thing with ASP.NET Web Forms, but it's less straightforward.[1] With ASP.NET MVC, you get it for free. You'll see more of these conventions throughout Part II, "Building an Application."

---

1. http://weblogs.asp.net/scottgu/archive/2009/10/13/url-routing-with-asp-net-4-web-forms-vs-2010-and-net-4-0-series.aspx

Extensible Architecture

Striking a balance between conventions and extensibility is tricky for web frameworks. If too many conventions are prescribed, they can restrict you from extending the framework when you need to do so. The opposite is also true: if no conventions are set, then your team has to continue to reinvent the wheel.

ASP.NET MVC strikes a pretty good balance. It comes with a powerful default view engine but makes it easy to extend or create your own. You'll learn about this in Section 6.2, *Building a Custom HTML Helper*, on page 123. ASP.NET MVC has a feature called *action filters* that you can extend to provide helpful features such as transaction support. You'll tackle this in Section 9.4, *Creating a Custom Action Filter*, on page 189. Because ASP.NET MVC's architecture has a single point of creation for all the controllers, you can extend it with *dependency injection*. Dependency injection decouples object behaviors, or, more specifically, the implementation of those behaviors. We pass the behavior to the constructor, effectively "injecting" it into the object. You'll see how to do this in Section 5.1, *IControllerFactory: Where Controllers Are Born*, on page 86.

Finally, ASP.NET MVC isn't tied to any single persistence framework (see the *Joe Asks...* on page 4 for more on persistence frameworks). In fact, it doesn't come bundled with one at all. This leaves room for you to choose the right tool for the job. In this book, you'll be using NHibernate, one of the most popular open source persistence frameworks. You'll see how to use NHibernate in Chapter 8, *Persisting Your Models*, on page 161.

Why Test-Driven Development?

Test-driven development (TDD) is a simple programming technique that *drives* your development by starting with a failing unit test. It's quickly becoming a standard practice on projects because TDD helps you feel more confident about your code. If you've never used TDD before, then Chapter 2, *Test-Driven Development*, on page 17 will show you how. With TDD, you'll spend much more time coding and much less time fiddling around with the debugger.

The other key advantage to this method is that it helps you learn a framework faster. Tests, when they pass, confirm that you've written a bit of code correctly, and you can even dig into the tests that the framework offers. Because ASP.NET MVC is open source, you're free to browse all of its unit tests to help you gain an even better understanding of it.

And if you're a seasoned test-driven developer who's embarking on learning ASP.NET MVC, this book will be your guide on how and what to test.

Who Should Read This Book?

This book was written for two audiences: Microsoft developers and non-Microsoft developers. The goal for both is the same: to learn how to build an ASP.NET MVC application based on development best practices.

For Microsoft developers with a long history of building applications using Microsoft frameworks, the emphasis on TDD might be unfamiliar to you. Almost all the code examples in this book have been written with TDD and are explained so that you can understand both how the tests work and how the ASP.NET MVC code works. Also, you'll learn about some tools and open source projects that can save you time when developing your ASP.NET MVC applications.

For non-Microsoft developers, you'll find the methods of testing familiar, but learning the language and the framework will be your primary focus. Although this book assumes a basic knowledge of the C# language, each tutorial explains line by line what the code is doing and why it is important.

Although you can develop VB .NET web applications with ASP.NET MVC, all the samples in this book are written in C#. If you're comfortable reading C# and translating for yourself, then you'll be fine using this book as your guide to ASP.NET MVC.

What's in This Book?

Part I of this book shows you how to build an ASP.NET MVC application and introduces you to the TDD approach.

Part II focuses on building a sample application. You will work through test-driving core components of ASP.NET MVC, as well as other essential frameworks that integrate with it. In Chapter 7, *Composing Views with Ajax and Partials*, on page 139, you will focus on working with jQuery.

Part III builds on the same application but introduces how to work with other frameworks. The database access in ASP.NET MVC is flexible, and you'll find out about NHibernate in Chapter 8, *Persisting Your Models*, on page 161. Also, you'll learn how to use the Castle Windsor container in Chapter 9, *Integrating Repositories with Controllers*, on page 177. To integrate with other applications, you'll also learn how to create Representational State Transfer (REST) web services in Chapter 10, *Building RESTful Web Services*, on page 199.

Part IV focuses on deployment, something that many of us struggle with. Chapter 12, *Build and Deployment*, on page 237 is dedicated to this subject. You'll also learn about nonfunctional requirements in Chapter 11, *Security, Error Handling, and Logging*, on page 219.

To get the most out of this book, it's highly recommended that you code through the problems while reading. Not only will this help you learn the concepts of the framework and experience the subtle differences in each test, but, more important, you'll master the test-driven discipline. This is a skill you'll take with you to every language you program in. Whether you are programming in C#, Java, or Ruby, knowing how to write tests will help you write high-quality code in shorter periods of time.

What's New in ASP.NET MVC 2.0?

Since version 1.0 of ASP.NET MVC was released in March 2009, the development team in Redmond has been working tirelessly at improving the framework in the 2.0 release. More evolutionary than revolutionary, these changes make view and model development easier. Let's talk quickly about the new features.

Strongly Typed HTML Helpers

These new helpers reduce errors at compile time as well as the number of lines of code in your views. The helper methods are an improvement over checking properties at runtime. For example, we'd do this in ASP.NET MVC 1.0 to render a textbox for a person:

```
Html.TextBox("Name");
```

This standard Html helper renders a textbox. It's linked to the Name property of the model so that when it's filled out, the model itself is updated. In ASP.NET MVC 2.0, you do it like this:

```
Html.EditorFor(person => person.Name);
```

Here the EditorFor() renders a textbox for the Person model and checks for the presence of the Name property at compile time. Compile-time checking alerts you early to typos that break your code. It also helps if you rename properties of models that are referenced in views.

```
Html.EditorFor<Person>(person => person);
```

EditorFor() can also check for all the properties of the Person and render them all for editing. In this case, the lambda expression we pass is the whole model, not just a single property. You'll get to use the DisplayFor() helper methods in Section 1.3, *MVC in Five Minutes: Building Quote-O-Matic*, on page 9.

Templated Views

Templated views build on what strongly typed view helpers allow us to do. With ASP.NET MVC 2.0, you can now create generic view templates that let you postpone customizing views. This works well for prototyping applications, such as when your pages need just enough information to get feedback from your customer to know whether you're on the right track. Building your own templates is as simple as creating a view under the View/Shared directory named after the controller's action. Instead of creating a view per model to show or create details, ASP.NET MVC can fall back on your templated views. You'll look at this feature in Section 4.3, *Adding Thoughts with Templated Views*, on page 71.

Data Annotations

Data annotations are a way to mark up your models with validation rules. For example, if you wanted to make sure that a user's name was no longer than twenty-five characters, you could add this attribute:

```
[StringLength(25, ErrorMessage="Invalid Length")]
public string Name {get; set;}
```

The attribute **StringLength** specifies a length of a maximum of twenty-five, and the ErrorMessage value will be the message you display to the user if they input a name that is too long or short. You'll see more of this in Section 6.4, *Adding Validations Using ModelStateDictionary*, on page 131.

Other Features

Areas, asynchronous controllers, and Html.RenderAction() are other useful new features in ASP.NET MVC 2.0. Because they're more advanced or specialized, they won't be covered in this book. Areas extend the way files are organized in an ASP.NET MVC project and are aimed at larger web applications (see Phil Haack's blog[2] for a tutorial on how to use them). Asynchronous controllers are for long-running tasks that can be run in parallel. Finally, Html.RenderAction() provides a more efficient way for HTML to be written to the response.

Online Resources

At the website for this book, http://pragprog.com/titles/jmasp, you'll find the following:

- You'll find the source code for all the snippets used in this book, including the full codebase for the sample application from Parts II and III. You can find the final solution in the GetOrganizedFinal folder when you unzip it.
- You'll find an errata page, where you can post errors you find in the current edition.
- You'll find a discussion forum where you can communicate with me and other ASP.NET MVC developers directly.

In addition, once you get to the end of the book, Section 12.3, *That's All, Folks*, on page 256 will give you some additional online resources to sites where you can further your learning.

Feel free to use the source code in your own applications. However, keep in mind that not all the examples in the book are fit for production code, because some are there to help you learn only. If you're reading the ebook version of this book, you can download and play with the code by clicking the little gray rectangle before the code listings.

Let's get started with a high-level overview in Chapter 1, *Getting Started with ASP.NET MVC*, on page 3, where we'll build a simple web application. Following that, in Chapter 2, *Test-Driven Development*, on page 17, we'll learn the basics of this more efficient form of development. With that knowledge, we'll be able to tackle building a full-featured end-to-end sample application for the rest of the book.

---

2. http://haacked.com/archive/2010/01/12/ambiguous-controller-names.aspx

Part I

Fundamentals

Chapter 1

Getting Started with ASP.NET MVC

In this chapter, you'll get your feet wet by exploring the basics of the ASP.NET MVC framework. You'll find out how ASP.NET MVC works differently than traditional ASP.NET. You'll also learn how to install MVC and the related software you'll need for the rest of the book. Finally, you'll get hands-on and build a single page web application called Quote-O-Matic.

Let's start by exploring what makes ASP.NET MVC such a powerful web development tool.

1.1 How ASP.NET MVC Works

ASP.NET MVC represents a simpler, more testable framework for developing web applications in Microsoft .NET.

When people reference the acronym MVC, they are most likely referring to the software design pattern. Model-View-Controller is a user interface design pattern that separates display, data, and flow of control into different objects (MVC was documented in *Design Patterns: Elements of Reusable Object-Oriented Software* [GHJV95] under the name Observer). The view represents the screen and user input, the controller acts to coordinate the input/output from the view, and the model is the data structure that is passed between the two. The pattern helps separate the display, interaction, and data logic.

\\// Joe Asks...

What Is a Persistence Framework?

Generally speaking, a persistence framework is a library used to simplify accessing and storing information. In practice, this means how we write our code to communicate with the relational database management system (RDMS). The current trend in the industry is to use object-relational mapping (ORM) persistence frameworks. These are abstract things such as tables, columns, and rows, and they allow us to work primarily with objects. Popular open source ORMs for .NET include NHibernate and iBATIS.NET. Microsoft also provides both the Entity Framework and LINQ to SQL as supported ORMs that can easily work with MVC. In this book, we'll use NHibernate since it's one of the most mature ORMs for .NET.

In ASP.NET MVC, the pattern is slightly different. Every request is served by a controller; for example, http://localhost/ShoppingCart will be directed to the ShoppingCartController. The controller then makes some changes to the model and selects a view to display. The model for the example is the ShoppingCart itself, and it contains information about stuff you'd like to buy. The view then renders with the contents of the model. In ASP.NET MVC, views are .aspx pages that contain HTML markup mixed with server-side coding. For our example, the default view in the shopping cart example is Index.aspx.

In Section 1.3, *MVC in Five Minutes: Building Quote-O-Matic*, on page 9, we'll implement this basic flow for a sample application. Refer to Figure 1.1, on the facing page, which shows a typical MVC flow working together as a user visits the Quote-O-Matic home page.

From here on, we'll use the short form MVC to refer to ASP.NET MVC for the rest of the book. If we need to talk about the design pattern itself, we'll say so specifically—otherwise, assume we're talking about ASP.NET MVC.

First, the user types a URL into the browser and hits the Enter key. This creates a request to the web server that invokes the HomeController's default action, Index(). The controller then calls the logic within

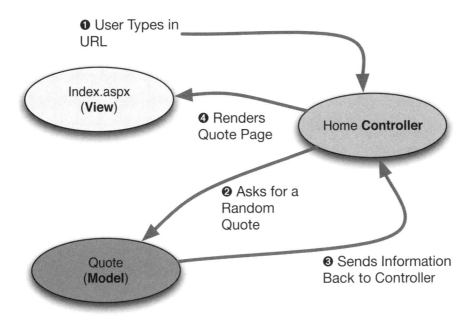

Figure 1.1: ASP.NET MVC REQUESTS ARE SERVICED BY CONTROLLERS.
THE CONTROLLER INTERACTS WITH A MODEL AND THEN RENDERS A VIEW.

the Quote class, which is the model in this example. The Quote will
return a random quote to the HomeController. Finally, the controller renders the default view, which is the Index.aspx file. The user sees the page
display in the browser.

For those familiar with ASP.NET Web Forms, there is a small learning curve when it comes to the way the programming model works in
MVC. For example, ASP.NET Web Forms tries to mask the fact that
we are dealing with HTTP, a stateless communication protocol. It does
this through the abstraction known as *web controls* and *code-behind*.
This leads to stateful information being stored in something known as
view state. MVC gets rid of view state and employs a more stateless
architecture.

With these MVC basics in mind, let's move on to installing MVC so that
you can see it in action.

MVC on the Web

The MVC design pattern is in extensive use by other web frameworks such as Rails, J2EE, Struts, Waffle, Django, and ErlyWeb, to name a few. Microsoft's ASP.NET MVC framework is a logical and major improvement over the open source MonoRail project, which also uses the MVC design pattern.* ASP.NET MVC has improved on Monorail's view engine, has more persistence layer options, and has official Microsoft support. Phil Haack (the guy who helped prototype ASP.NET MVC) and his team have taken the best of these frameworks and applied them to the development of ASP.NET MVC.

---

*. http://www.castleproject.org/MonoRail/

1.2 Installing MVC

You need the following software to develop applications in MVC:

- .NET Framework 3.5 with Service Pack 1 or newer
- Microsoft Visual Studio 2008 Service Pack 1 or newer
- ASP.NET MVC 2.0

The following software, although not required, is highly recommended for productive MVC development:

- Microsoft SQL Server 2005 Express or newer
- JetBrains ReSharper 4.5 or newer

Almost all the items in the previous lists are commercial software. However, all the software comes with at least a thirty-day (in some cases ninety-day) trial to get you up and running. It is also possible to develop with Visual Studio Express edition, which is free. If you do, you will not be able to use ReSharper, which means you'll have to rely on the tools that come with Visual Studio Express. Unfortunately, there are no open source alternatives to ReSharper, but some of the refactoring tools are now part of Visual Studio, and tools such as TestDriven.Net can assist you in running unit tests.

If you have Visual Studio 2010 installed or are planning to install it, then you're in luck because MVC 2.0 comes installed along with it. If you already have most of the software installed but are missing ASP.NET MVC, you can get the latest version[1] and run through the install wizard. Otherwise, if you don't have most of this software installed already, the quickest way to get there is to use the Microsoft Web Platform Installer.

Microsoft's Web Platform Installer

This tool simplifies the installation of the latest versions of .NET, Visual Studio Express, SQL Server Express, and ASP.NET MVC. First download the installer[2] and run through the setup. Once you have the installer running, you can select which components you want to install on the selection screen (Figure 1.2, on the next page). Under New Web Platform Extensions, select ASP.NET MVC 2.0. Under Web Platform and the subsection Databases, you can install the Express edition of SQL Server 2008. Finally, on the same Web Platform tab but under Tools, you can install the Express edition of Visual Studio 2008. After you've made all your selections, just click Install and grab several cups of coffee because this will take a long time depending on how many components you've selected.

I highly recommend that you start with the Professional version of Visual Studio. If you want to try before you buy, you can download the ninety-day trial of the full version of Visual Studio from the Microsoft Download Center. [3] If you want to use the latest version of Visual Studio 2010, at the time of this writing, the release candidate is available for download.[4] The commercial version gives you the ability to install plug-ins such as ReSharper. This book frequently references ReSharper's timesaving tools. Another popular plug-in is Visual SVN.[5] This plug-in will save you time and frustration every time you check in code to Subversion, a version control system. It's ideal to check in your code to the repository every ten to fifteen minutes, so Visual SVN will quickly become your best friend. Subversion is not covered in this book, but Mike Mason's *Pragmatic Version Control with Subversion* [Mas06] will get you up to speed.

With the core software installed, all that is left is ReSharper.

---

1. http://asp.net/mvc
2. http://www.microsoft.com/web/downloads/platform.aspx
3. http://msdn.microsoft.com/en-us/vcsharp/aa700831.aspx
4. http://msdn.microsoft.com/en-us/vstudio/dd582936.aspx
5. http://www.visualsvn.com/

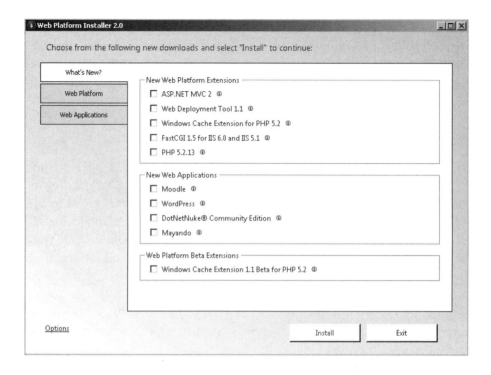

Figure 1.2: THE MICROSOFT WEB INSTALLER PLATFORM MAKES ASP.NET MVC AND RELATED COMPONENTS EASIER TO INSTALL AND KEEPS THEM UP-TO-DATE.

Plugging In ReSharper

Although it's not required to develop MVC applications, ReSharper can save you a lot of time. JetBrains offers a thirty-day evaluation of ReSharper.[6] Once you've installed ReSharper, you'll be able to use important navigation shortcuts. For example, hitting `Ctrl+N` brings up a code navigation window where you can type in the name of a **class**. While doing web development, we'll also frequently search for files using `Ctrl+Alt+N`. This helps in finding a web page or config file that you want to edit. Need to clean up and format your code? Then try hitting `Ctrl+Alt+F`, and watch your code instantly become easier to read. ReSharper is rich in refactoring and code generation tools as well. I'll introduce these time-savers as we move along. The price of the product

---

6. http://www.jetbrains.com/resharper/download/

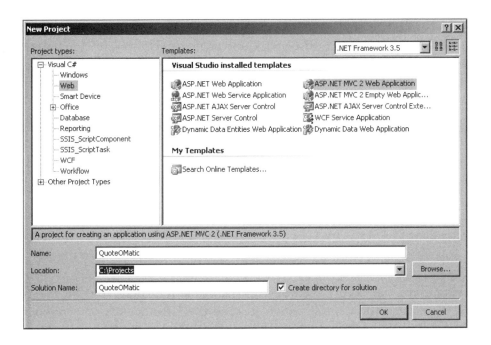

Figure 1.3: You can also create an empty MVC project that does not include the default controllers.

may seem hefty at first, but this tool quickly pays for itself in the time it saves you when navigating, formatting, refactoring, and generating code.

Now that you've seen how MVC works and you have it installed, it's time to take a test-drive. Next, we'll build a quick and dirty ASP.NET MVC application in all of five minutes.

1.3 MVC in Five Minutes: Building Quote-O-Matic

The easiest way to show off ASP.NET MVC quickly is to build an application that displays a model on the screen. Quote-O-Matic does just that. It randomly displays a famous quote every time you visit its home page. To start, we'll create a new MVC project in Visual Studio. We can see how this project wizard looks in Figure 1.3. For this project, we're not going to bother with unit tests. For now we just want to get our hands dirty with how things work.

To help solidify how MVC works, we'll now work through the same steps, showing the code involved. Controllers are composed of actions, which are C# methods accessed via a specific URL. The controller, in this example, performs the single action: Index(). This action obtains a random Quote object from the Quote **class**. Here's what it looks like:

```
gettingstarted/HomeController.cs
Line 1  [HandleError]
     2  public class HomeController : Controller
     3  {
     4    public ActionResult Index()
     5    {
     6      ViewData.Model = Quote.ChooseRandomQuote();
     7      return View();
     8    }
     9  }
```

Actions are executed based on the URL that was input by the user. Index() is also the default action in case the URL doesn't specify one (see more on these interactions in Chapter 5, *Managing State and Files with Controllers*, on page 81). Index() is using the Quote **class** to obtain a random quote on line 6. It assigns a special controller property called the ViewData.Model. We'll make use of this property when we start coding the Index.aspx file.

The last thing the controller does is return a view to be rendered. When the method View() is called without any parameters, MVC will search for a view that matches that action. In this instance, the action Index() looks for the file /View/Home/Index.aspx. This is an example of *convention over configuration*, because MVC does all the magic to translate the URL to the right method on a specific controller. This URL convention makes it easy for search engines to properly index your site and also makes it easy for users to remember their favorite URLs—all without having to configure a single XML file. That's convention over configuration in a nutshell. Before we get to the view, our action references the Quote object. Let's take a look at that now:

```
gettingstarted/Quote.cs
Line 1  public class Quote
     -  {
     -    private static Random randomizer = new Random();
     -
     5    private static List<Quote> FamousQuotes =
     -      new List<Quote>
     -        {
     -          new Quote{Author="Andy Warhol",
     -            Contents="In the future everyone " +
```

```
10        "will be world-famous for fifteen minutes."},
  -       new Quote{Author="Louis Hector Berlioz",
  -         Contents="Time is a great teacher, " +
  -           "but unfortunately it kills all its pupils."}
  -     };
15
  -   public string Contents { get; set; }
  -   public string Author { get; set; }
  -
  -   public static Quote ChooseRandomQuote()
20    {
  -       int randomIndex = randomizer.Next(FamousQuotes.Count);
  -       return FamousQuotes[randomIndex];
  -   }
  - }
```

This is a basic model that has the properties Contents and Author. Because we're interested in having numerous quotes for the site to produce randomly, we create a **static** list of FamousQuotes on line 5. Also, we add a simple randomizing function on line 19, which will return a random Quote every time we ask for one. This will get our controller code working.

Finally, we have to code the view. We store views as ASPX files in a directory named after the controller. In this case, the view we are working on for the Index() action is in the file Index.aspx. This file is mostly plain HTML and has a few helper methods from MVC to make it easier to produce text fields and buttons. We'll get to more of these in Chapter 6, *Enhancing Views with HTML Helpers and Master Pages*, on page 115. Our first cut at Index.aspx is shown here:

gettingstarted/Index.aspx

```
Line 1  <%@ Page Language="C#" MasterPageFile="~/Views/Shared/Site.Master"
  -      Inherits="System.Web.Mvc.ViewPage<Quote>" %>
  -     <%@ Import Namespace="Quoteomatic.Models"%>
  -
5       <asp:Content ID="indexTitle"
  -        ContentPlaceHolderID="TitleContent" runat="server">
  -        Quote-o-matic
  -      </asp:Content>
  -
10      <asp:Content ID="indexContent"
  -        ContentPlaceHolderID="MainContent" runat="server">
  -
  -        <h2>Random Quote</h2>
  -        <%= Html.DisplayFor(m => m) %>
15
  -      </asp:Content>
```

When we are inside a view file, we wrap the C# code with the **<%=** and **%>** syntax. This is the way to run code that renders HTML. This is similar to traditional ASP.NET, but we use this syntax more frequently in MVC because we're never using web controls. All MVC views are rendered through the view engine. An MVC view engine translates the markup and syntax in the view files into HTML that is ready for the browser. The default view engine is called *Web Forms*, and it uses the syntax that we used here. It is also the only view engine that we'll use throughout this book.

MVC does allow you to change or create your own view engine if for some reason the Web Forms view engine does not meet your needs. There are existing alternative view engines, such as NHaml,[7] NVelocity,[8] and StringTemplate,[9] that use different conventions and syntax than this. If your team finds that the default engine doesn't meet your needs, try exploring these existing alternatives.

On line 2, we specify that this view is strongly typed to the Quote **class**. This buys us compile-time checking when we use the Html.DisplayFor() method on line 14. This method looks through all the properties of the model—in our case Author and Contents—and prints their name and value. Although this gives us a nice place to start, we probably want to take this one step further to clean it up:

`gettingstarted/Index.aspx`

```
Line 1   <h2>Random Quote</h2>
     2   <blockquote>
     3   <b>&quot; <%= Html.Encode(Model.Contents) %> &quot;</b>
     4   <br />
     5   <span style="padding-left: 100px">
     6     <%= Html.Encode(Model.Author) %>
     7   </span>
     8   </blockquote>
```

Here we replace the DisplayFor() method with a couple of separate lines of code to format the quotation properly. We use Html.Encode() on line 3 to display the individual properties one at a time. This method can also help protect you from cross-site scripting (XSS) attacks by encoding the properties as text instead of HTML markup (see Section 11.1, *Preventing Cross-Site Scripting*, on page 221). We surround the Author's name with

---

7. http://code.google.com/p/nhaml/
8. http://sourceforge.net/projects/castleproject/files/NVelocity/1.1/CastleNVelocity-1.1.0.zip/download
9. http://code.google.com/p/string-template-view-engine-mvc/

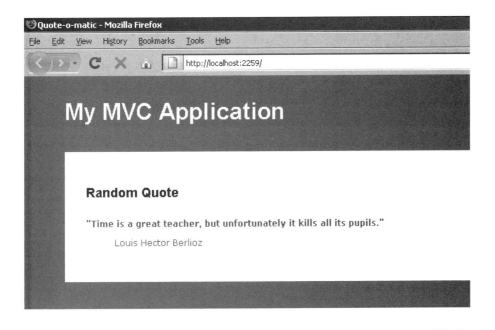

Figure 1.4: THE FINAL PRODUCT: QUOTE-O-MATIC

the HTML **span** tag. This is so we can shift the Author's name to the right on line 6 by applying a **style** attribute to it. Also, we add " to surround the Content with quotation marks.

The HomeController, the Quote (model), and the /View/Home/Index.aspx (view) all make up this simple example of MVC. Take a look at the end result in Figure 1.4. Next, let's see what is happening under the hood in MVC with Quote-O-Matic.

Flow of Control

MVC facilitates each web request in a similar way (Figure 1.5, on the next page). All requests that come into the web application will be caught by an Internet Server Application Interface (ISAPI) extension called aspnet_isapi.dll. One drawback of the framework as it stands right now is that the steps for configuring Internet Information Services (IIS), the staple Microsoft web server, vary depending on the version you are running. We'll cover these and other deployment woes in Chapter 12, *Build and Deployment*, on page 237.

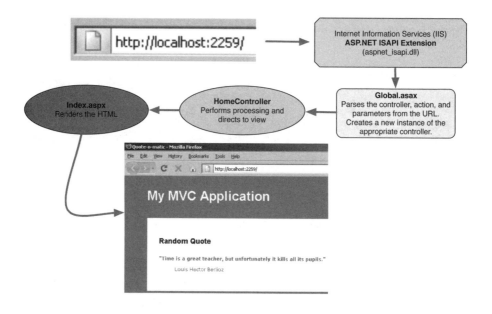

Figure 1.5: THE REQUEST PIPELINE FOR MVC IS SIMILAR TO ASP.NET, EXCEPT IT TRANSLATES THE URL INTO A CONTROLLER'S ACTION. DEPENDING ON WHAT THE ACTION DOES, IT WILL GENERALLY RENDER A VIEW.

After processing in the ISAPI filter, the request moves inside our MVC application. Requests are processed exactly like they are in traditional ASP.NET, through the Global.asax event BeginRequest(). This captures all the information from the URL, POST information, cookies, and so on, to allow a special class called the RouteTable to parse and delegate control to the appropriate controller (the sidebar on the facing page).

The router directs to the controller and action described in the URL. The default pattern to match is /{controller}/{action}/{id}?{querystring}. For example, a user navigates to http://localhost:2259/Home/Index. This is one of the key MVC conventions at work. This directs control through the RouteTable to the HomeController and the action Index(). The action then does some processing and assigns a model. The controller then decides which view to render. The convention is to match the name of the action to the name of the view. HomeController's action Index() will look in the directory /View/Home and select the file Index.aspx. The view renders, and the page is displayed to the user. The user is now free to make

Defining Custom Routes

MVC has the ability to define custom routes to make navigation, creating permanent links, bookmarking, and search engine optimization easier. Custom routes are good for declaring action parameters into the URL. You define routes in Global.asax by adding to the RouteTable through the MapRoute() method. For example, an action that requires a month, day, and year would look like this:

gettingstarted/Global.asax.cs

```
routes.MapRoute(
        "DateRoute",
        "{controller}/{action}/{month}/{day}/{year}/{id}"
);
```

The first parameter of MapRoute() is a unique name of the route. The second parameter defines a series of variables that will be matched to the input URL. {controller} and {action} are matched to their respective controller and action. The other variables need to match to the parameters of the action.

In this case, the action's signature would need to be ActionForDateRoute(int month, int day, int year, int id). There is an optional third parameter for MapRoute() for defining default parameters. We could extend our date route example so that the user doesn't type in a month, day, or year and can default to today's date.

We'll talk about how to test these routes in Section 5.3, *Testing Routes in MVC*, on page 97.

their next request. This flow of control is explained in more detail in Section 5.1, *IControllerFactory: Where Controllers Are Born*, on page 86.

Up Next

MVC is an important departure from traditional ASP.NET. With our first MVC application under our belts, it's time to learn some NUnit and how to test-drive code. MVC coupled with a good testing framework is a match made in heaven.

The test of a first-rate intelligence is the ability to hold two opposed ideas in the mind at the same time and still retain the ability to function.

► F. Scott Fitzgerald

Chapter 2

Test-Driven Development

Before we delve deeper into the workings of MVC, we'll touch on the basics of TDD. Understanding and using this technique helps us leverage one of the most important design features of MVC: testability. In this chapter, we'll go through a simple example of TDD by applying it to the age-old "Hello World" example.[1] If you already have a good understanding of TDD, feel free to skim or skip this chapter entirely.

2.1 TDD Explained

Test-driven development is a method developed by Kent Beck, author of *Extreme Programming Explained: Embrace Change* [Bec00]. It is a way to give you fast feedback about whether a piece of code works. Before there was TDD, the industry standard was to write unit tests long after the application code was complete. More commonly, you'd see lots of applications with no unit tests at all. This leads to many bugs over time, because there is no way of knowing whether new code has broken existing features. The difference that Beck introduces is to reverse this order by starting with a unit test and then writing the implementation. This approach became known as TDD. The phrase *test first* is used to describe the first step in the process of TDD where you start by writing a unit test that compiles but fails. The *test first* methodology can help drive out our code design and can reduce the occurrence of unused code, or *dead code*. Getting into the discipline of writing the test first reduces the chance of forgetting to write the test at all. It is also the approach we take for the rest of this book.

---

1. For those readers who would like to dive deeper into TDD with Microsoft .NET, I highly recommend *Pragmatic Unit Testing in C# with NUnit* [HT04].

Writing tests speeds up your development. That might seem counterintuitive at first. Adding a whole other set of test code to maintain appears to be more work, but it turns out the opposite is true. By writing tests for all the production code, you are building confidence that things are working as they're supposed to work. You also get quick feedback on the design of your objects, because the tests act as consumers of the code. Remember that each test is small—as short as one or two lines of code. Getting a test to compile and then fail quickly is the key to practicing TDD.

When all the tests are passing, you don't need to spend as much time debugging. Also, it means less manual testing to make sure you haven't broken an old page while changing a seemingly unrelated function. If tests are passing, you can confidently move forward to the next feature. The three different approaches to unit testing are illustrated in Figure 2.1, on the facing page.[2]

Let's use an analogy to illustrate the TDD cycle. Say you read an article on F#, a functional programming language that runs on the .NET Common Language Runtime (CLR), and it piqued your interest. You'd like to know more about F# but don't know where to start. You could buy a book on it, attend a conference that has talks on F#, or even consider going to a class on it. Although these are good ideas, most people neglect an important step: setting a goal. The Harvard School of Business conducted a study and found that the biggest differentiator between success and failure is strongly influenced by people defining a well-formed goal.[3] Do you want to be able to code in F#? Understand when to use a functional language? Be able to know how F# changes your application's architecture? Without a goal, it's hard to measure when you've been successful. A well-formed goal is something that you can define success criteria for. Suppose you said, "I want to be able to program in F#. I'll learn it by building a sample application." This defines the goal and the success criteria. It will be easy to tell when you have reached your goal.

Setting and achieving goals is just like TDD:

1. Write a test—define a goal.

2. Make it compile—understand the criteria for success.

---

2. This diagram was originally designed by Paulo Caroli (http://www.caroli.org/) and adapted for this book.

3. http://www.lifemastering.com/en/harvard_school.html

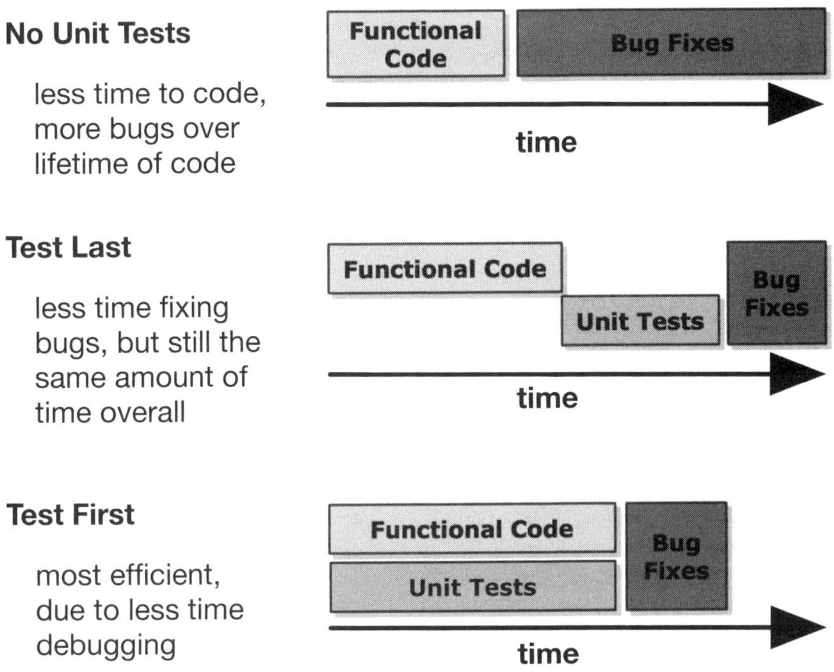

No Unit Tests

less time to code,
more bugs over
lifetime of code

| Functional Code | Bug Fixes |

→ time

Test Last

less time fixing
bugs, but still the
same amount of
time overall

| Functional Code | | Bug Fixes |
| | Unit Tests | |

→ time

Test First

most efficient,
due to less time
debugging

| Functional Code | Bug Fixes |
| Unit Tests | |

→ time

Figure 2.1: TESTING FIRST IS THE MOST EFFICIENT WAY TO DEVELOP APPLICATIONS. CODE THAT IS WRITTEN INSIDE A TEST IS CALLED *test code*, WHILE CODE THAT IS WRITTEN IN OUR APPLICATION IS CALLED *functional code*.

3. Run the test and make sure it fails—observe that the goal has not been met.

4. Write the *functional code*—try to achieve the goal.

5. Run the test again and watch it pass—observe that the goal has now been achieved.

The TDD cycle is illustrated in Figure 2.2, on the next page. First we write a test and get it to compile. Next, we run that test and watch it fail. The third step is to get that test to pass by implementing some *functional code*. The fourth step in the cycle is to *refactor*: to go back and improve the readability of the existing functional code *without changing the existing functionality*. One of the only ways to ensure you haven't changed the functionality is to have a complete unit test suite. If the process of changing the code changes the functionality, then it's not

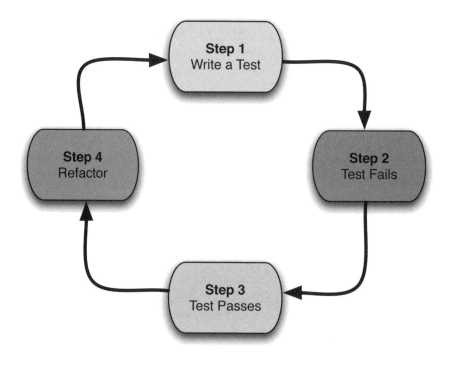

Figure 2.2: EACH REPETITION OF THE TDD CYCLE TAKES FROM FIVE TO TEN MINUTES.

refactoring—that's what we call adding new or unplanned features! After you perform any refactoring, you can rerun your test to make sure it's still passing and then start the process all over again.

One principle of refactoring is to follow the Don't Repeat Yourself (DRY) principle. DRY (coined by Dave Thomas and Andy Hunt in *The Pragmatic Programmer* [HT00]) reminds us to find duplicate code or simpler ways of expressing the intent of the code. We'll cover refactoring throughout this book, but our first exposure will be in Section 5.2, *Testing Authorization*, on page 93. Applying DRY helps us write more readable and maintainable code, but without a full suite of passing unit tests, refactoring is highly dangerous.

Before we can see TDD in action, we're going to need to install NUnit, an open source unit testing framework for .NET.

Joe Asks...

How Do I Justify TDD to My Project Manager?

Microsoft recently published a study quantifying the positive effects of using TDD.* The study shows that bugs and defects are reduced from 40 to 90 percent. If your project manager cares about a low bug count and wants empirical data, sharing this study with the person could help. The other interesting fact about the study is that Microsoft found that development time increased between 15 and 35 percent. Although this might seem like a lot, think about the cost of cycling back and fixing bugs, not to mention frustrating your customer. Remember, every time customers find a defect, it affects their overall confidence in your application.

The other major selling point for TDD from a management perspective is it naturally increases your software's flexibility. A codebase that has used TDD has a more decoupled architecture and a comprehensive automated test suite. For these reasons, adding new features is easier.

Finally, since management is often concerned with identifying and mitigating risks, TDD can be a godsend. Since TDD generally produces higher-quality code with fewer defects, it follows that it also reduces project risk.

---

*.   http://research.microsoft.com/en-us/projects/esm/nagappan_tdd.pdf

Installing NUnit

NUnit is one of the most popular testing frameworks used in .NET. It uses C# attributes to demarcate unit tests and a variety of simple assertion commands to make your tests fail and then pass.

NUnit is not the only test framework you can use for MVC. Visual Studio Unit Testing Framework, mbUnit,[4] and xUnit[5] are all acceptable alternatives. This book uses NUnit syntax, but translating the tests into a different .NET testing framework is fairly straightforward.

---

4.   mbUnit is unit testing framework, available at http://www.mbunit.com/.
5.   xUnit is an alternative to NUnit written by one of the original authors of NUnit, Jim Newkirk, available at http://xunit.codeplex.com/.

NUnit is downloadable either as a ZIP or as a Microsoft Installer (MSI) file.[6] The MSI installs NUnit into the Global Assembly Cache (GAC), allowing you to reference it more easily when creating a new unit test project in Visual Studio. However, the ZIP is the recommended download because for each project you want everyone to use same version of NUnit. So, create a Lib directory (an abbreviation for *Library*) in your solution to store important libraries like nunit.framework.dll and check it into source control management (SCM).

Throughout this book we'll reference the Lib folder as a way to store .dll libraries that our solution uses. As part of the completed solution in Parts II and III, you'll be able to see how the Lib folder stores files like nunit.framework.dll. You can find the final solution in the GetOrganizedFinal folder when you unzip it.

NUnit 2.5 has some nice additions. It includes a copy of PNUnit, which allows us to run tests on remote machines. This will let us use NUnit as part of performance testing. (There is an interesting video demonstration of PNUnit in action across six different machines simultaneously on its author's website[7])

That covers the concept. Let's now work through a simple TDD example.

2.2 Test-Driving "Hello World"

TDD is a simple practice that can be applied to complicated systems. TDD starts with a test that makes an assertion about what the *functional code* is supposed to do. A well-written test makes you ask yourself, *What do I need to do to get this test to pass?* To generalize, the answer is to create the simplest implementation to satisfy the condition of the test—no more, no less. Let's start with an example so you can see this in practice.

An NUnit test lives inside a test fixture class, and the framework allows you to mark a class as a fixture with the attribute [TestFixture]. The test itself is a regular method with return type **void** but marked with the [Test] attribute.

---

6. You can grab the latest copy of it from http://nunit.org.
7. http://www.codicesoftware.com/opdownloads2/oppnunit.aspx.

The code we'll work on first is the classic "Hello World" example with a small twist. Instead of outputting the information to the screen, we'll have a class's method return the magic words. We'll break this into several steps.

Writing a Test

First, we'll need to create a Visual Studio Class Library project called *HelloWorld*. Normally, we'll separate our tests and functional code, but for this first example let's just put both in the same solution. Second, we'll create our first unit test fixture:

tdd/WelcomerTest.cs

```
using NUnit.Framework;

[TestFixture]
public class WelcomerTest
{

}
```

Here we've created a new class file called WelcomerTest.cs that references nunit.framework.dll. We then added the attribute [TestFixture] to the class. Test fixtures hold many tests, and it's important to note that since we'll be testing the class Welcomer, we name the file WelcomerTest.cs. Now we need to add our first test:

tdd/WelcomerTest.cs

```
[TestFixture]
public class WelcomerTest
{
  [Test]
  public void Should_Say_Hello_World()
  {
    // your testing happens here
  }
}
```

Here we apply the [Test] attribute to our test method. Generally, the practice is to start the test with "Should..." because it forces us to think about the behavior of the class we are testing. In this example, it's *Welcomer Should Say Hello World*. Notice how we break the .NET convention of using capital letters for methods by separating each word with an underscore. We do this to make the test easier to read.

Up next we'll add a condition for testing:

tdd/WelcomerTest.cs

```
using NUnit.Framework;

[TestFixture]
public class WelcomerTest
{
  [Test]
  public void Should_Say_Hello_World()
  {
    Assert.AreEqual("Hello World", Welcomer.SayHello());
  }
}
```

What's needed now is some work on an assertion. NUnit has many different types of assertions that we'll use throughout this book. In this case, we use the AreEqual() method. The left side argument is always what we *expect*, while the right side is the *actual* output. Alternatively, you can use the newer syntax for writing assertions using the That() method. The same assertion reads as follows:

```
Assert.That("Hello World", Is.EqualTo(new Welcomer().SayHello()))
```

This newer style of assertion can be more natural to read as you go from left to right. Feel free to use the style you are most comfortable with; however, for the rest of this book, we'll use the older Assert.AreEqual() style because it's less verbose.

Either way we code our assertion, the test won't compile yet. This is because we have no Welcome class and no static method called Say-Hello(). Our next step is to add that code:

tdd/Welcomer.cs

```
public class Welcomer
{
  public static string SayHello()
  {
    return string.Empty;
  }
}
```

Our code now compiles by adding the method that returns an empty **string**. With the code compiling, we have the first step of the cycle done—we've written our first test. Now we want to make sure that when we execute the test, it will fail because we have yet to write the *functional code* to make it pass.

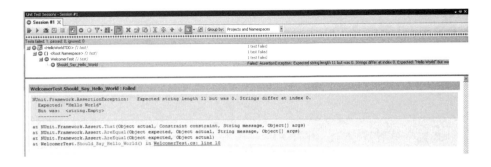

Figure 2.3: THE RESHARPER UNIT TEST RUNNER SHOWS WHICH TESTS ARE FAILING. ON YOUR SCREEN YOU'LL SEE THIS PROGRESS BAR APPEAR IN RED.

Watching the Test Fail

If you are using Visual Studio 2008 Professional, then using a plug-in to run tests is your best option. I highly recommend using ReSharper by JetBrains. In Section 1.2, *Plugging In ReSharper*, on page 8, we reviewed its features and key advantages. This tool helps us in many ways; it also has its own NUnit test runner. If you have ReSharper installed, you can see that the test is now failing (Figure 2.3). Otherwise, you can use TestDriven.Net: a free plug-in that lets you run and debug unit tests.[8] Alternatively, nunit-gui.exe comes packaged with NUnit and is another visual way to run your tests. If you're comfortable with the command line, you can also run tests using the nunit-console.exe utility like so:

```
C:\Program Files\NUnit 2.5.1\bin\net-2.0>
  nunit-console "C:\Projects\HelloWorldTDD\HelloWorldTDD.csproj"
```

The previous session assumes that you've created the HelloWorld solution in the directory Projects\HelloWorldTDD. It also assumes you have installed NUnit with an MSI. The command-line utility nunit-console.exe can run directly against Visual Studio project files, in this case HelloWorldTDD.csproj. Running tests from the command line also comes in handy when we're building and deploying our application. We'll talk about this in Section 12.2, *Adding Unit Tests to the Build*, on page 244.

---

8. http://www.testdriven.net/

Figure 2.4: A SUCCESS MESSAGE INDICATES THAT ALL THE TESTS ARE
PASSING. ON A COLOR SCREEN YOU'LL SEE A GREEN BAR.

As expected, the test fails, and the unit test runner shows the test is
failing. This completes the second step of the TDD cycle.

Getting the Test to Pass

Now we're going to switch over to the *functional code* to make this test
pass:

`tdd/Welcomer.cs`

```
public class Welcomer
{
  public static string SayHello()
  {
    return "Hello World";
  }
}
```

Hurray, the test passes (Figure 2.4)! We had to change the string that
SayHello() returns to be *Hello World*. We could refactor our code now to
see whether we can clean it up or reduce duplication, but it's looking
good the way it is. Now we can start the whole cycle again and write
another test for our next requirement.

TDD is more than just a way of testing your code. It is a way to drive
your design through small incremental steps. Some developers say that
TDD stands for "test-driven design," because writing tests first strongly
influences your application architecture to be more loosely coupled and
modular. This approach to design produces more flexibility and easier-
to-understand code.

Mastering TDD takes plenty of practice, and in this book you'll get a lot
of it. However, if you would like to learn even more about TDD, I highly
recommend Kent Beck's book *Test-Driven Development: By Example*

[Bec02]. Although the book uses Java and Python to work through examples, the principles apply to C# and ASP.NET MVC.

Up Next

With the basics of TDD in hand, it's time to get started using ASP.NET MVC. In the next chapter, we'll learn how to create, read, update, and delete a model in MVC.

Part II

Building an Application

Chapter 3

Getting Organized with MVC

Now that we understand TDD and the basics of MVC, we can start implementing the sample time management application we'll create throughout Parts II and III of the book: GetOrganized. This application will improve the speed and priority of how we get things done—it will help us get organized.

The first few chapters of Part II focus on how to use and test MVC controllers; the following chapters work through how to make the site look better using views and Ajax.

This chapter starts with an overview of what we'll be doing with GetOrganized in the upcoming chapters, and then we'll dive into test-driving MVC's create, read, update, and delete (CRUD) operations to create a simple to-do list.

3.1 Time Management with GetOrganized

GetOrganized is a web-based time management system inspired by ThinkingRock, an open source Java Swing application developed by Jeremy Moore. It helps you organize your thoughts and set up action items.[1] Both GetOrganized and ThinkingRock draw their inspiration from time management guru David Allen's book *Getting Things Done* [All02].

ThinkingRock's main screen illustrates the three steps of a *Getting Things Done* system (Figure 3.1, on the next page).

---

1. http://www.trgtd.com.au/

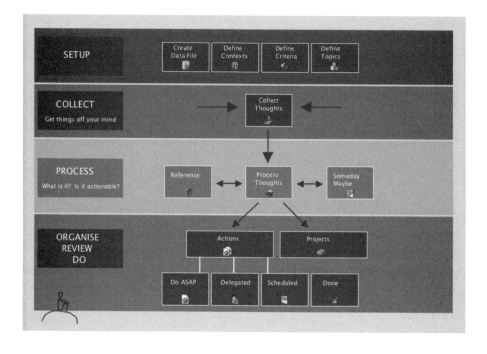

Figure 3.1: ThinkingRock helps you manage time with a three-step process: collect thoughts, process them, and implement actions.

1. Write down all the thoughts that are on your mind.

2. Process those thoughts, by either throwing them away or turning them into an action item.

3. Prioritize and complete the action items.

For the system to yield results, you commit a time every day and input your thoughts. These can be random and should have no concept of size, such as "Complete proposal for prospective client" or "Learn jQuery." Next, you categorize these thoughts into actionable or non-actionable items. Finally, you work through those action items in the form of a to-do list.

Let's get started by adding support for building a simple to-do list so that we can see all the things we need to work on.

3.2 Reading Data

Often the hardest thing to do when starting with TDD is to write the first test. This is especially true when a language or framework is new to us; the old pattern of writing the functional code first slips back, and before we know it, we're writing code with zero test coverage. TDD takes discipline, but we end up learning more and building greater confidence as we master it.

In the case of ASP.NET MVC, a good place to start is to test-drive the controller, because it's where so much of the application logic lives. Alternatively, you can start by test-driving your model, which we will do in Section 4.1, *Implementing Equals for Topic*, on page 61. In the end, you'll need to test both models and controllers independently.

Before we can start testing our controller, we need to create the MVC project GetOrganized.

MVC Project Structure

We installed MVC in Section 1.2, *Installing MVC*, on page 6, and this step is required before we can create a new MVC project. Once installed, we'll be able to create the solution GetOrganized with the MVC project name *Web*.

Although the project name *Web* is generic, you'll want to keep the project names simple to save screen real estate in the Visual Studio Solution Explorer. However, you'll want to modify the project properties to add a custom namespace by right-clicking the project properties. Then change the default namespace to *GetOrganized.Web*.

This is the first time we're looking at the project structure of an MVC project, so let's take a quick tour (Figure 3.2, on the following page).

By default Visual Studio generates an AccountController and HomeController. You can remove and replace these with your own code, but they give us a starting point for most web applications. The AccountController deals with user login, and the HomeController serves up the default MVC starter page. We'll touch more on the AccountController in Section 5.2, *Logging In*, on page 88.

Here's the rest of the structure:

- Content holds all images, CSS, and other static files.

- Controllers holds all your controller classes.

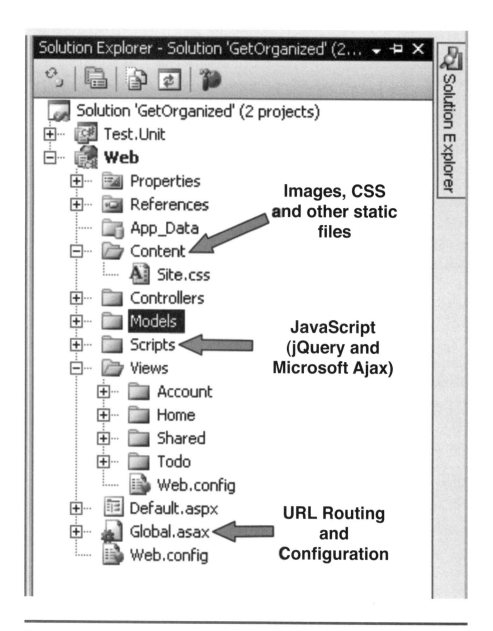

Figure 3.2: THE MVC PROJECT STRUCTURE HAS A WELL-DEFINED LOCATION FOR ALL FILES.

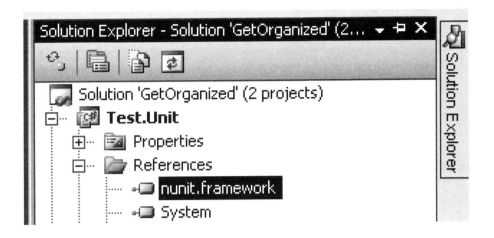

Figure 3.3: ADDING A REFERENCE TO NUNIT IS REQUIRED IN ORDER TO UNIT TEST.

- Models holds all your model classes.

- Views holds a subdirectory for each controller you create as well as a Shared folder for common components.

- Scripts has all a copy of jQuery and Microsoft Ajax support or any other JavaScript you create.

- Global.asax includes the routing and startup information for your application.

Our First Test

Let's get on with the business of writing our first controller test.

When creating tests, we generally create a new project, which produces a separate .NET assembly. We place our tests in that project so that test code never goes into production. We'll follow this convention by creating a project of the type Class Library, and we'll name it Test.Unit. Once it's created, make sure to add a reference to nunit.framework.dll, as shown in Figure 3.3.

This controller "should display a list of some to-do items." Hey, that sounds like a pretty good name for a test!

> ### ReSharper Tip: Class Navigation
>
> By naming all our test classes with the name *Test* at the end,
> rather than the start, it makes it easier to find the associated
> functional code with the test code. ReSharper has the code
> navigation shortcut `Ctrl+N` that helps us find classes in the solu-
> tion. When we type in TodoController, it will bring up the actual
> controller as well as the test, TodoControllerTest. ReSharper's
> code navigation allows an even shorter form by just typing in
> *TC* to bring us the same result.

To start, we need to add a test class, TodoControllerTest:

`gettingorganized/TodoControllerTest.cs`

```
using NUnit.Framework;

namespace Test.Unit
{
  [TestFixture]
  public class TodoControllerTest
  {
    [Test]
    public void Should_Display_A_List_Of_Todo_Items()
    {

    }
  }
}
```

We have our test skeleton, similar to what we did in Section 2.2, *Test-Driving "Hello World"*, on page 22. Now we'll fill it with an assertion.
The controller should display to-dos, so our assertion needs to verify
that to-do items load. However, this will generate a couple of compiler
errors, since neither a Todo class nor a TodoController exists. Let's work
on creating these classes first before we return to this test, starting by
creating a Todo model.

A model is a normal class. There are no special templates or wizards
like there are for views and controllers. To create a new model, right-
click the Solution Explorer, choose Add New Item, and select the Class
template.

An alternative way to solve our compiler problem would be to generate
the classes with ReSharper. While our mouse is over the compiler error

---

ReSharper Tip: Creating New Classes

While your mouse is over the Solution Explorer, hit `Ctrl+Alt+Ins`, and you'll be able to create and name a new class.

---

on Todo on line 5, we can use the ReSharper shortcut `Alt+Enter` to generate our missing Todo class (see the sidebar on page 45). This also works for controllers, but we don't get the generated template that MVC gives us.

For this new model, start by adding two properties, Title and Completed, and then add a default list of things to be done. This gives us a primitive way of saving our list. Static lists are *never* a good way to store information in real-world applications. We'll eventually replace the static lists in Chapter 8, *Persisting Your Models*, on page 161 when we introduce NHibernate.

Testing models is critical because they'll eventually hold important logic about how your system behaves. Since we're currently focusing on controller testing, let's deal with model testing a little later.

`gettingorganized/Todo.cs`

```
Line 1    namespace GetOrganized.Models
    -     {
    -       public class Todo
    -       {
    5         public static List<Todo> ThingsToBeDone = new List<Todo>
    -         {
    -           new Todo {Title = "Get Milk", Completed = false},
    -           new Todo {Title = "Bring Home Bacon", Completed = false}
    -         };
   10
    -         public bool Completed { get; set; }
    -         public string Title { get; set; }
    -       }
    -     }
```

Our first model has a List<Todo> and a couple of *auto properties*. Auto setters are a new C# 3.0 feature to reduce the amount of code required to have simple getters and setters. Instead of writing out public bool Completed {get {return completed;} } and then having to create the private boolean field completed, the *auto setter property* is shorter, as shown on line 11.

```
Todo.cs  TodoControllerTest.cs*

Test.Unit.TodoControllerTest

using GetOrganized.Models;
using NUnit.Framework;

namespace Test.Unit
{
    [TestFixture]
    public class TodoControllerTest
    {
        [Test]
        public void Should_Display_A_List_Of_Todo_Items()
        {
            Assert.AreEqual(Todo.ThingsToBeDone, new TodoController());
        }                                              Cannot resolve symbol 'TodoController'
    }
}
```

Figure 3.4: THERE WILL BE CLASSES THAT DON'T EXIST AS YOU WRITE YOUR TESTS. THIS IS A NORMAL PART OF TDD.

With the model in place, we've removed one of the compiler errors. However, we're still getting another one because there is no such thing as TodoController (Figure 3.4). Not to worry, this is a regular part of practicing TDD. You'll find yourself regularly inventing new classes to satisfy what you're testing. Eventually, you'll get to the point of a compiling and failing test.

To remove the compiler error, we'll create the TodoController. Creating a controller involves right-clicking the Controller folder, selecting Add Controller, and inputting the name of the controller. Make sure to check the "Add action methods for Create, Update, Delete, and Details Scenarios" box, because we'll use these stubs later. The code generated for the TodoController looks like this:

gettingorganized/TodoController.cs

```
Line 1  namespace GetOrganized.Controllers
     -  {
     -    public class TodoController : Controller
     -    {
     5      //
     -      // GET: /Todo/
     -
     -      public ActionResult Index()
     -      {
    10        return View();
     -      }
     -    }
     -  }
```

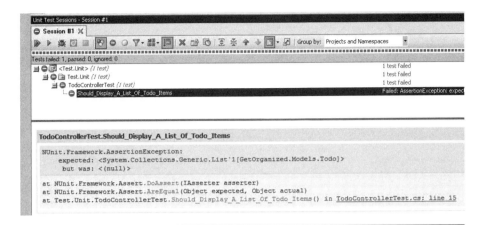

Figure 3.5: Should_Display_A_List_of_Todo_Items() is failing because the Index() action isn't meeting our expectations.

The helpful code comment on line 6 tells us that when we type in the URL http://localhost/Todo, we get the method that we're after. Note that Index() has a default route. The URL http://localhost/Todo/Index is equivalent to http://localhost/Todo, because this is specified in Global.asax.cs. Notice that the return value on the controller methods is an ActionResult object. Views use these objects for rendering purposes, but most important, they contain the model that we will attach to get this test to pass. ActionResults are covered in detail in Section 5.1, *Directing to Different Content Types with ActionResults*, on page 84.

To complete our assert statement, we'll need to compare apples to apples, or in this case to lists of Todo items. To achieve this, we need to cast ActionResult as a ViewResult object. The ViewResult class is a subtype of ActionResult that has a property called ViewData; this property is the key to passing the model between the controller and the view.

ViewData is a collection of objects. It has a special property called Model, which is where the model is set and accessed in the controller. We're expecting our controller to set our ViewData.Model to be our Todo list. For the code to compile, we'll need to add System.Web.Mvc to our references in the Test.Unit project. The code looks like this:

gettingorganized/TodoControllerTest.cs

```
Line 1   [Test]
     2   public void Should_Display_A_List_Of_Todo_Items()
     3   {
     4       var viewResult = (ViewResult) new TodoController().Index() ;
     5       Assert.AreEqual(Todo.ThingsToBeDone, viewResult.ViewData.Model );
     6   }
```

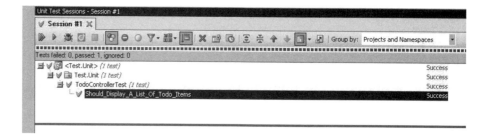

Figure 3.6: ADDING THE MODEL TO THE CONTROLLER MAKES OUR TEST
PASS.

Our code is compiling, and it's time to run the test and see whether it
fails. Our comparison is failing when we run the test (Figure 3.5, on the
preceding page). This means we've reached step 2 of the TDD cycle—
"Watch the test fail" (Figure 2.2, on page 20). To reach step 3—"Get the
test to pass"—we'll need to implement the Index() action to meet our
assertion.

Currently our Index() action simply returns a ViewResult and therefore
will fail. Let's wire up the model and get the test to pass (Figure 3.6):

```
gettingorganized/TodoController.cs
public class TodoController : Controller
{
  //
  // GET: /Todo/

  public ActionResult Index()
  {
    ViewData.Model = Todo.ThingsToBeDone;
    return View();
  }
}
```

Adding a View

Excellent, we've got our first passing test. But we still don't have anything the user can see. We need to add a view to complete the cycle.
Adding a view is similar to the process of adding a controller. Simply right-click anywhere in the controller's action code, and select Add
View (Figure 3.7, on page 42). We'll create a strongly typed view with
the template called List to generate the HTML that lists the List<Todo>
for us. The bottom of the dialog box is where we can specify the use of
a master page, which is a layout template for the whole site (we'll cover

master pages in Chapter 6, *Enhancing Views with HTML Helpers and Master Pages*, on page 115).

Here is a snippet of the code the view wizard generates:

gettingorganized/Index.aspx

```
<table>
<tr>
    <th></th>
    <th>
        Completed
    </th>
    <th>
        Title
    </th>
</tr>
<% foreach (var item in Model) { %>
<tr>
  <td>
    <%= Html.ActionLink("Edit", "Edit", new { /* id=item.PrimaryKey */ }) %> |
    <%= Html.ActionLink("Details", "Details", new { /* id=item.PrimaryKey */ })%> |
    <%= Html.ActionLink("Delete", "Delete", new { /* id=item.PrimaryKey */ })%>
  </td>
  <td>
    <%= Html.Encode(item.Completed) %>
  </td>
  <td>
    <%= Html.Encode(item.Title) %>
  </td>
</tr>
<% } %>
</table>
```

The view here simply iterates over the model, in this case a List<Todo>, and renders its contents. Note that MVC builds up all the correct headings and properties for you, but as of this release, it never automatically determines your ID key. In one of the following examples, we'll need to tweak the commented-out code to get it to work. For now, however, this works for our purposes of displaying the Todo items. If you are using Visual Studio 2010 and .NET 4.0, there is a different syntax for enclosing the HTML helpers that you'll see in the view:

```
<%=   //.NET 3.5 syntax   %>
<%:   //.NET 4.0 syntax   %>
```

This new syntax available to .NET 4.0 applications will automatically encode the contents as HTML, which will protect your site from cross-site scripting. We'll talk more about this in Section 11.1, *Preventing Cross-Site Scripting*, on page 221.

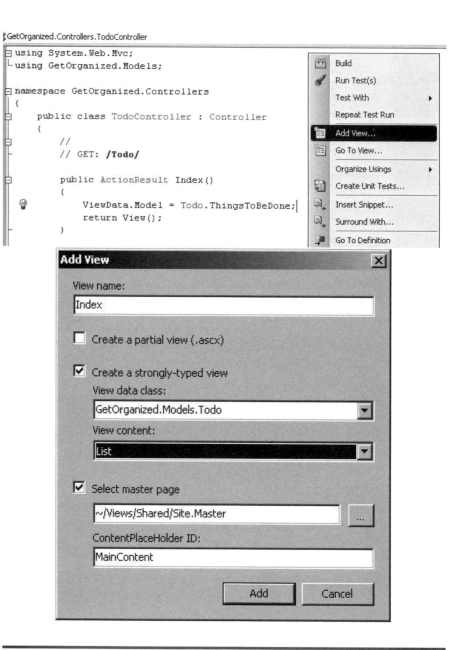

Figure 3.7: The Add View Wizard allows you to choose the model and view template you want to generate.

Zero Unit Testing for the View

We don't have a unit test for the view. This is because we'd need to assert against the HTML Document Object Model (DOM), which makes unit testing difficult. Generally, testing the view requires a browser or headless browser such as *Celerity*.[2] This is a much bigger investment of effort to unit test a single view, so we leave the UI elements to be tested by other frameworks such as Watir (or Watin in .NET) and Selenium RC.[3]

These are valuable tools and are a key component to application development best practices, but they are not required to test-drive code. Keep this in mind when customizing views and adding logic to them, because your unit tests will never cover them.

The design goal of our view is to be dumb. If we start seeing a large number of if/else statements in them, it's time to extract an *HTML helper* class that we can test-drive more easily. We can also consider moving the logic to the controller if it has more to do with interaction than display (we'll cover HTML helpers in depth in Section 6.2, *Colorizing a Drop-Down List*, on page 123, and we'll show an example of an open source grid HTML helper in Section 6.5, *Replacing Web Controls with Advanced HTML Helpers*, on page 134). If you really want to enforce the view to have minimal logic, consider using the alternative StringTemplate view engine.[4]

Let's look at the fruit of our labors by hitting ⌜F5⌝ or by clicking the Play icon (Figure 3.8, on the following page). By default, the first page you'll see is the HomeController's Index() action. To see the TodoController's action, you'll need to type in the URL http://localhost:4586/Todo. The port number *4586* will vary based on your Visual Studio settings, so replace that port number with whichever appears for you. The browser will now show you a working list of Todos.

Next up, we'll see how to add a new Todo.

---

2. Celerity is a Ruby-based browser that doesn't render graphically. Find out more at http://celerity.rubyforge.org/.
3. Watir, Watin, and Selenium RC are all examples of UI/acceptance-level testing frameworks. Watir is available at http://wtr.rubyforge.org/, Watin is downloadable at http://watin.sourceforge.net/, and Selenium RC is at http://seleniumhq.org/projects/remote-control/.
4. http://code.google.com/p/string-template-view-engine-mvc/

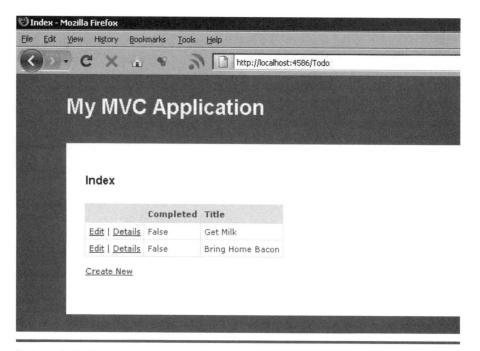

Figure 3.8: To-do items are now showing in a list on the Index.aspx page.

3.3 Creating a To-Do

We have a couple of to-dos on our list, but we're going to need to be able to add to that list if it's to be of any use. Unlike listing models, creation is a two-step process. The first is an HTTP GET request to load the create screen. The second is an HTTP POST to send the filled-out model back to be saved.

Taking the user to the create screen is the first step. We need to write a test to assert that when the Create() action is requested, it loads the Create.aspx view:

```
gettingorganized/TodoControllerTest.cs
Line 1  [Test]
    2   public void Should_Load_Create_View()
    3   {
    4     var viewResult = (ViewResult) new TodoController().Create();
    5
    6     Assert.AreEqual(string.Empty, viewResult.ViewName);
    7   }
```

Since this is a ViewResult and there is no model, all we want to check is that the action is invoking the proper view. On line 6, we assert

> ## ReSharper Tip: The Magic Keys
>
> If you're going to learn only one ReSharper shortcut, `Alt+Enter` is the one to know. `Alt+Enter` does more than just fix compiler errors. Affectionately known as the *magic keys*, this shortcut improves productivity. When you use the shortcut, ReSharper will give you a drop-down list of options of common operations you might be thinking about doing, such as changing a method from public to private or generating a **null** check on a variable. You can also use it to prompt you for code conventions, such as replacing your local typed variable definitions with the **var** keyword.

the view's name is properly being redirected to View/Todo/Create.aspx. Under normal circumstances, this kind of test is not helping all that much, since this is testing an MVC convention. The strange thing about the convention is that MVC's viewResult.ViewName property shows an empty string when the convention is followed, not the actual path to the View/Todo/Create.aspx view. If we were directing to a nonstandard view like CreateTodoWithOtherBits.aspx, then the test makes a lot more sense. We're testing it here for completeness and to show how it's done. Now let's make it pass:

`gettingorganized/TodoController.cs`

```
// GET: /Todo/Create

public ActionResult Create()
{
  return View();
}
```

There is little to this implementation since we've autogenerated the method stubs using the MVC template wizard. By default it will pass our test. This action simply directs the result to the Create.aspx view. It does this by convention, sending it the view with the same name as that of the controller and action. If we were sending it to our fictitious CreateTodoWithOtherBits.aspx, then we could do so by calling View("CreateTodoWithOtherBits").

Moving onto step 2, let's write a test to assert that we can add to the list. Remember: our first task is to get something compiling and failing.

```
gettingorganized/TodoControllerTest.cs
```

```
Line 1   [SetUp]
    -    public void setup()
    -    {
    -      Todo.ThingsToBeDone = new List<Todo>
    5        {
    -          new Todo {Title = "Get Milk"},
    -          new Todo {Title = "Bring Home Bacon"}
    -        };
    -    }
   10
    -    [Test]
    -    public void Should_Add_Todo_Item()
    -    {
    -      var todo = new Todo {
   15        Title = "Learn more about ASP.NET MVC Controllers" };

    -      var redirectToRouteResult =
    -        (RedirectToRouteResult) new TodoController().Create(todo);

   20      Assert.Contains(todo, Todo.ThingsToBeDone);
    -      Assert.AreEqual("Index",
    -        redirectToRouteResult.RouteValues["action"]);
    -    }
```

Here we create a new Todo model and invoke the Create() method on the controller. Line 22 of the test asserts that the collection ThingsToDo now contains this new item. The compiler gives us an error saying that the signature Create(Todo item) does not exist. Let's go ahead and create one. We'll also need to add System.Web.Routing to our project references to get this code to compile.

We're currently using a static List of Todo items (we won't learn about NHibernate until Chapter 8, *Persisting Your Models*, on page 161). This means we'll have to introduce a setup fixture with the [SetUp] attribute on line 1. This attribute tells NUnit to run a method *before* every [Test]. We want this setup to run before every test because it will reset the static list to its original state.

Similarly, another attribute called [TearDown] runs *after* every [Test]. Both [SetUp] and [TearDown] help us make sure our unit tests are free of side effects from the previous test, as in the case of creating, updating, or deleting. We assert that the action redirect occurs by casting the Action-Result as a RedirectToRouteResult and checking the contents of its collection on line 22.

The object RedirectToRouteResult has a collection of values for how to route the request. Remember, the format that MVC consumes is http:

//localhost/controller/action. The RouteValues collection contains all that information in a key-value relationship. RouteValues["action"] gives us the {action} segment of the URL. The MVC framework uses this information to redirect the browser (this will be explained in more detail in Section 5.1, *IControllerFactory: Where Controllers Are Born*, on page 86).

We now have a failing test, and now we need to make it compile. We'll do this by adding a new action called Create() in the TodoController:

```
gettingorganized/TodoController.cs
Line 1  // POST: /Todo/Create

  -     [HttpPost]
  -     public ActionResult Create(Todo todo)
  5     {
  -       try
  -       {
  -         // TODO: Add insert logic here
  -
 10         return RedirectToAction("Index");
  -       }
  -       catch
  -       {
  -         return View();
 15       }
  -     }
```

We've copied the implementation from the signature Create(FormCollection collection) into our Todo signature. As of this release, MVC generates controllers by default with the FormCollection parameter for retrieving model objects. Instead, we'll employ *model binding*, a cool MVC feature that uses the model themselves as method parameters. You'll see an example of the FormCollection signature later in Section 4.2, *Using the FormCollection and TempData Objects*, on page 65.

For the application to work, we'll need to delete the FormCollection signature of the Create() method. Otherwise, MVC will complain about an ambiguous reference. You'll also notice that MVC generates a **try** and **catch** block that swallows all exceptions. Do not do this with your production code, because it makes it hard to figure out what went wrong when exceptions are thrown (see the *Joe Asks. . .* on the following page).

Notice that we've added a special attribute [HttpPost] to line 3. This is an action filter, covered in Section 5.1, *Extending Actions with Action Filters*, on page 82. This action filter tells the MVC framework to allow only HTTP POST methods (we'll talk more about the other HTTP methods in Chapter 10, *Building RESTful Web Services*, on page 199). This allevi-

Joe Asks...

Why Is Swallowing Exceptions Bad?

If you throw any error such as a database error, having a catchall **try** and **catch** block will hide that error and proceed as if everything is OK. The generated stubs for Create, Edit, and Delete all render a view when any error is thrown. This is bad because in all of those actions it will try to render the Index.aspx page when the models are probably not loaded properly. This will translate in hard-to-understand stack traces, like NullPointerException somewhere on the view, when the error originated much earlier.

```
try
{
  // TODO: Add insert logic here
  return RedirectToAction("Index");
}
catch
{
  return View();
}
```

Catching exceptions is a good thing; just don't swallow all exceptions. It's a best practice to accompany all **catch** blocks with a typed exception like this:

```
catch(SomeException e)
{
  //do something with exception
}
```

Later in Section 6.4, *Adding Validations Using ModelStateDictionary*, on page 131 you'll learn how to use an **if** and **else** instead of a **try** and **catch** block.

ates ambiguity, because there are several Create() method signatures. The signature without any parameters—in this case the Create()—is the action that maps to the first time the creation page loads.

The test compiles but fails. This completes the second step of the TDD cycle: write a failing test.

Getting the test to pass is as simple as adding the variable todo to the collection in the controller:

gettingorganized/TodoController.cs

```
Line 1   // POST: /Todo/Create

    -    [HttpPost]
    -    public ActionResult Create(Todo todo)
    5    {
    -      try
    -      {
    -        Todo.ThingsToBeDone.Add(todo);
    -        return RedirectToAction("Index");
   10      }
    -      catch
    -      {
    -        return View();
    -      }
   15    }
```

Here we simply add the parameter to the Todo.ThingsToBeDone on line 8. You will see the positive effect the preceding code has in the Unit Test Runner output. The test now passes.

This looks like a good time to check out our handiwork. However, we've yet to generate the view to see it. Let's right-click the controller code and select Add View. This time we'll create a view with the type Todo using the *Create* template. This template generates the following code:

gettingorganized/Create.aspx

```
Line 1   <h2>Create</h2>

    -    <%= Html.ValidationSummary("Create was unsuccessful.
    -      Please correct the errors and try again") %>
    5
    -    <% using (Html.BeginForm()) {%>
    -    <fieldset>
    -      <legend>Fields</legend>
    -      <div class="editor-label">
   10       <%= Html.LabelFor(model => model.Completed) %>
    -      </div>
```

```
          <div class="editor-field">
            <%= Html.TextBoxFor(model => model.Completed) %>
            <%= Html.ValidationMessageFor(model => model.Completed) %>
15        </div>
          <div class="editor-label">
            <%= Html.LabelFor(model => model.Title) %>
          </div>
          <div class="editor-field">
20          <%= Html.TextBoxFor(model => model.Title) %>
            <%= Html.ValidationMessageFor(model => model.Title) %>
          </div>
          <p>
            <input type="submit" value="Create" />
25        </p>
        </fieldset>
        <% } %>
```

On line 20, we create an HTML input tag with Html.TextBoxFor(model => model.Title). These will be tied back to the model through model binding when we HTTP POST to the Create() action.

Notice how on line 4, we return an Html.ValidationSummary. This property is populated only when a model fails validation. For example, if our Todo is missing a title, a message will be displayed instructing the user to fill one in (we'll cover model validation in Section 6.4, *Adding Validations Using ModelStateDictionary*, on page 131).

It doesn't make sense to have a Completed field for this view, so let's remove it and take a look at what we have done so far (Figure 3.9, on the next page). We can now create Todo items, and once they're added successfully, we are sent back to the list of Todos that were being displayed before.

Now we'll see how to delete a model. For GetOrganized, we want to scrap a Todo.

3.4 Deleting: Creating an Action Without a View

Deleting records without using HTTP POST is a very bad thing. It breaks the protocol's convention to use an HTTP GET to modify or delete information (see the *Joe Asks...* on page 52). However, for right now we just want to put a delete link on the index page. The proper convention for this is to perform an asynchronous call using HTTP POST and Ajax. We'll cover that in Section 7.1, *Deleting with HTTP POST*, on page 141.

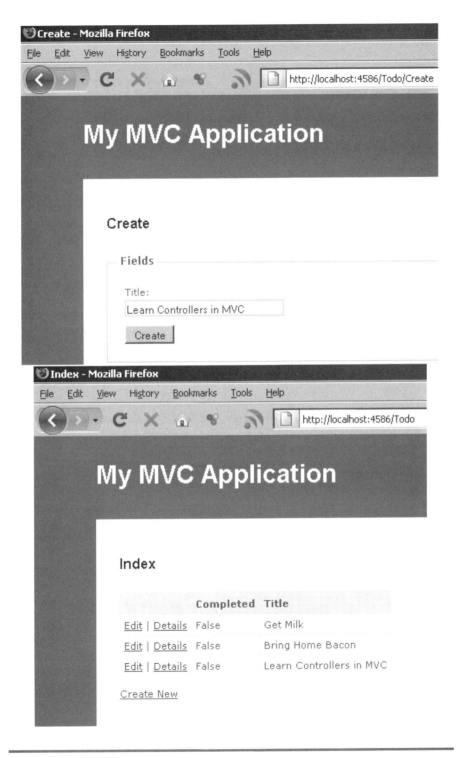

Figure 3.9: ADDING A TODO BRINGS US BACK TO THE INDEX PAGE.

Joe Asks...

Why Delete Only with HTTP POST or DELETE?

As we discuss in Chapter 10, *Building RESTful Web Services*, on page 199, following the semantics make it easier for other programmers to use your application.

Another good reason is to protect against search engines modifying content on your site. Imagine if you left the delete links accessible by Google, only to find out on Monday morning that all your data has been killed by a search engine. Most search engines use HTTP GET exclusively to crawl the Web, so having an HTTP GET that deletes content isn't going to leave much of a site to browse!

So, use HTTP POST when modifying content, and avoid this embarrassment. We'll work through this in Section 7.1, *Deleting with HTTP POST*, on page 141.

In the meantime, to simplify things, we'll break this convention temporarily. We will perform a delete with an HTTP GET. The first thing we'll need to do is to add another test for deleting a Todo.

gettingorganized/TodoControllerTest.cs

```
Line 1  [Test]
        public void Should_Delete_Todo_Item()
        {
          var mistakeTodo = Todo.ThingsToBeDone[0];
     5
          var redirectToRouteResult = (RedirectToRouteResult)
            new TodoController().Delete(mistakeTodo.Title);

          Assert.IsFalse(Todo.ThingsToBeDone.Contains(mistakeTodo));
    10    Assert.AreEqual("Index",
            redirectToRouteResult.RouteValues["action"]);
        }
```

This action test looks similar to the one used on Create() except we're going to assert that the mistakeTodo is *not* in the list on line 9. We'll also perform a redirect to the Index() action on success. The interesting bit about Delete() is that we don't have a Delete.aspx view to redirect to. Once we delete something, we redirect to the list of Todo items.

The following is the controller code to get the test to pass:

`gettingorganized/TodoController.cs`

```
// GET: /Todo/Delete/Title={name of todo}

public ActionResult Delete(string title)
{
  Todo.ThingsToBeDone.
    RemoveAll(todo => todo.Title == title);

  return RedirectToAction("Index");
}
```

Note that MVC's default signature for the Delete() action has the [Http-Post] attribute—you'll need to remove this for the page to work. You'll also need to replace the FormCollection with the Title of the Todo. Finally, you'll modify the link to the Delete() action on the Index.aspx view. We can do this by changing the following line:

`gettingorganized/Index.aspx`

```
<%= Html.ActionLink("Delete", "Delete", new { item.Title } ,
  new { onclick="return
    confirm('Are you sure you want to delete this?');" }) %>
```

Here we use the ActionLink() method on HTML to generate a link to the Delete() action. The final parameter of ActionLink() lets us set HTML attributes on the element, such as **style** and **class**.

Notice how the link's last parameter is passed a new { item.Title }. This uses a .NET 3.0 feature called *anonymous types*. Essentially, you are passing in a new class with a property Title that has the value of item.Title. *Anonymous types* provide a simple way to create objects we'll only ever use once. We'll use *anonymous types* throughout this book and in particular when using HTML helper methods.

Because we don't want people just deleting by accident, we add the **onclick** attribute. This prompts users with a confirmation box before it submits the HTTP GET request by adding the code new { onclick ="return confirm('Are you sure?');" }. Here's a look at the modified Index.aspx code:

`gettingorganized/Index.aspx`

```
Line 1  <table>
   -    <tr>
   -      <th></th>
   -      <th>Completed</th>
   5      <th>Title</th>
   -    </tr>
```

```
     <% foreach (var item in Model) { %>
     <tr>
       <td>
10       <%= Html.ActionLink("Delete", "Delete", new { item.Title },
           new { onclick ="return confirm('Are you sure?');" }) %> |
         <%= Html.ActionLink("Edit", "Edit",
           new { /* id=item.PrimaryKey */ })%> |
         <%= Html.ActionLink("Details", "Details",
15         new { /* id=item.PrimaryKey */ })%>
       </td>
       <td>
         <%= Html.Encode(item.Completed) %>
       </td>
20     <td>
         <%= Html.Encode(item.Title) %>
       </td>
     </tr>
     <% } %>
25   </table>
```

We are now able to browse the application and remove items that shouldn't be there. On line 13, we see the default MVC template for List pages is to have a commented-out Id.PrimaryKey. We rarely name our primary key field like that—normally it is just Id. For Todo, we're instead using Title as the primary key. We're doing it this way so you can see how extensible MVC is in the next section.

Later we will talk about adding antiforgery tokens (see Section 11.1, *Guarding Against Cross-Site Request Forgery Attacks*, on page 223) to help prevent unauthorized users from removing records. Now that we've seen how to delete a record, we'll move on to learning to mark Todo items as complete.

3.5 Updating: Marking a To-Do as Complete

Similar to Create(), Edit() is composed of two parts. The first loads a screen with the model details for editing. The second submits the modifications to be saved. We therefore have two tests to write, because Edit() doesn't just load a blank page like Create() did—it loads an existing item.

The convention for getting the details or editing a model is to pass in an Id, which is a unique integer. For example, the conventional URL for editing is http://localhost/Todo/Edit/1, where *1* is the Id of the Todo.

We'll have to deviate from convention, because our Todo doesn't have an Id field. To avoid ambiguous references, we'll delete the existing Edit(int id) signature and replace it with our own. Instead of loading by Id, we want to load our model by Title. Let's write a test for this:

`gettingorganized/TodoControllerTest.cs`

```
[Test]
public void Should_Load_A_Todo_Item_For_Editing()
{
  var editTodo = Todo.ThingsToBeDone[0];

  var viewResult = (ViewResult) new TodoController().Edit(editTodo.Title);

  Assert.AreEqual(editTodo, viewResult.ViewData.Model);
}
```

This test has more in common with the Index() test, because we're putting data into the view for display. By casting the result as a ViewResult, we ensure that we are never redirecting to another page or action. Now let's implement the code to get this to pass:

`gettingorganized/TodoController.cs`

```
//
// GET: /Todo/Edit/somethingToDo
public ActionResult Edit(string title)
{
    ViewData.Model =
      Todo.ThingsToBeDone.Find(todo => todo.Title == title);
    return View();
}
```

The test passes, and all we needed to do is a quick Find() on our ThingsToBeDone collection using the passed-in Title of the Todo.

Now we'll generate the view for this action. We use the wizard to add a strongly typed view of the template Edit. The edit page is displayed, as in Figure 3.10, on the next page. Let's move on to editing the ActionLink() on the Index.aspx page so we can get to this new Edit.aspx view, as shown here:

`gettingorganized/Index.aspx`

```
<%= Html.ActionLink("Edit", "Edit", new { item.Title }) %> |
```

With the link in place, we'll now create the test for editing a Todo. The test will look similar to the Create() test, except this time we will load *Get Milk* from our model and then edit it.

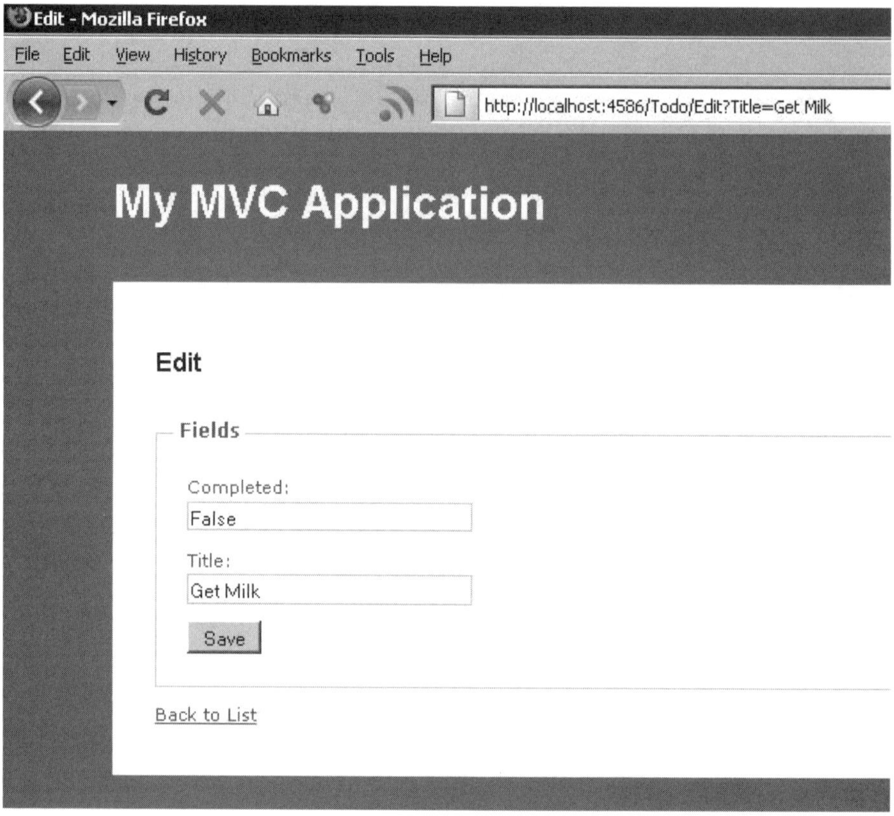

Figure 3.10: EDIT.ASPX, AS IT IS GENERATED BY MVC

gettingorganized/TodoControllerTest.cs

```
[Test]
public void Should_Edit_Todo_Item()
{
  var editedTodo =  new Todo { Title = "Get A LOT MORE milk" };

  var redirectToRouteResult =
    (RedirectToRouteResult)
      new TodoController().Edit("Get Milk",editedTodo);

  Assert.Contains(editedTodo, Todo.ThingsToBeDone);
  Assert.AreEqual("Index",
    redirectToRouteResult.RouteValues["action"]);
}
```

This is very similar to the Create() test except for some string name changes. Next, let's create a signature for Edit(string oldTitle, Todo todo). The reason we'll use the variable name oldTitle instead of just title will become obvious in our next step when we modify Edit.aspx to work properly. For now we'll just get the test to pass.

gettingorganized/TodoController.cs

```
// POST: /Todo/Edit/somethingToDo

[HttpPost]
public ActionResult Edit(string oldTitle, Todo item)
{
  try
  {
    Todo.ThingsToBeDone.
      RemoveAll(aTodo => aTodo.Title == oldTitle);
    Todo.ThingsToBeDone.Add(item);

    return RedirectToAction("Index");
  }
  catch
  {
    return View();
  }
}
```

Nothing revolutionary here—we're just finding the Todo in the list, removing it, and then adding the edited item. The trickery comes in the Edit.aspx view where we now need to define another property to use for the oldTitle parameter. It looks something like this:

gettingorganized/Edit.aspx

```
<%= Html.Hidden("oldTitle", Model.Title %>
```

This line generates an <input type="hidden" title="oldTitle" value="Bring Home Bacon" /> in the HTML, allowing us to keep the original title of the Todo item. This prevents confusion with the new edited title, which will be posted in as the action's parameter when we click Submit. So long as oldTitle matches the name of the variable in the Edit() method signature, we've ensured we're editing the correct model. Let's look at the results of this last set of tests in the browser.

That completes our first run through MVC using TDD. We've covered the basics of CRUD operations with a few slight modifications, in this case breaking the conventions int Id and deleting with an HTTP GET along the way (see the *Joe Asks...* on page 52). We now have a basic

GetOrganized application to make to-do lists of all the things we need to get done!

Up Next

We've woven the fundamentals of TDD and MVC together to complete CRUD operations. TDD increases our confidence that our application is working as expected. It also helps us learn MVC by breaking it down into smaller pieces.

Next up, we'll practice more TDD and MVC while introducing more context around our GetOrganized application. We'll use the JavaScript library jQuery to enhance the appearance of our site, and we'll learn how to deal with temporary data between requests with TempData.

The wise sees knowledge and action as one; they see truly.
► Bhagavad Gita

Chapter 4

Working with Controllers

We've learned the basic CRUD operations in MVC, and now it's time to go beyond that. Once you've covered the simple cases, you'll start to notice the need for more tests as well as an understanding of additional parts of the framework to accomplish them. In this chapter, we'll step up our game and introduce several new TDD techniques and MVC features. We'll extend how we use controllers and beef up the testing coverage that goes along with creating new controllers.

We'll start by learning a necessary part of practicing TDD: how to implement Equals() for our model objects. We'll also work on integrating jQuery, the popular JavaScript library, to make our web pages a bit flashier.

When it comes to controllers, we'll walk through using both FormCollection and TempData to create more complex models. To help with prototyping parts of our site, you'll learn about a new MVC 2.0 feature called *templated views*. This feature will allow us to create a default view for all controllers, which eventually can be replaced with a customized view. Finally, we'll talk about how to have a controller pass control to another controller.

In the previous chapter, we created a Todo list. We'll now work on building GetOrganized's "collect thoughts" functionality. Recording a thought will also involve assigning a Topic to it in order to help organize what you need to get done. So, before we can make a thought, we'll first need a way to create topics.

4.1 Creating Topics

Every thought has a category of what it relates to. Examples might be Work, Personal, Business Ideas, or Professional Development. This helps us keep track of all the things we need to get done in our busy lives.

The model of a Topic will consist of a topic name and a color. The color will visually distinguish topics from one another. Our first test will be to verify that a list of topics can be displayed when the view is rendered:

workingWithControllers/TopicControllerTest.cs

```
Line 1   [TestFixture]
         public class TopicControllerTest
         {
           [Test]
    5      public void Should_Have_List_Of_Topics_With_Name_And_Color()
           {
             var topic = new Topic {Id = 1, Color = Color.Red, Name = "Work"};
             var model =
               ((ViewResult) new TopicController().Index()).ViewData.Model;
   10        Assert.AreEqual(topic, ( (List<Topic>) model)[0]);
           }
         }
```

The code here is similar to how we listed TodoController back in Section 3.2, *Our First Test*, on page 35. We set up the expectation that the model will be assigned when we call the action Index() on line 9. The next line then asserts that the Topic is the same as we expected.

This test does not yet compile. We need to implement the TopicController and Topic classes. If we try to follow the same implementation as we did with TodoController, we're going to run into a problem. It's not wrong to implement the TopicController and the TodoController the same way, because the real problem rests with the Topic class.

The test will fail because we are asserting that a Topic is equal to another Topic. By default all classes, including Topic, do not know how to do that. If you've implemented the Equals() method before, then this concept might not be new to you. Overriding Equals() is a common side effect of working with TDD in .NET.

Think of our application like an onion with the controller code on the outside. You write a test for the first layer of the onion, but that makes you realize you need the second layer, or in this case the model. However, to get the test for the second layer working, you need to comment out the first layer because all the code is in the same assembly, and you need to get your test to compile. This means at this point it's OK to comment out the first test. Let's work on the model test first.

To get our TopicController test to pass, we need to implement the Equals() method on Topic.

Implementing Equals for Topic

C# objects all inherit from the base class Object. Object has an important method called Equals() that compares whether two objects occupy the same space in memory. Most of the time, as in the case of our Topic object, we are more interested in whether the values of two objects are the same.

For example, if two Topics have the name Work and the color red, then we'd expect them to be equal. Properties or fields need to match—this is called *value equality*—and that's why one of the reasons TopicController will fail (if we hadn't commented it out already). Topic is missing a *value equality* implementation.

Right now a Topic cares only whether it shares the same location in the computer's memory. This is called *reference equality*. Reference and value are two aspects of implementing equals. There are four in total:

- Null check. Has the object you are comparing been initialized?

- Reference check. Does it occupy the same space in memory?

- Type check. Is it made from the same class?

- Value check. Do all properties or fields match?

In the interest of brevity, we're only going to test-drive the value component. However, it's important to implement all four components for your production code, because you want to make sure all four of the previous questions are answered. Imagine if you were comparing a Cat and a Dog that both had the same name. If you relied only on *value equality*, your program would say they were the same. But if you implement a type check, then your code will know that the two are different. Also, remember that on most projects we end up generating the equals methods much of the time (see the sidebar on page 64).

To create our first model test, we'll add a new folder named Models to place the files in. Let's write a test for *value equality*.

workingWithControllers/TopicTest.cs

```
Line 1   [TestFixture]
    -    public class TopicTest
    -    {
    -      private Topic workTopic;
    5
    -      [SetUp]
    -      public void Setup()
    -      {
    -        workTopic = new Topic { Id = 1,
   10          Color = Color.White, Name = "Work" };
    -      }
    -
    -      [Test]
    -      public void Should_Be_Equal_By_Value()
   15      {
    -        var anotherWorkTopic = new Topic {Id = 1,
    -          Color = Color.White, Name = "Work"};
    -        Assert.AreEqual(workTopic, anotherWorkTopic);
    -      }
   20
    -      [Test]
    -      public void Should_Not_Be_Equal_By_Value()
    -      {
    -        var personalTopic = new Topic { Id = 2,
   25          Color = Color.Red, Name = "Personal" };
    -        Assert.AreNotEqual(workTopic, personalTopic);
    -      }
    -    }
```

TopicTest contains two separate tests, one where the two objects are the same, and the other where the two objects are different. New here, we're using the [Setup] attribute on line 6. We run [Setup] before each [Test]; we use it to refactor tests to share common code. In this case, we want to share the Topic Work across both tests. This is a good example of applying the DRY principle to your test code. The first test, Should_Be_Equal_By_Value(), compares two objects that are of the same value. The second test, Should_Not_Be_Equal_By_Value(), asserts that two Topics of different values aren't equal. Let's make these tests pass:

workingWithControllers/Topic.cs

```
Line 1   public class Topic
    -    {
    -      public static List<Topic> Topics = new List<Topic>
    -      {
    5      new Topic {Id = 1, Color = Color.Red, Name = "Work"},
    -       new Topic {Id = 2, Color = Color.Blue, Name = "Home"}
    -      };
    -
```

```
     public int Id { get; set; }
10   public Color Color { get; set; }
     public string Name { get; set; }

     public override bool Equals(object obj)
     {
15     // reference equality check
           // if (ReferenceEquals(this, obj)) return true;
       // type equality check
       // if (obj.GetType() != typeof (Topic)) return false;

20     var other = obj as Topic;

       return other.Id == Id
         && other.Color.Equals(Color)
         && Equals(other.Name, Name);
25   }

     public override int GetHashCode()
     {
       return Id; //required for assisting with collections
30   }
   }
```

Inside the Equals(), we cast the incoming object as a Topic on line 20. We do this so we can compare all the fields on line 22. This makes both our tests pass. We aren't testing the null or reference checks, but the implementations are provided in comments. We're also required to override GetHashCode() to help support collections, such as List<Topic>. An alternative way to implement Equals() is to use the ReSharper shortcut (see the sidebar on the next page). Let's get back to getting the controller test to pass.

Making TopicController Pass

We have a working Equals(), so we can get back to implementing the controller by getting our TopicControllerTest to pass.

workingWithControllers/TopicController.cs

```
public class TopicController : Controller
{
  //
  // GET: /Topic/

  public ActionResult Index()
  {
    ViewData.Model = Topic.Topics;
    return View();
  }
}
```

ReSharper Tip: Generating Equals

ReSharper can generate code in several ways. Using the shortcut Alt+Ins when you're inside the class text editor opens a dialog box with options for what kind of code you'd like to generate. One of the most useful generators that ReSharper has is the *Equality* generator. The generator dialog box asks you which fields you want to include in the Equals() and GetHashCode() methods.

Because ReSharper uses a good algorithm and it's not code you wrote yourself, you can skip test-driving Equals() if you are using this feature. If test code coverage is a concern and you're using NCover,* apply the [IgnoreFromCoverage] attribute on both the Equals() and GetHashCode() methods.

---

*. http://ncover.sourceforge.net/

This code is similar to the TodoController in Section 3.2, *Our First Test*, on page 35. We assign a model to a list of Topics and then render a view.

Before generating a view for this action, let's step back to our Topic. Right now we're using System.Color to store the exact color we want to display. HTML uses hex values to render colors, so we need to convert this. Let's write a test to validate that our model is capable of this:

workingWithControllers/TopicTest.cs

```
[Test]
public void Should_Convert_Color_To_Hex_Value()
{
  var aShadeOfRedTopic =
    new Topic { Color = Color.FromArgb(0, 208, 0, 0)};
  Assert.AreEqual("#D00000",
    aShadeOfRedTopic.ColorInWebHex());
}
```

We want to assert that the shade of red we've created is converted to the equivalent red color for the browser to read. Now let's make it pass:

workingWithControllers/Topic.cs

```
using System.Drawing;

//omit class definition

public string ColorInWebHex()
{
  return ColorTranslator.ToHtml(Color);
}
```

ReSharper Tip: Using Statements

Another helpful feature of the "magic key" `Alt+Enter` is the ability to bring in **using** statements for us. Simply put your cursor over the text that is in causing the error, and hit `Alt+Enter` to bring in the appropriate using statement.

To get this code to work, we'll use the class ColorTranslator, which translates the color into a hex value that browsers can use. This class comes from the .NET standard library and can be referenced by including System.Drawing (see the sidebar on the current page). Our test is now passing, and we're ready for the view.

In this case, we'll want something more than the default generated view. Since we're dealing with the property Color, we can actually display a color as opposed to just the color's name. The default view templates don't work for nonprimitive types, such as System.Color. This means you'll often modify view files to make them render all the information in the model.

Remember when generating the view to make it a strongly typed view of type Topic and set View Content to List. This creates the view file Views/Topic/Index.aspx, and we'll modify it as follows:

`workingWithControllers/Index.aspx`

```
Line 1   <td style="color: white;
     2      background-color: <%= item.ColorInWebHex() %>">
     3   <%= Html.Encode(item.Name) %>
     4   </td>
```

On line 2, we set the background of the Topic's Name to match its Color.

That takes care of displaying Topics, but now we need to be able to create them.

4.2 Using the FormCollection and TempData Objects

Up until now we've relied on MVC's model binding to translate complex objects, such as Todo, from the view back to the controller. Sometimes, as in the case of our Topic model, this default binding doesn't work for us. This is because Topic has a System.Color inside it. This is a *nonprimitive* type that does not map back easily like a string or int would.

Luckily, MVC has a class called FormCollection that will help us map the Topic's color into a new object. We'll also use TempData for the first time; it allows us to store information for one round-trip in the session (see the *Joe Asks...* on the facing page).

workingWithControllers/TopicControllerTest.cs

```
[Test]
public void Should_Create_Topic_And_Notify_The_User()
{
  var professionalDevelopment = new Topic {Id = 3,
    Color = ColorTranslator.FromHtml("#000000"),
    Name = "Professional Development"};

❶  var formValues = new FormCollection();
  formValues.Add("Id", professionalDevelopment.Id.ToString());
  formValues.Add("Name", professionalDevelopment.Name);
  formValues.Add("Color",
    professionalDevelopment.ColorInWebHex().Trim('#'));

  var controller = new TopicController();

  var result = (RedirectToRouteResult) controller.Create(formValues);
❷  Assert.Contains(professionalDevelopment, Topic.Topics);
❸  Assert.AreEqual("Index", result.RouteValues["action"]);
  Assert.AreEqual("Your topic has been added successfully.",
❹    controller.TempData["message"]);
}
```

❶ The class FormCollection represents a collection of keys and values that comes in the page request. By default when we generate a controller, the Create and Edit action methods use these instead of the model binding (this binding is talked about more in detail in Section 10.2, *Sending XML in the Request Using Model Binding*, on page 206). Because we have a nonprimitive type such as Color, which doesn't have a setter for a hex value like #FFFFFF, we can use the FormCollection to make sure it's translated properly. We do this with the help of ColorTranslator in System.Drawing. We also need to Trim() the # off because the color picker widget, which we'll use in the Create view, does not add that character to the output.

❷ Here we ensure the Topic is actually added to our model's static list.

❸ The controller redirects to the Index() action successfully.

❹ This is the first time we've used TempData. It's a collection of objects accessed and stored by a unique string called the Temp-

> ### Joe Asks...
> #### What Is a Session?
>
> Sessions are present in almost all web frameworks. They are a way of storing information between requests by the same user. Generally, the information tends to be temporary and small because of the technical cost that comes along with them. A shopping cart is a good example of data that would be stored in the Session.

DataDictionary. This collection stores information in the user's Session for this request and the next one only (see the *Joe Asks...* on this page). Because we're testing the controller outside the web environment, the controller does not invoke this mechanism for storing information in a web session.

We need to ensure that the success message is displayed properly. We're just putting it in TempData so that after the redirect we will still have it. TempData is a powerful mechanism to pass information to the next request, such as a success message.

To get this test to pass, we'll implement the following code:

workingWithControllers/TopicController.cs

```
Line 1   //
         // POST: /Topic/Create

         [HttpPost]
    5    public ActionResult Create(FormCollection collection)
         {
           var newTopic = new Topic();
           newTopic.Id = Convert.ToInt32(collection["Id"]);
           newTopic.Name = collection["Name"];
    10     newTopic.Color =
             ColorTranslator.FromHtml("#" + collection["Color"]);

           Topic.Topics.Add(newTopic);
           TempData["message"] = "Your topic has been added successfully.";
    15     return RedirectToAction("Index");
         }
```

On line 5, we have a signature of the method that has a FormCollection. This comes into use starting on line 8 where we assign all the values from within the FormCollection to a new Topic. Once fully constructed, we want to add a message to TempData that the Topic was successfully added on line 14. The test now passes.

Next, we'll see how to create a view for this. This view will be different: we'll make our color selector more visually interesting than just a drop-down list by using a JavaScript library called jQuery.

4.3   Adding a Little Color with jQuery

Creating a drop-down with a thousand colors doesn't seem like a good option, nor does letting people specify any color they want (because some might not exist). So, it's time to introduce a little jQuery to help us with this problem.

jQuery is a popular open source JavaScript library that comes prepackaged with ASP.NET MVC. It helps us make prettier and more interactive web pages. jQuery is also very helpful in adding Ajax support to our sites. jQuery is supported by multiple web frameworks.

If you have never used or heard of jQuery before, I suggest taking a look at http://jquery.com because lots of tutorials are available online. For a more in-depth reference, *jQuery in Action* [BK10] is a good resource. However, our usage is going to be fairly trivial, and a basic knowledge of JavaScript will be enough to continue.

jQuery has a host of plug-ins that allow us to leverage other people's work. There is a simple and easy-to-use color wheel plug-in called ColorPicker.[1] Download and add the colorpicker.js file to your /Scripts/ directory. Next, add colorpicker.css to your Content directory to add the styling. Also, add the images folder and its contents to your Content directory.

You'll have to do a find and replace in the colorpicker.CSS file to change the directory that the images are located in. Replace ../images/ with ../content/images/.

Before we get to generating the Create view—/Views/Topic/Create.aspx— we'll add some code to wire up the color picker in the site's master layout file Site.Master.

---

1.   http://www.eyecon.ro/colorpicker/

> **Speeding Up Your Pages with jQuery**
>
> Recently Microsoft announced the Content Delivery Network (CDN), which allows you to link your site's jQuery file directly to its Edge network. This can increase the speed of your site, especially if the traffic comes from all around the world. Adding a jQuery reference to the CDN looks like this:
>
> ```
> <script
>   src="http://ajax.microsoft.com/ajax/jquery/jquery-1.4.1.min.js"
>   type="text/javascript">
> </script>
> ```

`workingWithControllers/Site.Master`

```
Line 1  <head>
        <!-- omitted other scripts -->
        <link href="<%=ResolveUrl("~/Content/colorpicker.css) %>"
         rel="Stylesheet" type="text/css" />
5
        <script type="text/javascript"
          src="<%=ResolveUrl("~/Scripts/jquery-1.4.1.js") %>">
        </script>
        <script type="text/javascript"
10        src="<%=ResolveUrl("~/Scripts/colorpicker.js") %>">
        </script>
        <asp:ContentPlaceHolder ID="Head" runat="server" />
        </head>
```

This is the first time we'll touch the Site.Master file. You can find it in the Views/Shared directory. It is responsible for the general layout of the site. On line 7, we add references to the JavaScript and CSS files here so that all views inherit and have access to them. The code we add to the Site.Master fits into the head section of the document, which is where CSS files must be referenced (see the sidebar on the current page for an alternative way). The method ResolveUrl() is used in conjunction with the ~ symbol to properly resolve the URLs of these static resources. For example, if you're deploying locally to the http://localhost/GetOrganized virtual directory, the code would still work if you were at http://localhost. We'll discuss master pages in more detail in Section 6.3, *Simplifying Page Layouts with Master Pages*, on page 127. For now it's important to add a ContentPlaceHolder element on line 12 so that we can inject other scripts we need into the **head** element of the HTML document.

Now generate the /Views/Topic/Create.aspx view, and add the following lines inside the ContentPlaceHolder:

`workingWithControllers/Create.aspx`

```
Line 1  <asp:Content ID="Content1" ContentPlaceHolderID="Head"
          runat="server">
          <script type="text/javascript">
          $(document).ready(function()
     5    {
            $('#Color').ColorPicker(
            {
              onSubmit: function(hsb, hex, rgb)
              {
    10          $('#Color').val(hex);
              },
              onBeforeShow: function()
              {
                $(this).ColorPickerSetColor(this.value);
    15        }
          })
          .bind('keyup', function()
          {
          $(this).ColorPickerSetColor(this.value);
    20    });
        });
        </script>
      </asp:Content>

    25  <asp:Content ID="Content1" ContentPlaceHolderID="MainContent"
          runat="server">
          <div class="editor-label">
            <%= Html.LabelFor(model => model.Color) %>
          </div>
    30    <div class="editor-field">
            <%= Html.TextBoxFor(model => model.Color) %>
            <%= Html.ValidationMessageFor(model => model.Color) %>
          </div>
        </asp:Content>
```

Lines 3 to 22 contain the snippet of code that comes with the Color-Picker plug-in to make it work with a particular textbox field. We place this inside the asp:Content element that matches with the ContentPlace-Holder named head. HTML helpers generate an HTML **id** attribute based on the name of the variable. In our case, we're wiring up the color picker to the element with the **id** Color. This will make the color picker work, allowing you to select any color in the spectrum.

So, we have your Topic being managed with a fancy color picker, as well as implementing Equals(). Now it's time to introduce another feature of

MVC 2.0, templated views, which help reduce the number of views we need to implement while we're at the prototyping stage of application development.

Adding Thoughts with Templated Views

We now have topics set up. Our next feature is to collect our thoughts. We want to display thoughts as a list. Since we've already covered how to list models, we'll introduce a new way of rendering them in views.

In MVC 2.0, templated views let us define a generic way of displaying data without having to generate a custom view for it. But before we can get to templated views, we'll need to test-drive our controller:

workingWithControllers/ThoughtControllerTest.cs

```
[TestFixture]
public class ThoughtControllerTest
{
  [Test]
  public void Should_List_Thoughts_When_Index_Is_Called()
  {
    var result = (ViewResult) new ThoughtController().Index();

    Assert.AreEqual(Thought.Thoughts, result.ViewData.Model);
  }
}
```

By now these kinds of controller tests are starting to look familiar. We expect that the model is of type List<Thought>, and the name of the view to be rendered is called Index. To make the test pass, we'll need to implement our Thought model.

workingWithControllers/Thought.cs

```
public class Thought
{
  public static List<Thought> Thoughts = new List<Thought>
  {
   new Thought{
    Id = 1,
    Name = "Learn c# 3.5",
    Topic = Topic.Topics.
      Find(topic => topic.Name == "Work")},
   new Thought{
    Id = 2,
    Name = "Build a Killer Web Application",
    Topic = Topic.Topics.
    Find(topic => topic.Name == "Home")}
  };
```

```
    public int Id { get; set; }
    public Topic Topic { get; set; }
    public string Name { get; set; }
}
```

The Thought model has three properties: Id, Topic, and Name. It also has a **static** list of Thoughts filled with some sample data. With a Thought defined, we can now try to make the test pass:

workingWithControllers/ThoughtController.cs

```
public class ThoughtController : Controller
{
  //
  // GET: /Thought/

  public ActionResult Index()
  {
    ViewData.Model = Thought.Thoughts;
    return View();
  }
}
```

Similar to previous lists (such as Topic and Todo), we assign the collection List<Thought> to the ViewData.Model. On to rendering a view for this action. This time we'll use a templated view instead of generating another strongly typed view.

Templated views are added to the Views/Shared directory. If you're familiar with Rails, they act as a type of scaffolding, allowing us to get a page up and running with basic information. For our example, we'll be creating an Index.aspx in the Shared directory for our Index() action to use. If we want to build a strongly typed view later, MVC will simply ignore the file in the Shared directory.

Let's look at a snippet of the Index.aspx templated view:

workingWithControllers/Shared/Index.aspx

```
Line 1  <h2>Index</h2>
    -   <table>
    -     <% var modelList = (IEnumerable) Model; %>
    -     <% foreach (var item in modelList) { %>
    5     <tr>
    -       <td>
    -         <% ViewData["item"] = item; %>
    -         <%= Html.Display("item") %>
    -       </td>
    10    </tr>
    -     <% } %>
    -   </table>
```

On line 3, we cast the Model to an IEnumerable. This makes sure we're dealing with a list, which we then run through for each item it has.

Once we're inside the **foreach** loop, we assign the item to the ViewData on line 7. We'll use the Display() method to render the contents of the item, or in this case the Thought on line 8. We can't use the strongly typed methods in templated views, because they require that the model also be typed. Using the nongeneric helper method Display() lets us render any model we throw at it.

Using templated views to prototype pages allows us to focus on getting early feedback about our application. Later you can revisit those pages to improve the design and make them more usable.

After displaying a list of Thoughts, let's now work on creating them.

Populating a Drop-Down List

Doing a brain dump of Thoughts is an important step in getting things done. To create a Thought model, we're going to need a list of Topics. This is most easily done with a drop-down menu.

Let's start by writing a test to assert that a list of Topics is accessible when we're trying to create a Thought:

workingWithControllers/ThoughtControllerTest.cs

```
Line 1  [Test]
        public void Should_Provide_A_List_Of_Topics_For_Creating_New_Thoughts()
        {
          var expectedListItems =
     5      Topic.Topics.ConvertAll(topic =>
              new SelectListItem
              {Text = topic.Name, Value = topic.Id.ToString()});

          var result = (ViewResult)new ThoughtController().Create();
    10
          var firstTopic =
            ((List<SelectListItem>) result.ViewData["Topics"])[0];
          Assert.AreEqual(expectedListItems[0].Value, firstTopic.Value);
          Assert.AreEqual(expectedListItems[0].Text, firstTopic.Text);
    15  }
```

It's good to remember that the ViewData can be populated with things other than the model. In this case, we're adding a new key called View-Name["Topics"]. Unfortunately, the SelectListItem does not implement Equals, so we cannot compare the actual lists and have to resort to comparing individual values on line 12. Here we convert the Topic **class** into a SelectListItem class using the ConvertAll() method.

To make this test pass, we could implement ThoughtController as follows:

workingWithControllers/ThoughtController.cs

```
Line 1  public ActionResult Create()
     2  {
     3    ViewData["Topics"] = Topic.Topics.ConvertAll(topic =>
     4      new SelectListItem {
     5      Text = topic.Name, Value = topic.Id.ToString()
     6      });
     7    return View();
     8  }
```

On line 3, we convert the Topics into SelectListItems and assign it to the ViewData. This makes our test pass.

Now we'll generate the Views/Thought/Create.aspx view. The Create.aspx view for a Thought is a little different from the Topic because we're not just picking a random color but a set list of Topics themselves. The HTML helper class has a method DropDownList() that creates a drop-down of items for display. We need to populate ViewData with a list of Topics so that it is available to the view.

The following is a snippet of the file that relates to the drop-down list:

workingWithControllers/Thought/Create.aspx

```
<p>
  <label for="Topic">Topic:</label>
  <%= Html.DropDownList("Topic.Id",
    (List<SelectListItem>) ViewData["Topics"])%>
</p>
```

The first thing to note is one of the parameters of the DropDownList is Topic.Id. Use this notation to reference properties of other properties, such as how Thought has a property Topic() that has the property Id. We also see that we had to cast the ViewData["Topics"] as a collection List<SelectListItem>.

That takes care of the view and allows us to have our drop-down filled with the topics we input earlier.

Since we've already covered creating models a few times before for both Todo and Topic, it's time for you to strike out on your own. Try test-driving the second part of the create action of the ThoughtController. Maybe try adding another an attribute to Thought, such as how much it's bugging you. You can check your answers against the final solution of GetOrganized in the GetOrganizedFinal directory in the downloadable code.

Now we can move on to learning how to get controllers to pass control directly to another controller. This is our final feature of this chapter: converting thoughts into actions.

4.4 Controllers Talking to Controllers

After you've finished the brain dump of Thoughts, you need to move into an action plan. The process of *Getting Things Done* [All02], according to David Allen, is to decide on whether a Thought is actionable. If something is actionable, then it's going to have to have a well-defined outcome and take you more than five minutes to complete. An action also must be completable in the near future.

If the Thought is actionable, then we'll convert it to a Todo item. Otherwise, we'll either delete it, save it for future reference, or set it as a reminder for some future date when we could perhaps complete it.

For now, we will work on processing an actionable thought. In Section 6.1, *Processing Thoughts Take II: Actionable or Maybe Someday*, on page 116, we'll work on the other pathways.

Displaying a Thought for Processing

We need to display a single thought so that we either action it or not. The idea is not to go in any order. This means avoiding a list of Thoughts and picking which one we're going to process. Instead, we'll start with the oldest Thought, which reduces procrastination. No more avoiding the Thoughts like "fill in time sheets for last week." The first test is to grab a thought for display.

workingWithControllers/ThoughtControllerTest.cs

```
Line 1   using System.Linq;

         public class ThoughtControllerTest
         {
   5       [Test]
           public void Should_Display_First_Thought_When_Processing_Thoughts()
           {
             var expectedThought = Thought.Thoughts.First();
             var result = (ViewResult) new ThoughtController().Process();
  10         Assert.AreEqual(expectedThought, result.ViewData.Model);
           }
         }
```

Because we're using Language Integrated Query (LINQ) in our test code, we add a reference on line 1. LINQ uses extension methods to enhance the capabilities of IEnumerable classes. The LINQ property we use here is First on line 8. This pulls the first item from the list of Thoughts (see the sidebar on page 78). The rest of the test should seem familiar. To make the test pass, we'll try the following:

```
workingWithControllers/ThoughtController.cs
//
// GET: /Thought/Process

public ActionResult Process()
{
  ViewData.Model = Thought.Thoughts.First();
  return View();
}
```

Here we assign the model to be the first element of the Thought collection. This means we need a view. This view will be customized from the template that MVC generates for us. We can start with the default Details template. Here is what your page might look like:

```
workingWithControllers/Process.aspx
Line 1  <h2>Process Thoughts</h2>
     -  <fieldset>
     -    <legend>Thought</legend>
     -    <p>
     5      <b><%= Html.Encode(Model.Name) %></b>
     -    </p>
     -    <p>
     -      Topic:
     -      <%= Html.Encode(Model.Topic.Name) %>
    10    </p>
     -  </fieldset>
     -  <% using (Html.BeginForm("Convert", "Todo")) {%>
     -  <fieldset>
     -  <legend>Actionable</legend>
    15  <p>
     -    <%= Html.Hidden("Name", Model.Name) %>
     -    <%= Html.Hidden("Topic.Id", Model.Topic.Id) %>
     -    Well Defined Outcome:<%= Html.TextBox("Outcome") %>
     -  </p>
    20  <p>
     -    <input type="submit" value="Create Action" />
     -    </p>
     -    </fieldset>
     -  <% } %>
```

On line 2, we create a heading for the page to include the name of the Thought and its associated Topic. On the second part of the page, we create a new HTML **form** tag on line 12. The HTML **form** will post to the URL http://localhost/Todo/Convert. This action will create a new Todo from the Thought. The information is posted as hidden fields with the Hidden() method on line 16. The text field Outcome is passed as a regular parameter, unlike the other two fields that will bind to the Todo model.

Now for the conversion itself.

Converting a Thought into a To-Do

Once we've found a Thought that is actionable, we need to turn it into a Todo. Most of the work of creating a new Todo is already done. However, we need to account for the new properties we've just added, such as Outcome and Topic. Our next test will be to work on the conversion action in the TodoController. After the conversion is complete, we end up redirecting to the ThoughtController's action Process() instead of going to a Convert.aspx view. This is the first time we'll see a controller talking to another controller in MVC:

workingWithControllers/TodoControllerTest.cs

```
Line 1   [Test]
         public void Should_Convert_A_Thought_To_A_Todo()
         {
           var expectedTodo = new Todo
     5     {
            Title = "Build a killer web site",
            Outcome = "Site has 100 visitors per day",
            Topic = Topic.Topics[0]
           };
    10
           var thought = new Thought
             {Name = "Build a killer web site", Topic = Topic.Topics[0]};

           var result = (RedirectToRouteResult) new TodoController().
    15       Convert(thought, "Site has 100 visitors per day");

           Assert.Contains(expectedTodo, Todo.ThingsToBeDone);
           Assert.IsFalse(Thought.Thoughts.Contains(thought));
           Assert.AreEqual("Process", result.RouteValues["action"]);
    20     Assert.AreEqual("Thought", result.RouteValues["controller"]);
         }
```

We are testing that the new Convert() action takes a Thought as well as a Outcome. On line 4, we define the Todo we're expecting. We perform the conversion on line 15. After that, the assertion on line 17 ensures that the old Thought is deleted, and a new Todo is there.

> **Edge Cases and Unit Testing**
>
> You might have wondered while writing this code, what happens when you've run out of Thoughts and the list is empty? In this case, we'd write another test that specifies that condition and make the code work for it. For example, you might redirect the user to the main page of the application and post a warning to TempData saying that there are no more thoughts to process.
>
> We call this an *edge case*. Using TDD helps you work through these cases one at a time. Having a full suite of tests that covers all the edge cases ensures your code is evolving without producing as many defects.

To deal with the new properties, we're first going to have to modify the Todo **class**:

workingWithControllers/Todo.cs

```
public class Todo
{
// ...
// add new fields
public string Outcome { get; set; }
public Topic Topic { get; set; }
// ... implement equals
}
```

We needed to modify our original Todo to allow for the new fields, as well as implement the Equals() method (omitted from the earlier code). Here we added two new fields to the Todo class: Outcome, a **string**, and a Topic. This lets us map the fields over from a Thought.

Now, on to the TodoController's Convert() action:

workingWithControllers/TodoController.cs

```
Line 1  public ActionResult Convert(Thought thought, string outcome)
   -    {
   -      var newTodo = new Todo
   -      {
   5        Title = thought.Name,
   -        Outcome = outcome,
   -        Topic = Topic.
   -        Topics.Find(topic =>
   -          topic.Id == thought.Topic.Id)
   10     };
```

What Is Refactoring?

Back in Chapter 2, *Test-Driven Development*, on page 17, we introduced the TDD cycle of "red, green, refactor." We haven't touched on an actual refactoring until now. Refactoring is a way to change our code to reduce duplication, make it more readable, and enhance extensibility. Following the DRY principle, we try to avoid rewriting the same code twice. However, if you don't have unit tests, how do you know the refactoring has not changed the behavior or created a bug?

Most refactorings are reversible. For example, Extract Method (ReSharper shortcut `Ctrl+Alt+M`) can be reversed with Inline Method (ReSharper shortcut `Ctrl+Alt+N`). *Refactoring: Improving the Design of Existing Code* (FBB+99) is an excellent reference for this topic and applies to any language you work in.

```
      CreateTodo(newTodo);

      Thought.Thoughts.RemoveAll(thoughtToRemove =>
15        thoughtToRemove.Name == thought.Name);

      return RedirectToAction("Process", "Thought");
    }

20  private void CreateTodo(Todo todo)
    {
      Todo.ThingsToBeDone.Add(todo);
    }
```

Converting the incoming Thought to the Todo means mapping the properties over. We created a private method called CreateTodo() on line 20 because it would have produced a duplicate line with the TodoController's Create() method. This is a good example of refactoring (the sidebar on the current page). Using the DRY principle, we're reusing the same create logic in both the Convert() and Create() actions. We remove the converted Thought on line 15.

Finally, on line 17, we have the controller talking to another controller. The magic method RedirectToAction() has an additional parameter that specifies we want it to go to a different controller. We can now convert our Thoughts into Todos. In Section 6.1, *Processing Thoughts Take II:*

Actionable or Maybe Someday, on page 116, we'll add more ways of processing Thoughts while learning new ways to customize our views.

Up Next

We've learned how to move beyond CRUD operations and started driving out our GetOrganized sample application. We also practiced test-driving controllers and learned about testing the Equals() method. In the next chapter, we'll continue our focus on controllers and see how they are the centerpiece of ASP.NET MVC. We'll learn about how to manage the state and transfer of information with the HttpSession object and upload and download files.

*The best years of your life are the ones in which you decide
your problems are your own. You do not blame them on
your mother, the ecology, or the president. You realize that
you control your own destiny.*
  ▶ Albert Ellis

Chapter 5

Managing State and Files with Controllers

Controllers are the heavy lifters of the MVC framework. We use them to coordinate all activity between the user and the model. Up to this point we have implemented controllers, but we haven't covered all of their capabilities. There are a few tricks we have yet to learn that will help us develop web applications more efficiently. In this chapter, we will learn about the additional features of controllers: action filters, HttpSessionState, and file manipulation.

GetOrganized needs to restrict access to certain pages. Action filters will help us do that. We'll also need to keep track of what our users are doing while they are logged in by using HttpSessionState, and we'll see how to attach files to our Thoughts. We'll use MVCContrib,[1] an open source project that offers many enhancements to the MVC framework, to help improve the readability of our controller tests.

We have already learned that controllers direct models to views, but now we're going to look at how they can help us manage state and other external resources like files. Let's begin by looking at how controllers fit into the overall picture of the MVC framework.

5.1 Enabling Filters and Results with Controllers

Understanding how action filters and results work will help you see how controllers are created and how control is passed to them within MVC.

---

1. http://www.codeplex.com/mvccontrib

The controller is the entry point of our program and acts as the coordinator between the model and one or more views. From the request input from the browser, the controller takes the appropriate action. Each action interacts with a model and determines which view or other controller to send the response to. Since actions are where we spend a lot of time testing and coding, it is no surprise that MVC has built extension points into the framework in the form of action results and filters.

In this section, we'll learn how filters can help us roll up common functionality, such as security, into easy-to-apply labels to our actions. We'll also work through how action filters can make returning non-HTML resources such as files simpler than ever. Finally, we'll touch on how to leverage the HttpContext and store information from request to request.

Extending Actions with Action Filters

Action filters are C# attributes that you can apply to the controller or its actions. These filters perform an operation before the action is executed. Action filters are an example of *declarative programming*, aptly named after declaring what we want to accomplish up front.

We saw our first action filter, [HttpPost], in Section 3.3, *Creating a To-Do*, on page 44. We'll now see in depth how they work and when we use them. For example, an alternative to [HttpPost] is as follows:

controllers/ActionFilters.cs

```
[AcceptVerbs(HttpVerbs.Post)]
public ActionResult Create(Todo item)
{
    // create Todo here
}
```

In this case, the action filter is the [AcceptVerbs] attribute, and it's applied to the Create(Todo todo) action. Another example of an action filter is the [Authorize] attribute. You add this filter to controllers to restrict access so only users who are logged in can use it. An example of this is as follows:

controllers/ActionFilters.cs

```
[Authorize]
public ActionResult SecureMe()
{
    // users cannot get here unless they are logged in
}
```

> \\// **Joe Asks...**
> ~£
> ∼ **When Do I Use Output Caching?**
>
> Caching at the output level is normally reserved for things like the web application's home page. Home pages generally don't change based on individual user information and so are safe to output cache. Caching keeps a copy of the output that was generated from the first request. That makes the second request render a lot faster. However, you don't want to use caching for every action. For example, if you have an action that uses specific information from a user's profile, then caching would show other users' information.
>
> Output caching is not the only form of caching. Caching data is another way to speed up page load times. Once we start working with NHibernate in Chapter 8, *Persisting Your Models*, on page 161, we'll automatically get a certain level of data caching by default. If you want to really get serious about data caching, you should read more about the second-level caching available to NHibernate with the open source server memcached.*
>
> ---
> *. http://www.cnblogs.com/RicCC/archive/2007/10/13/NHibernate-Memcached.html

Action filters contain generic behavior that you can reuse on multiple actions. For example, another useful action filter to be aware of is [HandleError], which redirects the user in case of exceptions. We'll talk more about that in Section 11.2, *Using an Action Filter to Handle Errors*, on page 228.

The action filter [OutputCache] (see the *Joe Asks...* on this page) caches requests and improves performance of frequently requested actions. In Chapter 11, *Security, Error Handling, and Logging*, on page 219, we'll create our own action filters by inheriting from the class FilterAction. In this chapter, we'll learn to apply the [Authorize] attribute in Section 5.2, *Logging In*, on page 88.

We can also author our own action filters. This is something that we'll do in Section 9.4, *Creating a Custom Action Filter*, on page 189. Writing custom action filters is another reason why MVC is such an extensible framework.

Action filters are just one piece of the puzzle. To round out our understanding of controllers, you need to know about ActionResults.

Directing to Different Content Types with ActionResults

As we learned in Section 3.2, *Our First Test*, on page 35, action results are the return type of controllers. So far we've learned how to render a view and redirect to another action. This covers two subtypes of Action-Result, the abstract class that all controllers use as their return type.

The ViewResult is a subtype we've used to direct to a view that displays information, such as the Index() action on the TodoController. Here is an example of an action returning a ViewResult:

controllers/ActionResults.cs

```
public ActionResult Display()
{
  return View(ModelToDisplay);
}
```

What's interesting here is we've introduced a shortcut for how to set a model that is different than covered in the previous chapters. Instead of ViewData.Model = ModelToDisplay, we can accomplish the same thing with View(ModelToDisplay).

The second subtype of ActionResult is the RedirectToRouteResult. This result redirects control to another action or a different controller altogether. Here is a sample of using RedirectToAction():

controllers/ActionResults.cs

```
public ActionResult Redirector()
{
  return RedirectToAction("DifferentAction","DifferentController");
}
```

Notice that the first argument of RedirectToAction(string action, string controller) is the action we want to send the control to, and the second is the controller. We can omit the second argument if we want to stay within the same controller, like going from Create() to Index() on the successful creation of a model. In both cases, we never create an action result directly using return new RedirectToRouteResult{ //...}. Instead, we use methods that are available from the base Controller, which all controllers inherit from.

MVC offers many other types of action results. The most useful action results are as follows:

- JsonResult: Returns models in JavaScript Object Notation (JSON)
- ContentResult: Returns plain text
- FilePathResult: Returns a file from a path on the server
- FileStreamResult: Returns a file from a stream

Joe Asks...

When Would I Use JSON?

JSON is a helpful format to allow JavaScript libraries such as jQuery to manipulate objects, as opposed to using XML or HTML. Using JSON allows us to focus on becoming proficient in JavaScript, instead of having to master XPath. An object like Thought renders in JSON as follows:

```
var thought = {
        "Id": 0,
        "Topic": {
                "Id": 1,
                "Color": {
                        "R": 255,
                        "G": 0,
                        "B": 0,
                        "A": 255,
                        "IsKnownColor": true,
                        "IsEmpty": false,
                        "IsNamedColor": true,
                        "IsSystemColor": false,
                        "Name": "Red"
                },
                "Name": "Work"
        },
        "Name": "Learn C# 3.5"
}
```

Accessing the object within JavaScript with JSON becomes much easier with thought.Topic.Color, instead of using XPath to access the same field like this:

```
document.evaluate("thought/Topic/Color", document, null,
        XPathResult.ANY_TYPE, null)
```

JsonResult is useful for Ajax requests and often works with the ContentResult (these action results will be covered in Chapter 7, *Composing Views with Ajax and Partials*, on page 139). Most Internet applications need to allow users to download files, and MVC does this with FilePathResult and FileStreamResult. FilePathResult uses files located on the file system of the web server; we will use them in Section 5.5, *Manipulating Files*, on page 107. FileStreamResult takes any output stream, such as streaming a file out of the database.

Some action results are useful in specific situations but not used as frequently:

- JavascriptResult: Returns a JavaScript file
- FileContentResult: Returns a file as binary data
- EmptyResult: Returns nothing

JavascriptResult can aggregate all our application's JavaScript into one simple file reference. This is handy if there are a lot of jQuery plug-ins, each having a separate JavaScript file. Instead of having to add a large head section to your HTML file, imagine just using one with the help of this action result.

FileContentResult is a specialized kind of file return where you must return a Byte array, perhaps for graphics manipulation. Generally, we're better off using the FileStreamResult because it is faster and friendlier to our web server's memory usage.

EmptyContent is for rare situations where you would like to return something directly to the HttpResponse, such as when serving some static HTML fragment. Doing this short-circuits the normal pattern of MVC and is not recommended unless there is absolutely no alternative.

Although these are the default action results that come with MVC, the reason that the framework designers created ActionResult as an abstract class was for extensibility by developers like us. In Chapter 10, *Building RESTful Web Services*, on page 199, we'll see how to use MVCContrib's XmlResult to return XML from an action.

IControllerFactory: Where Controllers Are Born

It's helpful to understand how web requests are processed, because it puts the IControllerFactory in the context of the request pipeline. When a request comes in from the browser, it is handed off to the web server and passed through the UrlRoutingModule.

This module creates an MVCRouteHandler where the request gets executed in the method ProcessRequest(). This method gets a reference to the IControllerFactory interface responsible for creating an instance of our controller and calling the controller's Execute() method. Execute() is where our actions are called.

The other main function of the MVCRouteHandler is that it hooks up the HttpSessionState so we can use it between requests to store information

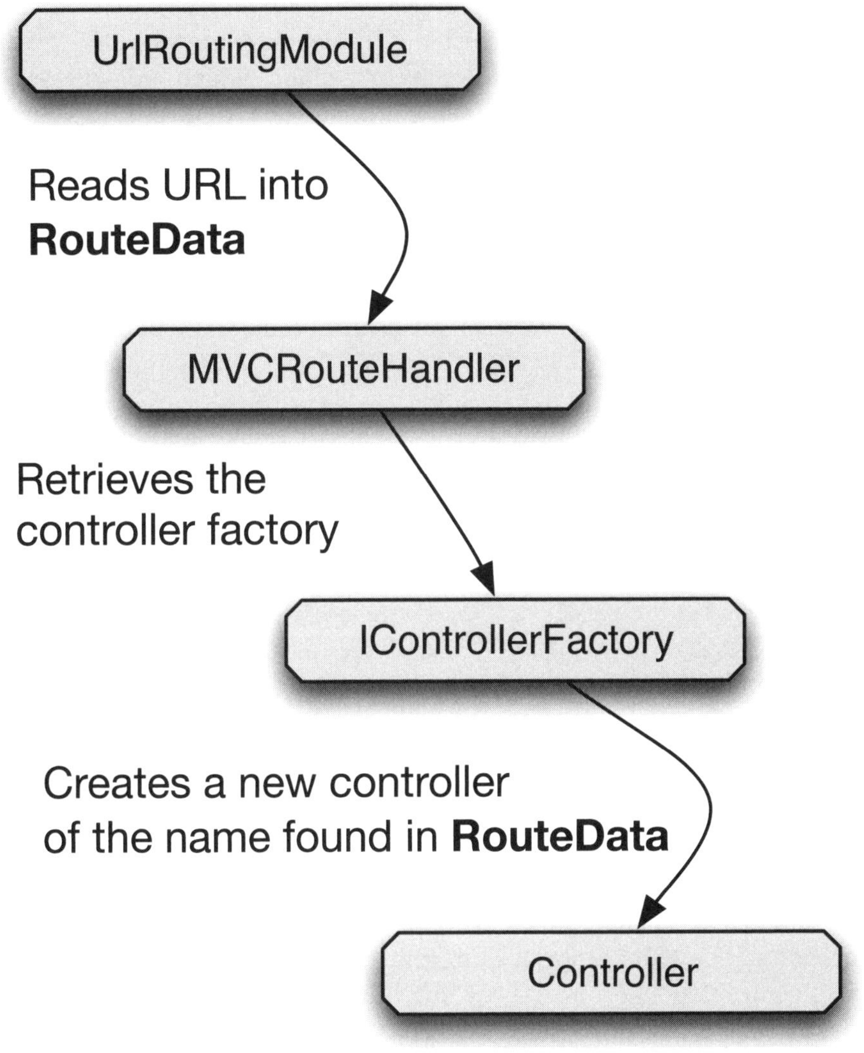

Figure 5.1: CONTROLLERS ARE CREATED BY THE ICONTROLLERFACTORY BASED ON A NAME INSIDE THE URL.

unique to each user. Controllers populate and manipulate HttpSession-State. These types of interactions between controllers and HttpSession-State will be covered in Section 5.4, *Storing Information in Memory*, on page 97 (see Figure 5.1).

The birthplace of a controller is the DefaultControllerFactory, which implements the IControllerFactory interface. The factory knows what type of controller to create using the RouteData class, which was set when the UrlRoutingModule ran earlier. For example, http://localhost/Todo parses Todo to create a new instance of type TodoController.

This factory interface allows us to extend how controllers are built; this extensibility helps us implement dependency injection. We'll cover this topic in Section 9.2, *Using Inversion of Control with the IControllerFactory*, on page 181 when we use MVCContrib to inject the database layer into controllers.

The term Inversion of Control (IoC) is mentioned a lot these days; it has become synonymous with dependency injection. We pass the behavior to the constructor, effectively "injecting" it into the object, as in new SomeController(IDatabaseConnector connector). The actual logic for the database is injected into SomeController. This helps us test each class separately.

Let's look at how action filters help add a user login to our application.

5.2 Logging In

We will apply some of this theory back into our code. Every web application has a login page, unless you have a central authorization service such as Active Directory handling that for you. For GetOrganized, we don't want other users to access our thoughts and to-do lists (like our boss finding out we are planning on asking for a well-deserved raise). For these next few features, we'll work with action filters as well as the standard Microsoft Membership API to implement the feature of logging in.

Out-of-the-Box Authentication

MVC gives us rudimentary security installed by default in the AccountController. We can administer all this from the ASP.NET Web Site Administration Tool. We'll set up our database so that we can save user information permanently, and we'll also learn how to use the action filter [Authorize] to prompt users to log in on secured pages.

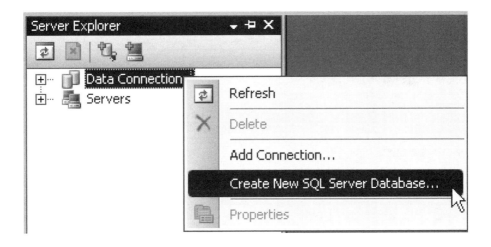

Figure 5.2: RIGHT-CLICKING DATA CONNECTIONS WILL ALLOW YOU TO CREATE A NEW DATABASE.

Set Up SQL Server for the Membership Provider

We're going to take a small detour from working with controllers to get our database set up. This isn't an MVC-specific requirement, but it is a feature of ASP.NET that takes only a few steps to configure.

If you've installed SQL Server Express, the MVC framework creates a database that stores user credentials as well as roles and groups. Simply rename the database file from aspnetdb.mdf to GetOrganized.mdf.

If you've installed the full version of SQL Server, you'll need to do the extra steps outlined in this section. It's important to cover the next steps even if you have only the Express edition, because most production environments are going to use the Enterprise version of SQL Server. Therefore, you should be aware of how to properly configure your application to work with it.

First we'll need to create a new database called GetOrganized for the application. This is done from either within Visual Studio on the Server Tools tab or through SQL Server Management Studio. In Figure 5.2, we can see how to do this from Visual Studio. This opens a wizard that asks for the SQL Server's name (localhost), authentication type (Windows), and name of the database (GetOrganized).

We also have to modify the Web.config file with the proper connection string.[2] Here is an excerpt from Web.config where the connection string has been replaced by our new one:

```
<connectionStrings>
        <add name="ApplicationServices"
            connectionString="data source=localhost;
            Initial Catalog=GetOrganized;Integrated Security=SSPI;"
            providerName="System.Data.SqlClient"/>
</connectionStrings>
```

The parts of the connection string that are more important to note are the data source and Initial Catalog. The data source is the network location of SQL Server, in this case localhost. The Initial Catalog is the name of the database, and we've set it to GetOrganized. Next, we need to generate the tables and (yuck!) stored procedures necessary to have the membership API to work. In Section 11.1, *Customizing the ASP.NET Membership Provider*, on page 224, we'll work through replacing those stored procedures using NHibernate.

Test-driven developers' biggest complaint about stored procedures is that they impair testing because business logic ends up in the data layer. It is also hard to test large stored procedures and simulate database-specific features such as triggers. Sometimes, we cannot avoid them because of other restrictions, and they've been used successfully in many projects. However, development will go faster if you use regular SQL queries and commands, because these are much easier to test. Better yet, use a framework like NHibernate, and avoid writing SQL altogether.

If this is the first time you are using SQL Server since it was installed, you'll need to enable a Named Pipes communication configuration. This is because we're using Windows authentication to connect to the database, and this is not allowed over TCP/IP. We use a program called Configuration Manager to do this (see Figure 5.3, on the facing page). It is found under the Windows Start menu and SQL Server tab.

Now it's time to fill the database with tables and stored procedures to support logging in, as well as users' roles.

We'll need to use the command-line program aspnet_regsql.exe, so open a command window using the Visual Studio command prompt shortcut.

---

2. A helpful resource to find the proper connection string is http://www.connectionstrings.com.

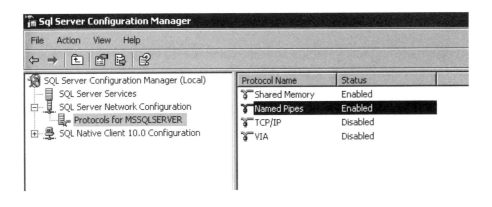

Figure 5.3: Configuring Named Pipes is required for using command-line SQL.

This useful utility can repair ASP.NET, as well as manage the ASP.NET authentication database. There are several options to this command, but we will use only three to get this job done. The -A mr adds both the membership (m) and the role (r) schema to the database. The -d Get Organized specifies the database to use; -E authenticates with the current Windows account.

```
Setting environment for using Microsoft Visual Studio 2008 x86 tools.

C:\Program Files\Microsoft Visual Studio 9.0\VC>
  cd C:\WINDOWS\Microsoft.NET\Framework\v2.0.50727

C:\WINDOWS\Microsoft.NET\Framework\v2.0.50727>
    aspnet_regsql -A mr -d GetOrganized -E

Start adding the following features:
Membership
RoleManager
........
Finished.
C:\WINDOWS\Microsoft.NET\Framework\v2.0.50727>
```

If you're unfamiliar with using the command-line tool, don't worry. We're first going to run a command called cd to change directories to the .NET runtime for the 2.0 version of the framework. This is where aspnet_regsql.exe is located. We then need to execute aspnet_regsql.exe to build the database and stored procedures so that authentication works.

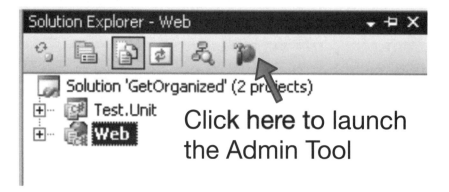

Figure 5.4: CLICKING THE GLOBE AND HAMMER ICON LAUNCHES THE ADMINISTRATION WEBSITE.

aspnet_regsql.exe has other uses as well, such as fixing up corrupted installations of ASP.NET. If for some reason you installed Visual Studio before you installed Internet Information Services (IIS), this utility can fix that as well.

It is also useful to generate a SQL script that we can run on different environments by replacing the -d option with -sqlexportonly file name.sql.

Once the database is configured properly, fire up the ASP.NET Web Site Administration Tool by clicking the icon in the Solution Explorer in Visual Studio (see Figure 5.4). You will use this site to administrate your ASP.NET MVC application.

After it launches, navigate to the Security tab. This tab is where we administer both users and roles. The site is for more than just managing security, since it allows us to modify other application settings, such as our connection string. However, most of the time it's just as easy to modify the Web.config file directly.

Remember that any data we modify here is only good for our local database. If we are setting up roles and users for an application, a SQL script is the right place for those items to be stored. This ensures that every database where we install our application is consistent.

 Joe Asks. . .

What Is the Difference Between Authentication and Authorization?

Authentication is the process of identifying that someone is who they say they are. For example, is jonathan19 really Jonathan McCracken? Authentication takes the form of a login screen or a token, often a browser cookie, that is passed back in every request.

Authorization means who can see or do what. Does jonathan19 belong to the group Administrators that is allowed to edit the main page of the site? Authorization takes the form of groups or roles that control what operations and data are exposed to their members.

Adding the (Authorize) Attribute

Let's secure our pages by adding the (Authorize) action filter to the TodoController. We apply the (Authorize) attribute to the controller or its actions. Here we are applying it to the entire controller:

controllers/ActionFilters.cs

```
[Authorize]
public class TodoController : Controller
{
  //rest of class goes here
}
```

When we try to access any URL starting with Todo, such as /Todo/Create, we are redirected to the login screen. Registering for the site is done through the site itself or through the ASP.NET Web Site Administration Tool. The AccountController, generated with every new MVC application, is set up to handle registration, login, "remember me" functionality, and password reset. Back in Section 3.2, *Our First Test*, on page 35, we talked about generating unit tests for these features.

Testing Authorization

Although it is tempting to just apply the attribute [Authorize] on controllers we want to protect, it is still a best practice to have unit tests cover this. Better yet, we are going to drive it from our unit tests. Testing C# attributes requires the use of the System.Reflection namespace, because they are accessible only in this way. Reflection is useful to access methods, fields, and attributes of classes through inspecting the Type of the member at runtime. To write our first test, we'll need to use the TodoController type and read off all of its attributes, looking for the System.Web.Mvc.AuthorizeAttribute.

controllers/TodoControllerTest.cs

```
[Test]
public void Should_Be_Logged_In_To_Do_Anything_With_Todos()
{
  typeof (TodoController).GetCustomAttributes(false).
    ToList().ForEach(Console.WriteLine);
}
//Output is:
//System.Web.Mvc.AuthorizeAttribute
```

As shown in the example, the secret of reflection is the typeof() keyword or alternatively GetType(), a method on every instance of an Object in C#. Either of these will give us the same list of operations to access members of that type, in this case the TodoController. After acquiring the type of the class, we use the method GetCustomAttributes(bool searchBase-Classes) to return a list that we convert to a List<object> of attributes we are looking for.

Let's move on to writing an assertion for this in the same test and removing the Console.WriteLine().

controllers/TodoControllerTest.cs

```
[Test]
public void Should_Be_Logged_In_To_Do_Anything_With_Todos()
{
  Assert.IsTrue(typeof (TodoController).
    GetCustomAttributes(false).
    Any(o => o.GetType() == typeof (AuthorizeAttribute)));
}
```

The test passes, because we already added the attribute to the TodoController. We had to use a little LINQ to filter the list by attributes using the Any() method. Note that we exercise the GetType() method since we have an instance of an object instead of a class where we use typeof().

This assertion looks like a prime candidate for reuse and therefore belongs in a new helper test class we'll name TestHelper. Using Re-Sharper to extract the method (Ctrl+Alt+M), we get the method into a form we can reuse locally.

controllers/TodoControllerTest.cs

```
[Test]
public void Should_Be_Logged_In_To_Do_Anything_With_Todos()
{
  AssertIsAuthorized(typeof (TodoController));
}

private static void AssertIsAuthorized(ICustomAttributeProvider type)
{
  Assert.IsTrue(type.GetCustomAttributes(false).
    Any(o => o.GetType() == typeof (AuthorizeAttribute)));
}
```

While refactoring the assertion into a method, we introduced a parameter to replace the typeof(TodoController) and made it reusable for other controllers. We gave it the type ICustomerAttributeProvider to ensure that only types with attributes assignable to them are passed in.

The next step is to move the method into its own **class**. We create the class TestHelper in a new folder called Helper. Then we'll use ReSharper to move the method there. ReSharper has the shortcut F6 for the Move refactoring. The gotcha with the ReSharper Move refactoring is that the member must be static.

controllers/TodoControllerTest.cs

```
Line 1   //Inside TodoControllerTest.cs
  -      [Test]
  -      public void Should_Be_Logged_In_To_Do_Anything_With_Todos()
  -      {
  5        TestHelper.AssertIsAuthorized(typeof (TodoController));
  -      }
  -
  -      //Inside TestHelper.cs
  -      namespace Test.Unit.Helper
 10      {
  -       public class TestHelper
  -       {
  -        public static void AssertIsAuthorized(ICustomAttributeProvider type)
  -        {
 15        Assert.IsTrue(type.GetCustomAttributes(false).
  -        Any(o => o.GetType() == typeof (AuthorizeAttribute)));
  -        }
  -       }
  -      }
```

Notice how in 5 we call our new TestHelper's static method AssertIsAuthorized(ICustomAttributeProvider type). Thanks to this refactoring, we will now be able to use this for all future authorization tests of controllers.

Taking this one step further, we can reuse what we've done for actions. We will write a test that covers both Create() and Create(Todo todo) that restricts them to logged-in users only:

controllers/TodoControllerTest.cs

```
[Test]
public void Should_Be_Logged_In_To_Create()
{
  TestHelper.AssertIsAuthorized(
    typeof(TodoController), "Create");
  TestHelper.AssertIsAuthorized(
    typeof(TodoController), "Create", typeof(Todo));
}

//...inside TodoController.cs we add [Authorize] to both methods

[Authorize]
public ActionResult Create() { // omitted }

[Authorize]
[HttpPost]
public ActionResult Create(Todo todo)  { // omitted }
```

Both assertions in our test are now producing compile errors. In order to get the code to compile, we overload AssertIsAuthorized(ICustomAttribute-Provider type, string action, params Type[]) to take the name of the action and its parameters. The C# keyword params allows us to pass zero or more of the same object and results in an object array, in this case a Type array. It's also interesting to note that when adding [Authorize] to the second Create(Todo todo), we now have multiple attributes. This is perfectly acceptable but can become unreadable if there are more than two. When that happens, it's a best practice to put them all on the same line.

Now let's get this test to pass:

controllers/TodoControllerTest.cs

```
public static void AssertIsAuthorized(Type type, string action,
    params Type[] parameters)
{
  AssertIsAuthorized(type.GetMethod(action, parameters));
}
```

The test passes, and all it took was using another method of reflection, GetMethod(). We were able to reuse our first TestHelper method and avoid further duplication of code. We now have a class that can test both controllers and their actions.

Now that we know a little about MVCContrib, let's see how it helps us test MVC routing.

5.3 Testing Routes in MVC

Routing is the backbone of MVC. We've seen how the friendly URLs map to controller actions and make it easy for search engines to index and for users to remember their favorite pages. Since we're working on covering our entire application with unit tests, it follows that we need to focus on testing these URLs. With a little help from MVCContrib, this becomes an easy task.

Let's briefly revisit our TodoController and its Edit() action. To test this route, we want to send the Title of the Todo we want to edit.

```
controllers/TodoControllerTest.cs
[Test]
public void Should_Route_To_Edit_Page_With_Title()
{
  "~/Todo/Edit?title=Get-A-LOT-MORE-milk".
    ShouldMapTo<TodoController>(x => x.Edit("Get-A-LOT-MORE-milk"));
}
```

MVCContrib allows us to write a simple route test like the previous one. We can test how the string ought to be parsed using just the string of the URL and the extension method ShouldMapTo(). The controller is specified in the ShouldMapTo() signature, and then we use the lambda expression to specify what action and parameters it needs to map to.

Using this method to test routes is a helpful way to make sure they are always working with each check-in. Route testing also comes into play when we start building web services in Chapter 10, *Building REST-ful Web Services*, on page 199. Routes for web services are important because you'll have other developers who are using them, which is another good reason to make sure they don't break.

With route testing complete, we can move on to learning to display a user's credentials in our pages through HttpContext.

5.4 Storing Information in Memory

Controllers interact with more than just views and models. They also work with an object called HttpContext. This important object is where the raw input and output for each request is stored. With HttpContext, you can manipulate directly the HttpRequest and HttpResponse classes, linking you into the input and output of a web request.

For example, say we want to output an HTML fragment, like in Section 5.1, *Directing to Different Content Types with ActionResults*, on page 84, as an EmptyResult. We access the class HttpResponse inside our controller's action like Response.Write("<p>HTML fragment"</p>");. Because MVC does a good job abstracting requests and responses from us, we are not going to touch them inside a controller most of the time. The significant classes inside HttpContext that we'll learn to use are HttpSessionState and the IPrincipal user.

In the previous section, we used IPrincipal without even knowing it. Every time a user authenticates, their information goes in the HttpContext under the property User. The user is stored in a class that implements IPrincipal, and in the case of form authentication is stored as a GenericPrincipal. This class holds the user's name and all of the roles the user belongs to. Accessing a user's information within a controller through the User looks like this:

```
controllers/SomeController.cs
public class SomeController : Controller
{
  public ActionResult DisplayUserInfo()
  {
    ViewData["UserName"] = User.Identity.Name;
    return View();
  }
}
```

Notice how we had to drop down one level deeper into User.Identity to get the user's login name. This is because all IPrincipals have an IIdentity embedded inside them. The IIdentity is who you are. Your IPrincipal is what you have access to (see the *Joe Asks...* on page 93).

Now let's test-drive access to the User property.

Test-Driving Authorization

We want to display "<username>'s Todos" on the to-do page. In the previous section, we set User.Identity.Name to ViewData("UserName") so we could display the name of the logged-in user. Let's test-drive this.

We first need to write a test to validate that the username is set to a logged-in user and then check that ViewData("UserName") is assigned to that user's name.

> ### Forms Authentication vs. Windows Authentication
>
> In the previous section, we covered Forms authentication, the default for MVC applications. Another popular authentication is *Windows authentication*, which uses who you've logged into your Windows machine as, as opposed to retyping information on the website. Most .NET intranet applications use Windows to handle authentication, because it saves employees time reentering their credentials. You can turn on Windows authentication by changing the Web.config file from this:
>
> ```
> <authentication mode="Forms"></authentication>
> ```
>
> to this:
>
> ```
> <authentication mode="Windows"/>
> ```

Our unit test would look like this:

controllers/TodoControllerTest.cs

```
Line 1  [Test]
   -    public void Should_Set_Logged_In_User_To_ViewData()
   -    {
   -      var todoController = new TodoController();
   5
   -      todoController.HttpContext.User =
   -        new GenericPrincipal(new GenericIdentity("Jonathan"), null);
   -
   -      var result = (ViewResult) todoController.Index();
  10
   -      Assert.AreEqual("Jonathan", result.ViewData["UserName"]);
   -    }
```

The test compiles, but there is a big problem here when we run the test. We get a NullReferenceException on line 7 because the HttpContext is null. Trying to set the HttpContext results in another stumbling block: it has no setter property. The only option we have is to stub out this object, but instead of doing this ourselves, our friends at MVCContrib have already done the heavy lifting for us.

Using MVCContrib's TestControllerBuilder to Test Controllers

Before we can improve our test, we'll need to install MVCContrib. There are two dynamic link libraries (DLLs) that we need to reference in our project from the download: MVCContrib.TestHelper.dll and RhinoMocks.dll. Rhino Mocks is an open source mocking and stubbing framework that

\\/
Ɔ¿Ɔ **Joe Asks...**
 ᴈ __Why Stub Your Objects?__

Stub objects, also known as *stubs*, are nonproduction imitations of the real object. They are useful when testing components in isolation—in this case separating HttpContext from TodoController, when we cannot easily create the dependent class. Since Http-Context exists only within the web server container, we use a stub that acts like it in its place. This lets us test TodoController without having to start up a web server.

is popular in .NET.[3] MVCContrib's TestControllerBuilder makes extensive use of Rhino Mocks to stub out the HttpContext.

MVCContrib's TestHelper library provides a few shortcuts in writing our assertions. It has its own extension method to the ActionResult to allow us to test the result without having to do the casting that we have up until now. For example, once these libraries are imported, the assertion we've used until now—var result = (ViewResult) todoController.Index()—can be replaced with todoController.Index().AssertViewRendered().

One of the most important components to MVCContrib is having access to a stub of HttpContext. To implement the test, we will have to use the crucial class TestControllersBuilder, which instruments our controller so that we can access the HttpContext. We add the TestControllersBuilder to the test that was failing by doing the following:

controllers/TodoControllerTest.cs

```
Line 1   [Test]
    -    public void Should_Set_Logged_In_User_To_ViewData()
    -    {
    -        var todoController = new TodoController();
    5        var builder = new TestControllerBuilder();
    -        builder.InitializeController(todoController);
    -        builder.HttpContext.User =
    -      new GenericPrincipal(
    -        new GenericIdentity("Jonathan"), null);
   10
    -        Assert.AreEqual("Jonathan",
    -      todoController.Index().
    -      AssertViewRendered().ViewData["UserName"]);
    -    }
```

---

3. RhinoMock's home page is http://ayende.com/projects/rhino-mocks.aspx.

Notice that on line 6, we call InitializeController(Controller controller) to set up the stub on HttpContext. Instead of setting the context on the Todo-Controller itself, we set it on the builder. This gets rid of the null exception and allows us to add to the controller code to make this pass:

`controllers/TodoController.cs`

```
public ActionResult Index()
{
  ViewData["UserName"] = User.Identity.Name;
  ViewData.Model = Todo.ThingsToBeDone;

  return View();
}
```

Here we add the username to the ViewData from the HttpContext.

The assertion now passes because this code makes it work. Using AssertViewRendered(), an extension method of MVCContrib's TestHelper library, saves us from doing the casting. There are other useful extensions, including the AssertActionRedirect(), which replaces our usage of casting an ActionResult as a RedirectToRouteResult. Both of these clarify our tests and ultimately make them easier to write.

With the test passing, it's now time to add a little code to the /View/Todo/Index.aspx to finish off this feature. Here is a snippet of what that looks like:

`controllers/new_todo_index.aspx`

```
<asp:Content ID="Content2"
  ContentPlaceHolderID="MainContent" runat="server">

    <h2><%= ViewData["UserName"] %>'s Todos</h2>

    // ... rest of file remains the same
```

The view code is modified slightly to render the user's name right into the page heading. It's a better practice to only reference ViewData instead of directly accessing the Session, because it keeps other components out of the view.

The HttpContext is now fully testable using MVCContrib. We can move on to using it to implement some new functionality needed in our application that requires the use of HttpSessionState.

Adding a Summary of Activity Using the Session

You can access the HttpSessionState through the Session property inside any controller. Sessions are useful for storing information between requests about the same user. For example, a shopping cart with a

When Open Source Doesn't Apply

Sometimes we encounter a corporate policy or specific legal requirement that prevents us from using open source. Although this can be frustrating from a developer's point of view, we have to try to understand the business reason. Not all open source projects are equal in terms of recognition. For example, NUnit is widely accepted, whereas MVCContrib is relatively new to market.

Many open source projects do not have official vendor support. Often it's just a couple of developers coding in their spare time, and companies pay licenses for software because it's backed by a level of support. Companies feel they can turn to someone to fix bugs, or get help with using the tools, when they are paying for support. This is why, up until now, we have not used MVCContrib to solve all of our testing problems. But with the more difficult way to test controllers covered, we'll now introduce a easier way.

number of products in it is a classic example of information stored in HttpSessionState. You can add any object into the Session by assigning it, like Session["key"] = "someValue";, or you can retrieve it by typing var someVariable = Session["key"]. Be warned, though, that storing objects in Session is expensive in terms of both memory and application performance. Information that is a good candidate for the Session is both small in size and will be thrown away after the user logs out. Otherwise, you can consider storing it in the database.

Similar to User, Session is accessible via the HttpContext and requires the use of our new tool, TestBuilderController. We want to add a page to our application that gives us a summary of what to-dos have been added since we've logged in. Analogous to the way that online banking displays bills or transfers you've made during the session, GetOrganized will tell us what Todos we've added since we've logged in.

First we'll learn how to use the Session to track users' Todo activities.

Adding Todos to the SessionSummary

We're going create a new class, SessionSummary, to track to-dos that have been added. This class will attach to the Session. We'll create SessionSummary under the Model directory, because it will eventually have its own controller and views. The code for SessionSummary is as follows:

```
controllers/SessionSummary.cs
Line 1  public class SessionSummary
    -   {
    -     public List<Todo> AddedTodos { get; private set; }
    -
    5     public SessionSummary()
    -     {
    -         AddedTodos = new List<Todo>();
    -     }
    -
   10     public bool Equals(SessionSummary other)
    -     {
    -       if (ReferenceEquals(null, other)) return false;
    -       if (ReferenceEquals(this, other)) return true;
    -
   15       //This Equals makes sure what's in the lists is
    -       // compared, not the reference
    -       equality on the List<T> itself
    -       if (other.AddedTodos.Count != other.AddedTodos.Count)
    -         return false;
   20
    -       for (int i = 0; i < other.AddedTodos.Count; i++)
    -       {
    -         if (!other.AddedTodos[i].Equals(AddedTodos[i]))
    -           return false;
   25       }
    -         return true;
    -     }
    -
    -     public override bool Equals(object obj)
   30     {
    -       if (ReferenceEquals(null, obj)) return false;
    -       if (ReferenceEquals(this, obj)) return true;
    -       if (obj.GetType() != typeof (SessionSummary))
    -         return false;
   35
    -       return Equals((SessionSummary) obj);
    -     }
    -
    -     public override int GetHashCode()
   40     {
    -         return (AddedTodos != null ? AddedTodos.GetHashCode() : 0);
    -     }
    -   }
```

This class has a list of Todo items, but since we have an uninitialized list when the object is created, we initialize AddedTodos in the constructor. You'll notice on line 17 that the Equals() method checks the contents of the list, not the reference to the list itself.

The next step is to write a test for TodoController's Create(Todo todo) to verify that after we create the Todo we also put it into the Session. This means going back to modify the old test Should_Add_Todo_Item(), from Section 3.3, *Creating a To-Do*, on page 44, to look like this:

```
controllers/TodoControllerTest.cs
[Test]
public void Should_Add_Todo_Item()
{
  var todo = new Todo
    {Title = "Learn more about ASP.NET MVC Controllers"};

  var sessionSummary = new SessionSummary();
  sessionSummary.AddedTodos.Add(todo);

  var todoController = new TodoController();
  var builder = new TestControllerBuilder();
  builder.InitializeController(todoController);

  todoController.Create(todo).
    AssertActionRedirect().ToAction("Index"));

  Assert.Contains(todo, Todo.ThingsToBeDone);
  Assert.AreEqual(sessionSummary,
    todoController.Session["SessionSummary"]);
}
```

Similarly to testing the User, we need to initialize a TestControllerBuilder to ensure we don't get a NullReferenceException when trying to access the Session.

Note that we use the method AssertActionRedirect() in conjunction with ToAction(string actionName) instead of doing an Assert.AreEquals(). This is another convenience method of MVCContrib that helps shorten and clarify our controller tests.

This test is now failing, and to get it passing, we'll need to modify the private method CreateTodo(). We want to make the change there so that when a Thought converts to a Todo, it is also added to the SessionSummary.

Adding the SessionSummary to the Session looks like this:

controllers/TodoController.cs

```
Line 1  private void CreateTodo(Todo todo)
   2    {
   3      Todo.ThingsToBeDone.Add(todo);
   4      if (Session["SessionSummary"] == null)
   5        Session["SessionSummary"] = new SessionSummary();
   6
   7      var summary = ((SessionSummary) Session["SessionSummary"]);
   8      summary.AddedTodos.Add(todo);
   9    }
```

This makes the test pass! Looking at this code, we'll see that we first check whether a Session has been stored in the key SessionSummary on line 4. This check is important to prevent a null object the first time a user adds a Todo.

The other code worthy of note is on line 7, where we cast the result from the Session to a SessionSummary that we expect. This is how to retrieve objects from the Session. We don't need to reassign the Session after we modify SessionSummary, because it updates by reference. Now that we have the Session populated with the information we need, we can display it to the user.

Displaying Session Information

Having all this information in the Session is the first step. The second step is to display the information to users of GetOrganized. In this case we're talking about to-do items, but often we'll have objects that require more than one screen to completely fill in. For example, if your user registration requires a lot of information, it might be split up into multiple screens. Using the Session to store the information until all steps are complete prevents against premature database calls.

Now let's display those Todos. We'll need a new controller to display our SessionSummary. Driving this from a test looks like this:

controllers/SessionControllerTest.cs

```
Line 1  [Test]
   -    public void Should_Display_SessionSummary_On_Index()
   -    {
   -      var summary = new SessionSummary {
   5        AddedTodos = {
   -          new Todo { Title = "Complete Management Report"}
   -          }
   -      };
   -
```

```
10    var sessionController = new SessionController();
      var builder = new TestControllerBuilder();
      builder.InitializeController(sessionController);
      builder.Session["SessionSummary"] = summary;

15    Assert.AreEqual(summary,
        sessionController.Index().AssertViewRendered().ViewData.Model);
    }
```

This test fails because we are not setting anything up in the model in
SessionController. The one thing that is different in this test is on line
13. We are setting up the expectation that there is information in the
session from a previous request. Let's get the test to pass:

controllers/SessionController.cs

```
Line 1  public class SessionController : Controller
2       {
3         public ActionResult Index()
4         {
5           if (Session["SessionSummary"] == null)
6             Session["SessionSummary"] = new SessionSummary();
7
8           return View(Session["SessionSummary"]);
9         }
10      }
```

The test bar is now green, and we also made use of the shortcut we
learned earlier on line 8 to pass the model in the View(). We perform a
similar check if the Session is null, like we did on TodoController's private
method CreateTodo().

Having a working controller that sets the model means we can display
the content using a simple typed view, as shown here:

controllers/Session_Index.aspx

```
<%@ Page Title="" Language="C#"
  MasterPageFile="~/Views/Shared/Site.Master" Inherits=
  "System.Web.Mvc.ViewPage<GetOrganized.Models.SessionSummary>"%>

<asp:Content ID="Content1" ContentPlaceHolderID="MainContent"
  runat="server">

    <h2>New Things You Have to Do</h2>
    <ul>
        <% foreach (var todo in Model.AddedTodos)
          {%>
          <li><%= Html.Encode(todo.Title) %></li>

        <%} %>
    </ul>
</asp:Content>
```

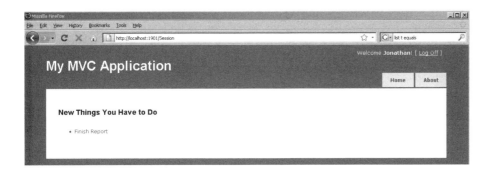

Figure 5.5: USE HTTPSESSIONSTATE TO DISPLAY INFORMATION THAT IS SHORT-LIVED, LIKE THE NEWLY ADDED TO-DOS SINCE LOGIN.

The view code iterates through the AddedTodos to display the items in an unordered list. This satisfies our need, and now we know what new todos we've added this session, as shown in Figure 5.5.

HttpContext can help with more than just session information. It can also be used to upload and download files. To do this, it collaborates with the action result FilePathResult.

5.5 Manipulating Files

A picture is worth a thousand words, and what better way to illustrate this than to have us upload sketches, diagrams, and photos when we create a new Thought in our application. We'll also need to view and download these images with the help of FilePathResult, an action result that streams a file from the web server to our desktop. In this section, we're going to deal with uploading an image and downloading it to be saved on our computer.

The following code is not production ready because of a security concern. When you allow users to upload files to your site, it's a best practice to have your web application save them to a directory that is not accessible over the Web. This allows you to preform some validations, such as a virus scan, before making it available for others to see. To simplify the learning here, these sorts of precautions have been skipped intentionally.

Upload Images to Our Thoughts

On the create screen, we're going to add a field to upload an image that we can review later. Before we modify /View/Thought/Create.aspx, we are going to extend the test of the Create(Thought thought) method in the ThoughtController. We should review what the old test does right now, prior to changing it:

controllers/ThoughtControllerTest.cs

```
[Test]
public void Should_Add_A_Thought_On_Create()
{
  Thought newThought = new Thought
  {
    Id = 3,
    Name = "Research big screen TVs",
    Topic = Topic.Topics.Find(topic => topic.Name == "Home"),
  };

  var result = (RedirectToRouteResult)
    new ThoughtController().Create(newThought);

  Assert.Contains(newThought, Thought.Thoughts);
  Assert.AreEqual("Index", result.RouteValues["Action"]);
}
```

The test adds a Thought to the ThoughtController, ensures it is added to the collection Thought.Thoughts, and redirects to the Index() action.

Now we will introduce a little more of Rhino Mocks than we have used previously. Because uploaded files are accessed via HttpContext.Request. Files, we have to stub out the files beyond what TestControllerBuilder is capable of doing. When we add new files and store them in a directory (in the upcoming example the UserContent directory), we need to make sure they are uniquely named. A primitive way of doing this is to randomly generate a number to prepend to the filename; for example, picture.jpg becomes 12345-picture.jpg. The modified test therefore ends up looking like this:

controllers/ThoughtControllerTest.cs

```
Line 1  [Test]
   -    public void Should_Add_A_Thought_And_Upload_An_Image_On_Create()
   -    {
   -      Thought newThought = new Thought
   5      {
   -        Id = 3,
   -        Name = "Research big screen TVs",
   -        Topic = Topic.Topics.Find(topic => topic.Name == "Home"),
   -      };
  10
```

```
     MockRepository mocks = new MockRepository();
     var file = mocks.Stub<HttpPostedFileBase>();
     Expect.Call(file.FileName).Return("bigscreen.jpg");
     Expect.Call(file.ContentLength).Return(12);
15   mocks.Replay(file);

     var thoughtController = new ThoughtController();
     var builder = new TestControllerBuilder();
     builder.InitializeController(thoughtController);
20   builder.Files["ImageAttachment"] = file;

     thoughtController.Create(newThought).
       AssertActionRedirect().ToAction("Index");

25   Assert.Contains(newThought, Thought.Thoughts);

     Assert.IsTrue(newThought.
       ImageAttachment.Contains("UserContent/"));
     Assert.IsTrue(newThought.
30     ImageAttachment.Contains("-bigscreen.jpg"));
   }
```

On line 11, we introduce the MockRepository from Rhino Mocks. This class generates new stubs or mocks. Since the interface to Request.Files is read-only, we create a stub from MockRepository that will fake out calls to HttpPostedFile, which is the file we are pretending to upload.

We need to receive a filename back, so on line 13 we use Rhino Mocks' method Expect() to stub the property FileName to return bigscreen.jpg. To finish off our stub, we call Replay(object obj) with HttpPostedFile. Replay(object obj) tells Rhino Mocks to execute the commands contained in the last Expect() statement.

With our stub HttpPostedFile configured, we use TestControllerBuilder to call the actual attachment on line 20. This means we are expecting to have an input tag with the name *ImageAttachment* on the page where we upload the file. To test the randomly added numbers to the filename, we have to do two separate AreEquals() calls on line 28. Another way to test random numbers is to inject the behavior through a provider that we can stub out, but in this case it's a simple enough workaround.

The test is now failing. Let's get it to pass:

controllers/ThoughtController.cs

```
Line 1   [AcceptVerbs(HttpVerbs.Post)]
         public ActionResult Create(Thought newThought)
         {
           newThought.Topic =
5            Topic.Topics.
```

```
          Find(topic => topic.Id == newThought.Topic.Id);

          HttpPostedFileBase file = Request.Files["ImageAttachment"];
          if (file.ContentLength != 0)
10        {
            int randomNumber =
              new Random().
              Next(100000, Int32.MaxValue);
            string imgUrl =
15            "UserContent/" + randomNumber
              + "-" + file.FileName;
            file.SaveAs(
              Server.MapPath("~/UserContent") + "/" +
                randomNumber + "-" + file.FileName);
20          newThought.ImageAttachment = imgUrl;
          }

          Thought.Thoughts.Add(newThought);
          return RedirectToAction("Index");
25      }
```

On line 8, we pull the file out of the Request.Files and ensure that someone has actually attached a file before we prepare to save it to the web
server. The Random class adds a six- to ten-digit number to the filename
we save on line 13. This helps prevent against name clashes, but to be
sure, we might have done a File.Exists before actually saving the file on
line 19 and attaching it back to the Thought.

Once you add the ImageAttachment to Thought, the test passes. We can
take a look at how to wire this up with our /View/Thought/Create.aspx:

`controllers/Thought_Create.aspx`

```
<form action="Create" method="post" enctype="multipart/form-data">
<fieldset>
  <legend>Fields</legend>
  <p>
    <label for="Id">Id:</label>
    <%= Html.TextBox("Id") %>
    <%= Html.ValidationMessage("Id", "*") %>
  </p>
  <p>
    <label for="Name">Name:</label>
    <%= Html.TextBox("Name") %>
    <%= Html.ValidationMessage("Name", "*") %>
  </p>
  <p>
    <label for="Topic">Topic:</label>
    <%= Html.DropDownList("Topic.Id",
      (List<SelectListItem>) ViewData["Topics"])%>
  </p>
```

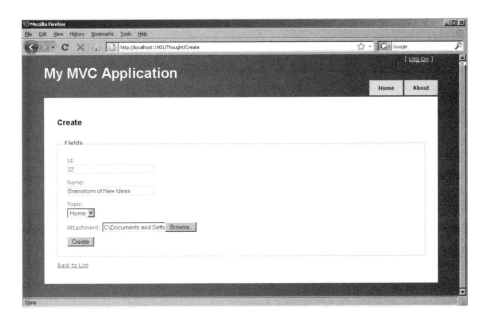

Figure 5.6: ADDING AN INPUT TAG OF THE TYPE FILE ADDS THE BROWSE OPTION TO ATTACH THE FILE.

```
<p>
  Attachment: <input type="file" name="ImageAttachment" />
</p>
<p>
  <input type="submit" value="Create" />
</p>
</fieldset>
</form>
```

Uploading files to a site involves modifying the HTML of the page to accept multipart form data. This means we need to remove the HTML.BeginForm() with coding our own form to have an encoding, enctype, of multipart/form-data. We also had to add the input field with the name ImageAttachment and the type file to line up with the string we are looking for on the controller side. We can see the code in action in Figure 5.6. Next we'll download and view our images.

Downloading with FilePathResult

Saving or displaying a file's contents is just as important as uploading it. GetOrganized needs to have the ability to display the attached images or download them when viewing a Thought. Since uploading is now working, we can now proceed to get the download going.

We'll want to write a test for a new action called Download(int id), which will return the FilePathResult. Our test will be as follows:

controllers/ThoughtControllerTest.cs

```
[Test]
public void Should_Download_File_With_Random_Number_Removed_From_Name()
{
  var expectedThought = Thought.Thoughts.First();
  expectedThought.ImageAttachment =
    "UserContent/232923-picture.jpg";

  var fileresult = new ThoughtController().
      Download(expectedThought.Id).
      AssertResultIs<FilePathResult>();

  //actual filename on web server
  Assert.AreEqual("~/UserContent/232923-picture.jpg",
    fileresult.FileName);

  //file name that user downloads
  Assert.AreEqual("picture.jpg",fileresult.FileDownloadName);
}
```

The key to this test is that we use another MVCContrib method, Assert-ResultIs<FilePathResult>(), to validate that we are returning a file to the output. The other two fields we'll assert are FileName, which represents the file on the web server itself, and FileDownloadName, the filename that is saved on the user's computer. In this test, we wanted to make sure that our random numbers are excluded from the download name because they really have no meaning to the user.

Let's move on to getting the test to pass:

controllers/ThoughtController.cs

```
//
// GET: /Thought/Download/5

public FilePathResult Download(int id)
{
  Thought thought = Thought.Thoughts.Find(x => x.Id == id);

  return File("~/" +
    thought.ImageAttachment, "application/octet-stream",
      Path.GetFileName(thought.ImageAttachment)
          .Split(new[] {'-'}, 2)[1]);
}
```

To return a FilePathResult, we use the File() method. We specify the physical path to the file on the web server, which we get from ImageAttachment, the content type of application/octet-stream, and the name we want to save the file as on the user's machine. To get the physical path of the file, we had to add ~/ to the path, because this marker signifies the root of the web application.

The Multipurpose Internet Mail Extensions (MIME) type is set to application/octet-stream to prompt the user to a download the file, as opposed to viewing the image in the browser. For example, a MIME type of image/jpg would render the same file in the browser as an image. In the final parameter of File(), we call Split() on the filename to remove the random numbers.

This causes the test to pass, but now we need to add a link to download our attached images on the /View/Thought/Index.aspx view:

```
controllers/Thought_Index.aspx
<% //inside View/Thought/Index.aspx %>
<td>
<%= item.ImageAttachment != null ?
  Html.ActionLink("Download Image", "Download", new { item.Id })
         : MvcHtmlString.Empty %>
</td>
```

Since not every Thought has an image attached to it, the link we place on the Index.aspx page needs to be dependent on whether the ImageAttachment property has been set (Figure 5.7, on the next page). After that check, we need to generate an action link to the Download() action and pass the Id of the Thought.

We can now upload and download images in GetOrganized. Most business users today are very familiar with email attachments and expect uploading and downloading to be part of their applications.

Up Next

We've built security using action filters and learned to download files with action results. We also know how to have the controller use HttpSessionState to store certain kinds of information. We will continue to leverage these features throughout our development of GetOrganized and in Part III, "Integrating with Other Frameworks," of this book.

Next up, we'll zoom in on how to make our views more visually appealing and reusable with the help of master pages, and we'll see a few more useful HTML helpers.

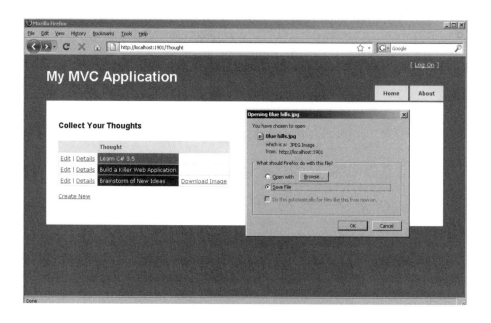

Figure 5.7: CHANGING THE **MIME** TYPE TO APPLICATION/OCTET-STREAM
PROMPTS THE USER TO DOWNLOAD OR OPEN THE FILE.

It is better to be beautiful than to be good, but it is better to be good than to be ugly.

▶ Oscar Wilde

Chapter 6

Enhancing Views with HTML Helpers and Master Pages

Building a successful web application requires excellent design and usability, not just killer functionality. Take Facebook, for example. When Facebook first came out, it had pretty much the same functionality as MySpace, but it was cleaner and more usable. Facebook's design focused on a simple three-column layout, while MySpace's had multiple tiles that allowed users to put whatever HTML markup on their home pages they wanted. Facebook gained popularity in part because MySpace's design was less usable.[1] Therefore, let's not neglect design; in this chapter, we'll work on making our sample application look good.

So far, we've used HTML helpers to render, create, and edit model data using common tags such as textboxes and drop-downs. GetOrganized currently leaves a lot to be desired in terms of style. In this chapter, we'll work on improving the look of the site with Cascading Style Sheets (CSS) and the implementation of master pages. We'll also work on building our own HTML helper to move presentation logic out of the view and into a testable class. This will feed into how to validate user inputs and display friendly, informative validation messages. Finally, we'll discuss advanced view helpers, which is the MVC analog of traditional ASP.NET web controls. All of these will make GetOrganized a more user-friendly application.

To start off, we'll work on learning a new HTML helper method to render radio buttons (Figure 6.1, on the following page).

---

1. See http://web.archive.org/web/20050101092643/http://www.myspace.com/. This link is very slow to load; you may have to try it several times.

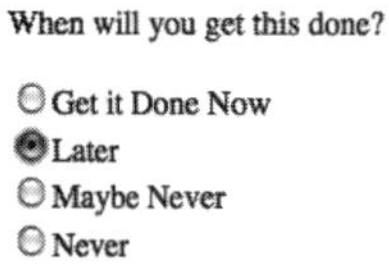

When will you get this done?

○ Get it Done Now
◉ Later
○ Maybe Never
○ Never

Figure 6.1: RADIO BUTTONS DISPLAY CHOICES IN A MORE VISIBLE WAY THAN A DROP-DOWN DOES.

6.1 Making Our Site Presentable with HTML Helpers

Sometimes we want to display a choice to a user that emphasizes a bigger consequence than a drop-down does. Radio buttons work well for this purpose, because they clearly show the user that they are making a choice between different paths. For GetOrganized, we want to emphasize the choice between a Thought and a Todo that we want to tackle later. When we left the ThoughtController class in Section 4.4, *Controllers Talking to Controllers*, on page 75, we were converting a Thought into a Todo. That works well for a Thought that maps easily to a single task, but we also want to be able to process big ideas and ideas that we want to tackle in the future. For example, converting the Thought "Build a compiler" into a single Todo doesn't make a lot of sense. That's a project that will take a considerable amount of our time, and right now we're busy enough learning MVC. However, if we think the idea will still interest us in the future, we will want to put it into a new Someday category. To build this feature, we need to modify the Process.aspx view by adding the choice of turning a Thought into a Todo or a Someday.

Processing Thoughts Take II: Actionable or Maybe Someday

First let's drive the conversion of a Thought through a test. To do this, we need to modify the Thought model slightly:

```
views/Thought.cs
```
```
Line 1  public class Thought
        {
          public static List<Thought> Somedays = new List<Thought>
          {
     5    new Thought{Name = "Learn Smalltalk",
            Topic = Topic.Topics.Find(topic => topic.Name == "Work")}
          };
```

```
      public static List<Thought> CurrentThoughts = new List<Thought>
10    {
      new Thought{Name = "Learn C# 3.5",
        Topic = Topic.Topics.Find(topic => topic.Name == "Work")},
      new Thought{Name = "Build a Killer Web Application",
        Topic = Topic.Topics.Find(topic => topic.Name == "Home")}
15    };

      public int Id { get; set; }
      public Topic Topic { get; set; }
      public string Name { get; set; }
20    public string ImageAttachment { get; set; }
    }
```

Instead of creating a class called Someday, we can add a list to store
our Somedays on line 3. We didn't create a new class here because a
Someday looks exactly like a Thought, except that we aren't going to put
it into action for a long time. The *single responsibility principle* of object-
oriented programming (see the *Joe Asks...* on the following page) tells
us that each class has a single job or function. It would be hard to
define a new job for a Someday that is different from a Thought; therefore,
we won't create a new class.

The variable name Thoughts is now ambiguous, so renaming it to Cur-
rentThoughts helps clear this up. We rename the collection Thoughts to
CurrentThoughts on line 9. Renaming is a common refactoring. With Re-
Sharper, we use the shortcut F2 to help us clarify the intent of a class.
After any refactoring, it's a good practice to run the whole test suite.

This makes sure everything still works before we proceed; remember
"red, green, refactor" back in Figure 2.2, on page 20?

Let's write a test inside ThoughtControllerTest, which looks like this:

views/ThoughtControllerTest.cs

```
[Test]
public void Should_Convert_A_Thought_To_A_Someday()
{
  Thought writeACompiler = new Thought { Name = "Write a Compiler" };
  new ThoughtController().MakeASomeday(writeACompiler).
    AssertActionRedirect().ToAction("Process");
  Assert.Contains(writeACompiler, Thought.Somedays);
  Assert.IsFalse(Thought.CurrentThoughts.Contains(writeACompiler));
}
```

> ### Joe Asks...
> #### What Is the Single Responsibility Principle?
>
> Often abbreviated as SRP, the single responsibility principle is one of five principles in SOLID object-oriented design.* SRP says that each **class** has only one responsibility. This is one test to see whether a **class** needs to be broken up into two or whether it deserves to exist at all. For example, if you have a **class** that you describe as "This class manages a user's address and how they log in and what they've bought recently...," then it's doing too much. Using the word "and" when describing your class is a code smell. Remember to keep SRP in mind because it helps keep your classes concise.
>
> ---
>
> *.   http://butunclebob.com/ArticleS.UncleBob.PrinciplesOfOod

Here we make two assertions to ensure that a Thought gets removed from CurrentThoughts and moved into Somedays. We then assert a redirect to the action Process() using the MVCContrib extension method AssertActionRedirect.ToAction(string actionName).

Let's get this test to pass by implementing the new method in Thought-Controller:

`views/ThoughtController.cs`

```
// POST: /Thought/MakeASomeday

[HttpPost]
public ActionResult MakeASomeday(Thought aThoughtToDoSomeday)
{
  Thought.Somedays.Add(aThoughtToDoSomeday);
  Thought.CurrentThoughts.Remove(aThoughtToDoSomeday);

  return RedirectToAction("Process");
}
```

The implementation of the method MakeASomeday() follows the assertions laid out in the test. We remove the new Thought from the Current-Thoughts collection and add it to the Somedays collection. We redirect to the Process() action to prompt the user to work on the next Thought.

We need to make this work for the view, so we'll modify the code in Process.aspx and introduce the radio button selector shown here:

```
views/Process.aspx
Line 1  Actionable: <%= Html.RadioButton("IsActionable",
   -       "Action", true, new {id = "actionRadio"}) %>
   -    Maybe Someday: <%= Html.RadioButton("IsActionable",
   -       "MaybeSomeday", false, new {id = "someDayRadio"}) %>
   5
   -    <div id="actionDiv">
   -    <fieldset>
   -    <legend>Actionable</legend>
   -    <% //... convert Todo form removed to shorten %>
   10   </fieldset>
   -    </div>
   -    <div id="someDayDiv">
   -    <% using (Html.BeginForm("MakeASomeday", "Thought")) {%>
   -    <fieldset>
   15   <legend>Maybe Someday</legend>
   -    <p>
   -       <%= Html.Hidden("Id", Model.Id) %>
   -       <%= Html.Hidden("Name", Model.Name) %>
   -       <%= Html.Hidden("Topic.Id", Model.Topic.Id) %>
   20      <input type="submit" value="Do it Someday" />
   -    </p>
   -    </fieldset>
   -    <% } %>
   -    </div>
```

First note the introduction of the radio button HTML helper method RadioButton(string propertyName, string valueOfSelection, bool isSelected). We add two radio buttons on line 2: one if the user thinks the Thought is actionable and the other if it's a maybe-someday activity. We introduce another important component to HTML helpers on these lines as new {id = "actionRadio"} is passed into the parameters. Using this syntax creates a unique **id** attribute when the page renders. This isn't exclusive to radio buttons. We can use the last parameter of HTML helpers to pass in any HTML attributes we want rendered. Another example is to pass in a CSS **class** attribute, which we'll do in Section 6.1, *Adding a Dash of CSS to HTML Helpers*, on page 121. If you are unfamiliar with CSS, a quick tutorial is available on Patrick Griffith's website.[2]

---

2. http://www.htmldog.com/guides/cssbeginner/

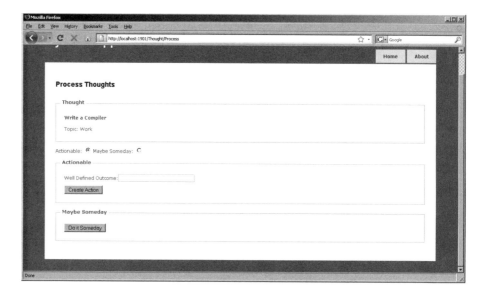

Figure 6.2: DISPLAYING BOTH DIVS HERE IS BAD USER DESIGN. LET'S USE JQUERY TO HIDE AND SHOW ONLY WHAT IS SELECTED.

We create two different HTML div tags on lines 6 and 12 to build up separate HTML forms for both scenarios. On line 13 in doItSomedayDiv, we wire up the form to point to the ThoughtController with the MakeA-Someday() action. After adding this, we can fire up the application and then move Thoughts into the collection of activities we'll take on Someday (Figure 6.2).

We now have a new problem: whichever radio button the user selects, two divs are displayed. To fix this, we pull out a little jQuery to make the page more usable.

Hide and Showing Divs with jQuery

Back in Section 4.3, *Adding a Little Color with jQuery*, on page 68, we inserted a color picker to GetOrganized. This time we're going to use jQuery to show either the actionable or the maybe-someday section based on which radio button is selected. If jQuery is totally unfamiliar to you, it will be helpful to read through the basics of selector, events, and effects in the tutorial at http://jquery.com.

For now, we want to hide the right div when the user clicks the Actionable or Maybe Someday button. The following is how this looks in our Process.aspx:

`views/Process.aspx`

```
Line 1  <asp:Content ID="Content2" ContentPlaceHolderID="Head"
     -    runat="server">
     -    <script type="text/javascript">
     -       $(document).ready(function(){
     5
     -         $("#actionRadio").click(function(){
     -           $("#actionDiv").slideDown();
     -           $("#someDayDiv").slideUp();
     -         });
    10
     -         $("#someDayRadio").click(function(){
     -           $("#actionDiv").slideUp();
     -           $("#someDayDiv").slideDown();
     -         });
    15       });
     -    </script>
     -  </asp:Content>
```

On line 2, we add our JavaScript to the head section of the page by using the content placeholder. We'll talk more about content placeholders later in this chapter in Section 6.3, *Simplifying Page Layouts with Master Pages*, on page 127. Next we define our standard jQuery block where our JavaScript code will execute:

```
$(document).ready(function(){ ... })
```

Both lines 6 and 11 are essentially inverses of the same function. They each start by wiring up the click event to their respective radio button. Next, we'll hide one div with **slideUp** and show the other with the **slideDown** jQuery effects. When we load up the page and click the radio buttons, we can now hide and show the right div for the job.

We're looking a lot better, but when the page first loads, we still see two boxes. Let's use a little CSS to hide both of these divs when the page first loads.

Adding a Dash of CSS to HTML Helpers

When we first wrote the code for Process.aspx in the previous section, we gave the divs specific names, and we can access them via jQuery.

To hide these divs when the page loads, we'll define two of the styles in our CSS, like so:

views/Process.aspx

```
<asp:Content ID="Content2" ContentPlaceHolderID="Head"
  runat="server">
  <style type="text/css">
    #actionDiv
    {
      display: none;
    }
    #someDayDiv
    {
      display: none;
    }
  </style>
  // ... omitted javascript ...
</asp:Content>
```

Instead of a **script** tag, we create a **style** tag to set up our CSS styles for the two divs. jQuery allows us to select elements by ID; CSS has the same feature. We define two styles: one for #actionDiv and the other for #someDayDiv. The **display** attribute for each is set to none. Note that most of the time we will extract our styles and JavaScript into separate files. To extract CSS into a separate file, all we need to do is insert the following code:

```
<link rel="stylesheet" type="text/css" href="FileName.css" />
```

Then remove the style tags and paste the contents into the new file. Similarly, for JavaScript, we just insert the HTML:

```
<script type="javascript" src="FileName.js"></script>
```

Now place the contents of our script into that file, and presto! Separating CSS and JavaScript into files makes them easier to read most of the time.

At the start of this chapter, we said we wanted to improve the look and feel of the site. This is most easily accomplished through CSS. By using the **id** and **class** HTML attributes while we program our views, we can then apply styles in a separate file for the whole site. Not only does this ensure consistency, but it makes it easy to tweak the visual look when all the styling is in one place.

We've talked about applying styles through the **id** attribute, but we also need to know how to use the **class** attribute. CSS classes act on every element in the HTML document that has the class="nameOfClass" attribute applied to it. Having CSS classes on our HTML helper allows us to customize the look and feel of the site. In the previous section, we learned about adding a parameter for the radio button with new {id = "nameOfId"}. Similarly, if we want to add a CSS **class**, we do it like new {@class = "className"}. Notice that we had to apply the special character @ because in C# **class** is a keyword that signifies a new object definition, which causes a compiler error.

Knowing more about how to use HTML helpers, we can now work on extending HTML helpers to build our own Color drop-down box. When we create a Thought and select its Topic, we visually associate a color with it.

6.2 Building a Custom HTML Helper

When developing applications, standard HTML helpers will meet a great number of our needs. However, there are often situations we have to extend them such as when we want to display standard input tags in slightly different ways, across more than one page. Traditional ASP.NET would have accomplished this through web or user controls. With MVC, we do this through custom HTML helpers. We will also talk about advanced HTML helpers in Section 6.5, *Replacing Web Controls with Advanced HTML Helpers*, on page 134.

Back in Section 4.2, *Using the FormCollection and TempData Objects*, on page 65, we used the ToHtml() method on ColorTranslator right inside the view. Since there are no unit tests covering views, this is never a good practice. We want to make our view code as simple as possible, so we wrap up such logic into separate view helpers. In this section, we'll extend the normal drop-down to display the colors of the Topics it contains.

Colorizing a Drop-Down List

Instead of tagging on to the Html class with an extension method, we are going to create our own class to avoid confusion. This advantageous approach keeps objects small and specific. It can be confusing to have everything extend Html as the application's codebase becomes larger. First we create a directory to hold our view helper. By convention we can add the directory ViewHelpers to give them a home. We can

now test-drive a ColorDropDownHelper by creating a test fixture called
ColorDropDownHelperTest:

```
views/ColorDropDownHelperTest.cs
```

```csharp
using GetOrganized.ViewHelpers;

[Test]
public void Should_Render_Colored_DropDown_Markup()
{
  var workTopic = new List<Topic> { new Topic {Id=1,
    Name="Work", Color= Color.Red} };
  Assert.AreEqual(
    "<select id=\"Topic_Id\" " +
    "name=\"Topic.Id\" style=\"background-color: transparent;\">"+
    "<option style=\"color: white; background-color: Red\" "+
    "value=\"1\">Work</option></select>",
    ColorDropDownHelper.Topic("Topic.Id", workTopic));
}
```

This test gives the actual HTML output that we want the HTML helper
to produce. In this case, we'll generate **select** and **option** tags populated
with information from the Topic we want. We expect that the result-
ing call to Topic(string propertyName, List<Topic> topics) will modify the **style**
attribute in the HTML to be the specific background color of that Topic.
If we pass in the workTopic with the Topic color of red, we will see an
option tag render in red. This test is now failing, so let's get it passing:

```
views/ColorDropDownHelper.cs
```

```csharp
public static class ColorDropDownHelper
{
  public static string Topic(string name, List<Topic> options)
  {
❶    var select = new TagBuilder("select");
❷    select.MergeAttribute("style", "background-color: transparent;");
    select.MergeAttribute("name", name);
    select.GenerateId(name);

❸    var optionBuilder = new StringBuilder();

    foreach (var option in options)
    {
      var optionTag = new TagBuilder("option");
❹      optionTag.MergeAttribute("value", option.Id.ToString());
      optionTag.MergeAttribute("style", "color: white; background-color: "
❺        + ColorTranslator.ToHtml(option.Color));
      optionTag.SetInnerText(option.Name);
      optionBuilder.Append(
❻        optionTag.ToString(TagRenderMode.Normal));
    }
```

```
❼      select.InnerHtml = optionBuilder.ToString();
       return select.ToString(TagRenderMode.Normal);
    }
}
```

This is a fairly large block of code, so we'll use the previous markers to guide us. First we'll use the TagBuilder class at marker ❶. This class generates the HTML relating to the tag we are using and includes some other helpful methods. That brings us to the ❷ marker where we use the MergeAttribute() to tack on the transparent background color. Firefox and other standards-compliant browsers like Opera and Safari require that this be set to transparent to allow users to see the colors that we are setting on individual drop-down options. However, there is still a problem with this helper because the currently selected option doesn't display the proper color. This could be solved using JavaScript, but for now we'll leave it to be fixed later. We also use the MergeAttribute() method to add the name attribute of the tag so that it wires up to the next HTTP POST. This is because forms take what is posted by name, never by ID. This method also renders properties such as Topic.Id into Topic_Id, replacing the dot with an underscore.

Let's move on to building up the options for our drop-down in marker ❸. We want to create a StringBuilder because the current TagBuilder that ships with MVC does not currently support nesting them together. We need to iterate through each Topic in the list to render an option tag. This is similar to what we did to create the **select** tag on the name attribute. We set the value attribute to the Id of the **option** tag in marker ❹. We then set each **option** to its Topic's background color using the converter method ToHtml() at marker ❺. After that we add the appropriate TagRenderMode at marker ❻. The output we use is set to Normal mode, which renders the tag with full start and end tags. For example, the select tag looks like <select><\select> in Normal mode. The other render modes are useful in different situations. For example, if we are making a tag that closes itself like an image tag, we can use SelfClose. If we have a tag that spans a larger part of the page like a div, we can use the StartTag and EndTag render options. Finally, we join the options we've built with the Select tag. Using InnerHtml in the Select tag, we assign all the options to be rendered inside in marker ❼.

This gets our test to pass, but we'll need to make some changes to the ThoughtController's Create() to make sure we no longer return a list of SelectItems.

We'll now modify the existing test:

```
views/ThoughtControllerTest.cs
```
```
[Test]
public void Should_List_Topics_When_Creating_New_Thoughts()
{
  var expectedList = Topic.Topics;
  var viewDataOfTopics = new ThoughtController().
    Create().AssertViewRendered().ViewData["Topics"];
  Assert.AreEqual(expectedList, viewDataOfTopics);
}
```

This code is simplified with the help of MVCContrib and the logic moved to the view helper. We now call an AssertViewRendered() and return a viewDataOfTopics to assert against the loaded list. Because we've now removed the need for SelectItems, the following implementation code is also reduced:

```
views/ThoughtController.cs
```
```
public ActionResult Create()
{
  ViewData["RealTopics"] = Topic.Topics;
  return View();
}
```

Not only is the test passing now, but it also has a much slimmer Create() method. All we do here is load the list of Topics into ViewData. Let's now move on to adding our HTML helper to the /Thought/Create.aspx view:

```
views/Create.aspx
```
```
Line 1  <%@ Page Title=""
    -     Language="C#" MasterPageFile="~/Views/Shared/Site.Master"
    -     Inherits="System.Web.Mvc.ViewPage<GetOrganized.Models.Thought>" %>
    -  <%@ Import Namespace="GetOrganized.Models"%>
    5  <%@ Import Namespace="GetOrganized.ViewHelpers"%>

    -  <asp:Content ID="Content1"
    -     ContentPlaceHolderID="MainContent" runat="server">
    -        <!-- form setup and the rest of the form omitted -->
   10        <p>
    -        <label for="Topic">Topic:</label>
    -                  <%= ColorDropDownHelper.Topic("Topic.Id",
    -          (List<Topic>) ViewData["RealTopics"]) %>
    -                  </p>
   15  </asp:Content>
```

Adding the import statement on line 5 references our new view helper and allows us to use it on line 12. With our drop-down complete, users of GetOrganized will be better able to categorize Thoughts into different Topics.

Let's move on to changing the layout of our site to make it look a whole lot nicer.

6.3 Simplifying Page Layouts with Master Pages

We first used a master page in Section 4.3, *Adding a Little Color with jQuery*, on page 68 when we added the jQuery JavaScript file to the head section of the HTML page. A *master page* is a common template for a group of views. We can think of it as a superclass that contains generic layout information for all our views. Master pages have been a feature of ASP.NET ever since 2.0 and are available in MVC as well. ContentPlaceHolder tags are key elements of a master page. They are defined areas of the page that are specific to each view. Placeholders are present in all the view code we've worked on so far; we just haven't gone into detail about how they work. To start, we'll spruce up GetOrganized's home page with the help of the Microsoft ASP.NET Design Gallery.

Using the ASP.NET Design Gallery

The ASP.NET Design Gallery is a collection of free designs for sites that take you beyond the blue-gray MVC layout.[3] Each layout contains at least a Site.Master master page and a Site.css CSS file. Most also contain additional images, view helpers, and JavaScript that help the site look even better. For GetOrganized, we're going to use the layout called Gray Round to give us rounded corners and a simple menu. Even though the template has a readme.txt file that explains the installation process, let's go through the process together.

First we need to download this layout and unzip it.[4] The structure of these templates includes both a C# and a Visual Basic version, but we are interested only in the C# version in the folder DesignTemplateCS. This template has a Site.Master file, a Site.css file, three images, and a custom HTML helper called MenuItemHelper. Before copying over the Site.Master file, we need to extract the three lines we added to include jQuery and the ColorPicker plug-in.

---

3. http://www.asp.net/mvc/gallery
4. http://www.asp.net:80/mvc/gallery/View.aspx?itemid=21

```
views/site.master.clip
```

```
<head>
<!-- omitted other scripts -->
<link href="../../Content/colorpicker.css"
  rel="Stylesheet" type="text/css" />

<script type="text/javascript"
  src="<%=ResolveUrl("~/Scripts/jquery-1.4.1.js") %>">
</script>
<script type="text/javascript"
  src="<%=ResolveUrl("~/Scripts/colorpicker.js") %>">
</script>
<asp:ContentPlaceHolder ID="Head" runat="server" />
</head>
```

Copy them to the clipboard for now. You'll paste them back in a few minutes after we move the whole template over. Bringing the template over means overwriting the following files:

- Site.Master goes in the Views/Shared directory.

- Site.css and the three image files go in the Content directory.

- MenuItemHelper goes in the ViewHelpers directory.

After copying all the files and including them in our Visual Studio solution, we paste the contents of the old master page back into the new Site.master. We also tweak it so it will work with our application:

```
views/Site.Master
```

```
Line 1   <%@ Master Language="C#"
     -      Inherits="System.Web.Mvc.ViewMasterPage" %>
     -   <%@ Import Namespace="Helpers" %>
     -   <!DOCTYPE html PUBLIC "-//W3C//DTD XHTML 1.0 Strict//EN"
     5      "http://www.w3.org/TR/xhtml1/DTD/xhtml1-strict.dtd">
     -   <html xmlns="http://www.w3.org/1999/xhtml">
     -
     -   <head>
     -   <meta http-equiv="Content-Type"
    10      content="text/html; charset=iso-8859-1" />
     -   <link href="<%=ResolveUrl("~/Content/colorpicker.css") %>"
     -      rel="Stylesheet" type="text/css" />
     -   <link href="<%=ResolveUrl("~/Content/Site.css") %>"
     -      rel="stylesheet" type="text/css" />
    15   <link href="<%=ResolveUrl("~/Content/colorpicker.css") %>"
     -      rel="stylesheet" type="text/css" />
     -   <script type="text/javascript"
     -      src="<%=ResolveUrl("~/Scripts/jquery-1.4.1.js") %>"></script>
     -   <script type="text/javascript"
    20      src="<%=ResolveUrl("~/Scripts/colorpicker.js") %>"></script>
```

```
     <asp:ContentPlaceHolder ID="Head" runat="server" />
     </head>

     <body>
25     <div class="page">

       <div id="header">
         <div id="title">
             <h1>Get Organized</h1>
30       </div>

         <div id="logindisplay">
           <% Html.RenderPartial("LogonUserControl"); %>
         </div>
35
         <div id="menucontainer">
           <ul id="menu">
             <%= Html.MenuItem("Home", "Index", "Home")%>
             <%= Html.MenuItem("My Todos", "Index", "Todo")%>
40           <%= Html.MenuItem("Thoughts", "Index", "Thought")%>
             <%= Html.MenuItem("Process Thoughts",
     "Process", "Thought")%>
           </ul>
         </div>
45     </div>

       <div id="main">
         <asp:ContentPlaceHolder ID="MainContent" runat="server" />

50       <div id="footer">
             GetOrganized &copy; Copyright 2010
         </div>
       </div>
     </div>
55   </body>
     </html>
```

First we make sure to paste the contents *above* the ContentPlaceHolder with the ID TitleContent on line 16. Put it above so that any jQuery placed in the head ContentPlaceHolder executes correctly. Then rename this placeholder to head on line 21 to ensure that our existing views continue to work properly. We replace the default title on every page with GetOrganized on line 29. MenuItemHelper, which generates a menu of links, is another cool thing we get with this template. We can add all the links to our existing controllers to the menu on line 38. The site is now looking spiffy, as shown in Figure 6.3, on the next page.

Before we move on, let's touch up our site's home page by modifying View/Home/Index.aspx. We'd like to add some more obvious links to the

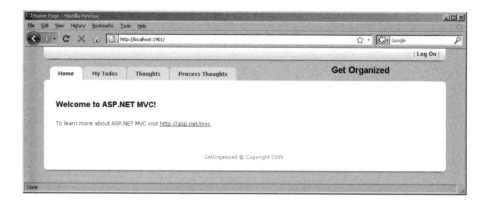

Figure 6.3: Applying an ASP.NET design takes about five to ten minutes, and the effect is dramatic.

page so users can quickly link to their Todo list, Thought creation, or the process Thought screen. To do this, we'll introduce the ActionLink() HTML helper method. To render the links on the home page, we do the following:

`views/Index.aspx`

```
Line 1   &#65279;<asp:Content ID="indexContent"
    -      ContentPlaceHolderID="MainContent" runat="server">
    -        <h2>Quick Links</h2>
    -        <ul>
    5        <li><%= Html.ActionLink("My Todos",
    -            "Index", "Todo") %></li>
    -        <li><%= Html.ActionLink("Input Your Thoughts",
    -            "Create", "Thought") %> </li>
    -        <li><%= Html.ActionLink("Process Thoughts into Todos",
   10            "Process", "Thought") %> </li>
    -        </ul>
    -      </asp:Content>
```

Notice how we use ContentPlaceHolderID="MainContent" to encapsulate the whole view. It will render inside the master page where Content-PlaceHolder is defined. On line 5, we use the method Html.ActionLink(string linkText, string actionName, string controllerName) to render three links to commonly used features of GetOrganized. We also remove the link to http://asp.net/mvc to make the site look more finished (Figure 6.4, on the facing page).

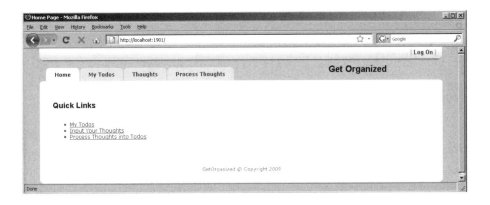

Figure 6.4: VIEWS CAN RENDER LINKS WITH THE HELP OF HTML.ACTIONLINK.

Now we'll deal with an key feature of every web application: field validation. We need to make sure end users properly input Todos into GetOrganized. Valid data is essential and often underestimated in web application development. Luckily, MVC helps us out here.

6.4 Adding Validations Using ModelStateDictionary

Validating end-user input happens on almost every page of a web application. Sometimes we want to make sure passwords don't contain special characters. Other times we want to ensure a phone number conforms to a certain format (such as xxx-xxxx). Because it is such a common thing to do, MVC provides a simple way of validating model objects through the ModelStateDictionary class. Any entry that does not conform to the rules we define adds the specific error to the dictionary. The dictionary is then available to be rendered by the view. We first saw validation crop up in our views back in Section 3.3, *Creating a To-Do*, on page 44, where we saw the Html.ValidationSummary tag. This tag displays a summary of all validation errors stored in the ModelStateDictionary. Let's learn how to use this class by applying validation logic in our Todo. We are going to make sure that the Title can be a maximum of twenty-five characters long.

Validation logic lives in the model. In this example, a Todo's Title needs to brief. We create the IValidatable interface and apply it to any model that requires validation.

```
views/IValidatable.cs
// a marker for Models that can be validated
public interface IValidatable
{
  void Validate(ModelStateDictionary state);
}
```

The interface has only one method, Validate(ModelStateDictionary state), which contains specific validations when we apply it to the Todo class. We save this class to the Models/Validation directory in the Web project to keep it separate from the actual model classes. Let's write a test to check for the validation logic on Todo:

```
views/TodoTest.cs
Line 1  [TestFixture]
   -    public class TodoTest
   -    {
   -
   5    [Test]
   -    public void Title_Length_Should_Be_To_Maximum_Of_25_Characters()
   -    {
   -      Todo longTodo = new Todo {Title="123456789ABCDEF123456789ABCDEF"};
   -      Todo twentyFiveCharacterTodo =
  10        new Todo{Title="123456789ABCDEF1234567"};
   -      Todo shortTodo = new Todo{Title="1234"};
   -
   -      Assert.IsFalse(IsValid(longTodo));
   -      Assert.IsTrue(IsValid(twentyFiveCharacterTodo));
  15      Assert.IsTrue(IsValid(shortTodo));
   -    }
   -
   -    private bool IsValid(IValidatable toValidate)
   -    {
  20      ModelStateDictionary state = new ModelStateDictionary();
   -      toValidate.Validate(state);
   -      return state.IsValid;
   -    }
   -
  25    }
```

This test covers three scenarios: too big (longTodo), just right (twentyFive-CharacterTodo), and small (shortTodo). After setting up the data, we run the first assertion on line 13, which calls up the private method IsValid(IValidateable toValidate) on line 18. We then call on the ModelState-Dictionary property IsValid() to see whether there are any errors within the model we just validated on line 22. This gives us a proper failing test once we add IValidatable to Todo.

Let's now get this to pass:

`views/Todo.cs`

```
Line 1  public class Todo : IValidatable
    -   {
    -     public string Title { get; set; }
    -
    5     public void Validate(ModelStateDictionary state)
    -     {
    -       if (Title.Length > 25)
    -         state.AddModelError("Title",
    -         "Name must not exceed 25 characters" );
    10    }
    -     //... omitted rest of class ...
    -   }
```

First we implement the IValidatable interface on line 5 and perform our validation. We have only one validation, which is to check that the Length of the Title is no longer than twenty-five characters. If this validation fails, we add an error to the ModelStateDictionary through its method AddModelError(string propertyThatIsValidated, string errorMessage) on line 9. As we start to add more validations, instead of relying on IsValid, we can check for the presence of the error message we were expecting to be thrown. This test is now passing, and we're ready to move on to modifying the TodoController to check that the model is valid. We add a test to the TodoControllerTest to test-drive this:

`views/TodoControllerTest.cs`

```
[Test]
public void Should_Display_Errors_When_Todo_Is_Not_Valid()
{
  var invalidTodo =
    new Todo {Title = "123456789ABCDEF123456789ABCDEF"};

  var modelState = todoController.Create(invalidTodo).
    AssertViewRendered().ViewData.ModelState;

  Assert.IsTrue(
    modelState.ContainsKey("Title length must be between 0 and 25"));
}
```

Here we simply want the Create() action to render the Create.aspx screen again when validation fails. We assert that the error with the key *Title* is in the ModelState. This style of searching for the presence of keys in the ModelState is helpful when we are unit testing additional validations independently, such as when we are checking that only hex values are entered for Color, for example.

Let's move onto the controller code:

```
views/TodoController.cs
```

```
Line 1   // POST: /Todo/Create
     -   [Authorize]
     -   [HttpPost]
     -   public ActionResult Create(Todo todo)
     5   {
     -     todo.Validate(ModelState);
     -
     -     if (ModelState.IsValid)
     -     {
    10       CreateTodo(todo);
     -       return RedirectToAction("Index");
     -     }
     -     else
     -     {
    15       return View();
     -     }
     -   }
```

We need to validate the model on line 6 by calling our IValidatable interface. Notice that we pass in ModelState, which is a ModelStateDictionary that exists inside every controller. This object will also be passed to the view to allow validation error messages to be displayed.

We replace our **try/catch** block with an **if/else** on lines 8 and 13 by calling ModelState.IsValid. This is a big victory since swallowing exceptions is never a good idea (see the *Joe Asks...* on page 48). Doing so makes it hard to determine what piece of code threw the exception.

Our Create.aspx view is already set up to display validation errors with an Html.ValidationSummary and several Html.ValidationMessage tags. These were generated when we used the create view template, so they don't need any changes. In Figure 6.5, on the next page, we see the validation error message telling us a Todo's Title is too long.

This covers a simple type of validation, but more complicated examples come up in real-world applications. We'll cover more sophisticated validations in Section 9.5, *Linking NHibernate and MVC Validations*, on page 192. For now we can move on to a more advanced type of HTML helper that comes with MVCContrib: the Grid.

6.5 Replacing Web Controls with Advanced HTML Helpers

There has been a huge investment in ASP.NET web controls over the past eight years. A lot of MVC's barrier to entry will be eliminated by

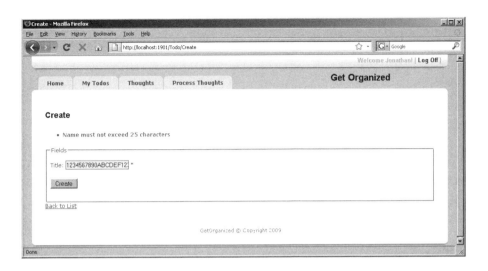

Figure 6.5: HTML.VALIDATIONSUMMARY DISPLAYS ALL THE ERRORS AT THE TOP OF THE PAGE. HTML.VALIDATIONMESSAGE PUTS AN INDICATOR NEXT TO THE FIELD THAT FAILS VALIDATION.

replacing them with more complex HTML helpers or what we'll call *advanced* HTML helpers. Advanced helpers are feature-rich and reusable across different applications, unlike standard HTML helpers. A custom HTML view helper is specific to one application like our Color drop-down, but an advanced helper is useful across many MVC applications. Advanced helpers start out as a custom HTML helper but evolve into a reusable component as its features become more complex. An example of an open source advanced view helper is the MVC-Contrib Grid, located in the MvcContrib.UI.Grid namespace. This component is analogous to the traditional ASP.NET GridView but extends the HTML helper to render it. Grids give us a way to list data in a tabular format, which is a common operation in most web applications. To demonstrate how this component works, we're going to reimplement our /View/Todo/Index.aspx view using the Grid.

There is a short Grid tutorial on the author Jeremy Skinner's blog.[5] The example we're using is similar to one that Jeremy explains in his blog. The Grid uses a concept called *method chaining*, which is common for domain-specific languages (DSLs). You might have seen this before

---

5. http://www.jeremyskinner.co.uk/2009/02/08/rewriting-the-mvccontrib-grid/

when working with jQuery selectors, where every selector returns an array to be operated on again:

`$("li").(".hidden")`

This jQuery returns an array of list elements and then selects elements inside that array that have the CSS class hidden. Chaining allows us to tack additional attributes or features onto an existing statement, eliminating the need for multiple statements. This can be awkward to use at first, but you'll quickly realize the benefits through a reduction of verbose code.

Before we can call Html.Grid, we need to reference the MVCContrib assembly in our project. Simply add the MvcContrib.dll file to the Web project in GetOrganized. Since we now have the reference, we can jump right into the /View/Todo/Index.aspx. We remove the existing table and iterate through a **foreach** loop with a single call to Html.Grid:

views/Todo_Index.aspx

```
Line 1    <%@ Import Namespace="GetOrganized.Models"%>
    -     <%@ Import Namespace="MvcContrib.UI.Grid"%>
    -
    -     <asp:Content ID="Content1" ContentPlaceHolderID="head"
    5        runat="server">
    -        <title>My Todos</title>
    -     </asp:Content>
    -
    -     <asp:Content ID="Content2" ContentPlaceHolderID="MainContent"
   10        runat="server">
    -        <h2><%= ViewData["UserName"] %>'s Todos</h2>
    -
    -     <%= Html.Grid(Model).Columns(column => {
    -           column.For(
   15              todo =>
    -              Html.ActionLink("Delete", "Delete", new {todo.Title})).
    -              Named("Delete").DoNotEncode();
    -            column.For(
    -              todo =>
   20             Html.ActionLink("Edit", "Edit", new { todo.Title })).
    -              Named("Edit").DoNotEncode();
    -            column.For(todo => todo.Title);
    -            })
    -          .Attributes(style => "text-align: center;")
   25      .Empty("You have completed everything. Congrats!")
    -      %>
    -
    -      <p>
    -          <%= Html.ActionLink("Create New", "Create") %>
   30      </p>
    -     </asp:Content>
```

Since there is no unit testing of the view, we can't test-drive this. However, we still have confidence because MVCContrib's Grid has been well unit tested by its authors. Note the reduction in line count on this view. We've gone from several pages of code to a short paragraph that does the same thing. We also see extensive usage of lambda expressions when defining columns in the Grid. We'll see a lot more of this in Section 8.3, *Mapping with Fluent NHibernate*, on page 166.

Before we can call the Grid, we add an import statement on line 2. This lets us call the Grid on line 13 where we pass it the model. The model must be of type IEnumerable<T> for the Grid to work. We then define columns with the method Columns(). This method takes a lambda expression for building all the columns we want. Here we want to define three: the delete link, the edit link, and the Title of the Todo.

For each column we use the method column.For() on line 14 to define what we want to render. On line 16, we render an HTML link just like we did previously, except we use the variable todo, which is defined in the column.For() method. We ensure that the HTML generated for the action link does not become encoded, which is the default behavior of the Grid. Line 17 overrides the encoding with the aptly named DoNotEncode() method. The other two columns follow a similar pattern.

We can also add HTML attributes to the columns on line 24, where we set the **style** to align the text of the columns to center. Another useful feature of the Grid is to display a message when there is no data in the list. On line 25, we call the method Empty() and pass it in the message we want displayed when the list is empty. The Grid renders both scenarios, one with a set of Todos (Figure 6.6, on the following page) and one without any (Figure 6.7, on the next page).

Advanced HTML helpers like the Grid simplify the task of displaying repetitive data. In the near future, more open source and commercial advanced HTML helpers will become available.

Up Next

We learned more about how to make our site look better through master pages. We also learned how to move logic from the view itself into either a custom HTML helper or an advanced one. We touched on adding validation to our models and having errors display on the view. In the next chapter, we'll continue learning about views by seeing how to use Ajax and partial views. Partials continue to improve the design and usability of our site while reducing duplicate code.

Figure 6.6: The MVCContrib Grid displays tabular data with minimal markup in the view.

Figure 6.7: Using the Empty() method takes care of situations when there's nothing in the list.

Far more thought and care go into the composition of any prominent ad in a newspaper or magazine than go into the writing of their features and editorials.

▶ Marshall McLuhan

Chapter 7

Composing Views with Ajax and Partials

Ajax and embedded apps (such as Flash) are changing users' browsing experience. In the Microsoft stack, you'll be using technologies such as Silverlight, Ajax, and a lot of JavaScript to develop rich Internet applications (RIAs) with code that executes on the user's browser. For example, the latest release of Firefox 3.5 supports the concept of worker threads. This lets you run JavaScript in the background similar to the way a desktop application does.

First we'll focus on improving usability through Ajax. MVC has several controller ActionResults that help with Ajax calls. MVC also comes bundled with jQuery, which has easy Ajax support. We'll then introduce partial views, which allow us to generate fragments of HTML. Partials reduce duplicate view code, as we'll learn in Section 7.3, *Using Partials to Reduce Duplication*, on page 149. GetOrganized is missing Ajax currently. To make the application feel more responsive, we'll be adding a few new features there. We'll also cover how to perform common Ajax operations that many applications require—including GetOrganized. We'll learn to delete models with the HTTP POST method without having to click a submit button. Also, one of the most commonly used Ajax features is to perform an autocomplete search, like Google Suggest does. We'll learn how to do that using a jQuery plug-in with MVC.[1]

---

1. I'd like to thank my colleague Joe Poon for helping develop the content in this chapter. It is based on a presentation that we did for a .NET user group in Calgary, Canada, in 2009. The slides and code are available for download on Joe's blog at http://joepoon.com/blog/2009/05/14/jquery-at-the-calgarynet-user-group/.

7.1 Working with Ajax

Before we work on deleting a Todo with HTTP POST, we're going to start with a few principles of Ajax development. This includes getting Visual Studio to display the jQuery API to help us with our syntax.

In a nutshell, Ajax is a browser-based technology that is called using JavaScript. It generally is used to update web pages without having to navigate to a new page or refresh an existing one. Ajax enriches the user's experience of a website by reducing the number of times a user refreshes the page and has to navigate to multiple pages to get something done. However, some browsers either do not support JavaScript or have disabled it for security reasons. Some mobile devices have yet to build in support for JavaScript libraries such as jQuery. This is why we need to take care to ensure that there is an alternative to Ajax to get the job done. Supporting less "rich" clients is often referred to as *graceful degradation*. Simply put, the web page will still work on browsers that may not support JavaScript or Ajax. Later in Section 7.2, *Finding It in a Snap with Autocomplete*, on page 145, we'll delve into this.

Most end users will be using Ajax, so dealing with graceful degradation presents the problem of duplicating your programming effort. To prevent having two separate implementations, we need to keep the code common. Luckily, MVC has the IsAjaxRequest() method available to you within each controller that can help you create a single implementation. Doing this avoids the creation of controller actions such as CreateWith-AJAX(), which does almost the same thing as Create() does.

Working with Ajax involves more JavaScript and jQuery than we have done so far. One way to help us with the syntax is to enable IntelliSense for jQuery. This is done by downloading a hot fix to Visual Studio 2008.[2] Enabling IntelliSense helps us move between C# and JavaScript with less stress on the brain. If jQuery is completely unfamiliar to you, take a look at http://jquery.com for tutorials and simple walk-throughs. If you're using Visual Studio 2010, there's no need to apply a hot fix.

Keeping in mind graceful degradation and having IntelliSense turned on, we can start working on our first Ajax feature in GetOrganized. We're going to delete a Todo by using an HTTP POST.

---

2. http://code.msdn.microsoft.com/KB958502/Release/ProjectReleases.aspx?ReleaseId=1736

Deleting with HTTP POST

The first Ajax operation we'll do will revisit the way we deleted Todos in Section 3.4, *Deleting: Creating an Action Without a View*, on page 50. We will now restrict that controller action to allow only HTTP POST. Starting out we'll just modify the action method shown here:

`ajax/TodoController.cs`
```
Line 1   // GET: /Todo/Delete/Title={name of todo}
    -    [AllowedVerbs(HttpVerb.HttpPost)]
    -    public ActionResult Delete(string title)
    -    {
    5      Todo.ThingsToBeDone.
    -        Remove(
    -        Todo.ThingsToBeDone.Find(todo => todo.Title == title));
    -
    -      if (Request.IsAjaxRequest())
   10        return new EmptyResult();
    -
    -      return RedirectToAction("Index");
    -    }
```

On line 2, we restrict the Delete() operation to HTTP POST. That was easy enough, but now our view /View/Todo/Index.aspx will have problems because it currently tries to delete via an HTTP GET. We also need to detect whether the call is made with Ajax on line 9. This prevents us from sending a redirect to a request that really needs no response at all. In this case, we want to return an EmptyResult because the Ajax request doesn't need any data to complete its operation.

Before we can implement our jQuery, we'll need to create another HTML helper. This is because in the View/Todo/Index.aspx view we use the Grid view component. The Grid only accepts a function for each table column, not hand-coded HTML. Our new HTML helper will create links, which are **anchor** tags with specific **id** and **class** attributes. An exercise to flex your NUnit skills is to write your own test for LinkHelper and see whether you can drive your own implementation. We'll place this helper with the others in ViewHelpers:

`ajax/LinkHelper.cs`
```
Line 1   using System.Web.Mvc;
    -    using System.Web.Routing;
    -
    -    namespace GetOrganized.ViewHelpers
    5    {
    -      public static class LinkHelper
    -      {
```

```
        public static string Link(this HtmlHelper helper,
          string linkText, string url, object htmlAttributes)
10      {
          var builder = new TagBuilder("a");

          builder.MergeAttributes(
            new RouteValueDictionary(htmlAttributes));
15        builder.Attributes.Add("href", url);
          builder.SetInnerText(linkText);

          return builder.ToString();
        }
20      }
      }
```

This HTML helper is similar to the one we created in Section 6.2, *Colorizing a Drop-Down List*, on page 123. The last parameter of the helper on line 9 allows us to pass in anonymous objects from our views. Back in Section 6.1, *Adding a Dash of CSS to HTML Helpers*, on page 121, we added a **class** or **id** attribute to an HTML helper. This lets us call the helper and add our own style:

```
Html.ActionLink("name","action", new { @class = "someCssClass"})
```

This saves us from having many overloading signatures for our helper. This way we can pass in whatever other attributes into the tag we need. To turn this object of attributes into something that TagBuilder can digest, we convert it to a RouteDictionary on line 14. Once converted to an IDictionary<string, object>, it is merged into the tag and can be rendered to the view. Since we have our HTML helper coded, we can move on to the main event—adding jQuery to our view that allows us to delete a Todo:

`ajax/Site.Master`

```
Line 1  <head>
    -   <meta http-equiv="Content-Type"
    -     content="text/html; charset=iso-8859-1" />
    -   <link href="../../Content/colorpicker.css"
    5     rel="Stylesheet" type="text/css" />
    -   <link href="../../Content/Site.css"
    -     rel="stylesheet" type="text/css" />
    -   <link href="../../Content/colorpicker.css"
    -     rel="stylesheet" type="text/css" />
    10  <script type="text/javascript"
    -     src="../../Scripts/jquery-1.4.1.js"></script>
    -   <script type="text/javascript"
    -     src="../../Scripts/colorpicker.js"></script>
    -
```

```
15   <script type="text/javascript"
       src="../../Scripts/jquery.autocomplete.js"></script>
     <link href="../../Content/jquery.autocomplete.css"
       rel="stylesheet" type="text/css" />

20   <script type="text/javascript"
       src="../../Scripts/jquery-ui-1.8rc3.min.js"></script>

     <script type="text/javascript"
       src="../../Scripts/jquery.livequery.js"></script>
25
     <asp:ContentPlaceHolder ID="Head" runat="server" />
     </head>
```

We'll be using several other jQuery plug-ins to get this chapter's code
to work. We've added them to the Site.Master so they're available to
all views. On line 16, we add three jQuery plug-ins: Autocomplete,[3]
jQuery-UI,[4] and Live Query.[5] Some plug-ins, like Autocomplete, come
with a CSS file to add the proper look when it's used. With the necessary JavaScript and CSS files referenced, we can then add the jQuery
we need to do an HTTP POST delete in the View/Todo/Index.aspx file:

> ajax/Index.aspx

```
Line 1   <%@ Page Title="" Language="C#"
         MasterPageFile="~/Views/Shared/Site.Master"
         Inherits="System.Web.Mvc.ViewPage<IEnumerable<Todo>>" %>
         <%@ Import Namespace="System.Drawing"%>
5        <%@ Import Namespace="GetOrganized.Models"%>
         <%@ Import Namespace="GetOrganized.ViewHelpers"%>
         <%@ Import Namespace="MvcContrib.UI.Grid"%>

         <asp:Content ID="Content1"
10         ContentPlaceHolderID="head" runat="server">
         <title>Index</title>
         <script type="text/javascript" language="javascript">
           $(document).ready(function() {
             $(".deleteTodoLink").click(function() {
15             var element = $(this);
               var todoTitle = element.attr("id");

               $.post(
               "Todo/Delete",
20             { title: todoTitle },
```

---

3. http://www.pengoworks.com/workshop/jquery/autocomplete.htm
4. http://jqueryui.com/download
5. http://plugins.jquery.com/project/livequery

```
           function() {
             element.closest("tr").
             fadeOut("slow", function()
           { $(this).remove(); });
25         }
         );
       });
     });
   </script>
30 </asp:Content>

   <asp:Content ID="Content2"
     ContentPlaceHolderID="MainContent" runat="server">
       <h2><%= ViewData["UserName"] %>'s Todos</h2>
35
       <%= Html.Grid(Model).Columns(column => {
            column.For(
                x =>
                Html.Link("Delete", "#", new { id = x.Title,
40                  @class = "deleteTodoLink" })).DoNotEncode();
            column.For(
                x =>
                Html.ActionLink("Edit", "Edit", new { x.Title })).
                Named("Edit").DoNotEncode();
45          column.For(x => x.Title);
            })
         .Attributes(style => "text-align: center;")
        .Empty("You have completed everything. Congrats!")
       %>
50
       <p>
           <%= Html.ActionLink("Create New", "Create") %>
       </p>
   </asp:Content>
```

The first thing to notice is that all of our jQuery code lives inside the
ContentPlaceHolder head at the top of the file. This keeps things more
cleanly separated and makes factoring our jQuery into a separate file
easier if we find it becoming too large.

We need to add a reference to GetOrganized.ViewHelpers on line 6. This
lets us use our new LinkHelper inside the Grid on line 39. Notice how
we use anonymous object initialization here to pass in a **class** and
id attributes. These attributes make using jQuery selectors easier to
determine which delete link is clicked. Let's get to the jQuery code itself.

On line 22, we select the element that is clicked through a jQuery selector using the keyword **this**. jQuery selectors return an array of HTML
elements, so in this case we are selecting the **anchor** tag. This allows us

to grab the **id** attribute, which is the Title of the Todo that we want to delete. We are now ready to perform our Ajax call. The $.post() on line 18 is how we instruct jQuery to make our HTTP POST call to the controller. This method takes three parameters. The first two are the URL and the querystring parameters that it will use to make the request. The last parameter takes a function that gives instructions of what to do when the HTTP POST has completed successfully. Here it removes the Todo row from the table by having it fade out slowly. To select the element that will be deleted, we call element.closest("tr") on line 22. We get the link's closest table row—the **tr** tag—and the column's parent. This selects the whole row we want to delete. On line 24, we remove the row from the HTML document using the remove() method and the jQuery fade() effect.

Running the program with F5 will now show that Todos delete with a nice fade effect. This helps visually indicate to users which items are deleted. Since we have a little more Ajax in our tool belt, it's time to add one of the most popular Ajax functions: autocomplete.

7.2 Finding It in a Snap with Autocomplete

When customers want to build search into a site nowadays, they probably want autocomplete. Search used to involve a lot of back and forth between screens or clicks to get the result you were looking for. With autocomplete, the search results are right there for you to read and to provide immediate feedback as you type.

For GetOrganized, it'd sure be nice to help jog our memory by searching for all the Thoughts we've input. Perhaps you've written an idea down with a lot of details but can't remember the exact title you want to find. Searching is not only a useful feature—it's also a way for us to learn how to implement autocomplete with jQuery and MVC.

A benefit to working in jQuery is the large number of high-quality plug-ins you can download and use. In Section 7.1, *Deleting with HTTP POST*, on page 141, we added the jQuery Autocomplete plug-in to the Site.Master so that it is available for use. There are numerous autocomplete plug-ins for jQuery, some of which are more advanced than the one we are using. For example, you might want to handle callbacks that return data in JSON instead of plain text. For that case, then JQ Autocomplete might better suit your needs.[6]

Before we can autocomplete with jQuery, we must implement a search in the ThoughtController. That means starting with a test.

`ajax/ThoughtControllerTest.cs`

```
[Test]
public void Should_Find_Thoughts_By_Text_Match_Case_Insensitive()
{
  var learnCsharp = Thought.CurrentThoughts[0];
  var contentResult = (ContentResult)
    new ThoughtController().Search("learn");

  Assert.AreEqual(learnCsharp.Name, contentResult.Content);
}
```

This test sets the expectation that we'll find the Thought called *Learn C# 3.5* based on the user typing in *learn*. This means that our search algorithm should be case insensitive. The other thing to note is that because we'll use this action with Ajax, more specifically a jQuery autocomplete plug-in, we need to return plain content to the response. We test for the presence of ContentResult on line 6. Let's get this test passing:

`ajax/ThoughtController.cs`

```
public ActionResult Search(string q)
{
  var searchResults = Thought.CurrentThoughts.FindAll(
  thought => thought.Name.ToLower().Contains(q.ToLower()));

  var autocompleteResults =
    String.Join("\n",
    searchResults.ConvertAll(g => g.Name).ToArray());

  return Content(autocompleteResults);
}
```

On line 1, we named our search parameter q. This is because the jQuery plug-in expects the parameter to be named that way. Normally it's not a good idea to name parameters with single characters because it makes it a lot harder for developers (yourself included) to understand a variable's or method's intent. We also make the search case insensitive on line 4. An easy way to do this is by making everything lowercase with the ToLower() method. Our search algorithm is very primitive; for more advanced text search, see the sidebar on page 151. The next step is to

---

6. http://www.devbridge.com/projects/autocomplete/jquery/

bring the results into a line-separated format on line 8. The Autocomplete plug-in wants each result on a new line, so we join all the Thought's Names using the String.Join() method. We take all of these results and send them back to the response with the Content(object result) method. The test passes, but we need a way to send users to the actual Thought they selected. Right now we can view a Thought only by Id. The next test will be to let us redirect a request that asks for a Thought by Name and send it to the /View/Thought/Detail/Id page.

ajax/ThoughtControllerTest.cs

```
Line 1  [Test]
2  public void Should_Find_Thought_By_Name_And_Redirect_To_Details_View()
3  {
4    var routeValueDictionary = new ThoughtController().
5      FindDetails("Learn C# 3.5").
6      AssertActionRedirect().RouteValues;
7
8    Assert.AreEqual("Details", routeValueDictionary["action"]);
9    Assert.AreEqual(1, routeValueDictionary["id"]);
10  }
```

This tests the ThoughtController action FindDetails(). On line 4, we use a RouteValueDictionary, which is a specialized Dictionary<string, object>. We are testing that the redirect to the details view has the corresponding Id associated with the Thought. The implementation of FindDetails() looks like this:

ajax/ThoughtController.cs

```
Line 1  //
-  // GET: /Thought/FindDetails?nameOfThought={name}
-
-  public ActionResult FindDetails(string nameOfThought)
5  {
-    var thought = Thought.CurrentThoughts.
-      Find(x => x.Name == nameOfThought);
-
-    return RedirectToAction("Details",
10    new { id = thought.Id });
-  }
```

With a simple lambda expression, we can find the associated Id of the Thought. On line 10, we direct to the details view. Note how we use anonymous object notation here to pass in the id to the method. This notation is used throughout MVC to make passing RouteValueDictionary data easier, like how we did for LinkHelper. The test is now passing, and it's time to implement our autocomplete jQuery.

```
ajax/Home_Index.aspx
```

```
Line 1   <asp:Content ID="indexHead" ContentPlaceHolderID="head"
    -       runat="server">
    -    <title>Home Page</title>
    -    <script type="text/javascript" language="javascript">
    5      $(document).ready(function() {
    -        $("#searchThoughtsTextBox").
    -          autocomplete("Thought/Search", { minChars: 1 });
    -        $("#searchButton").click(function() {
    -          window.location = "Thought/FindDetails?nameOfThought=" +
   10            escape($("#searchThoughtsTextBox")[0].value);
    -          });
    -      });
    -    </script>
    -    </asp:Content>
   15
    -    <asp:Content ID="indexContent" ContentPlaceHolderID="MainContent"
    -        runat="server">
    -      <!-- omitted quick link code -->
    -
   20      <h2>Search Thoughts</h2>
    -      <input id="searchThoughtsTextBox" name="title" type="text" />
    -      <input id="searchButton" type="submit" value="Find" />
    -    </asp:Content>
```

The first thing we need to do is actually add our textbox and submit button to support search on line 21. We talked about using graceful degradation earlier. Here we are in part satisfying the needs of non-JavaScript browsers, because we can type in the name of the Thought. To fully support graceful degradation for our search feature, we'd have to do more work than just this, but it's an important principle to keep in mind for production web applications.

Having the textbox on the page will allow us to hook up the jQuery Auto-complete plug-in on line 7. The plug-in takes numerous other options, but we're interested only in the basic usage. We'll supply the URL for it to perform an HTTP GET and {minChars : 1} to start "autocompleting" after the first character is typed in by the user. That's it for autocomplete, but we also want to be able to hook the submit button to redirect the browser to the Thought detail page. This one doesn't require jQuery but the plain old JavaScript window.location property on line 9. Instead of using the JavaScript getElementById(), we use a jQuery selector on line 10. Because all jQuery selectors return an array of objects, we use the first element of the array $(".class")[0] to get the element. The other JavaScript method, escape(), encodes the string into a URL. That's autocomplete in a snap (see Figure 7.1, on the next page)!

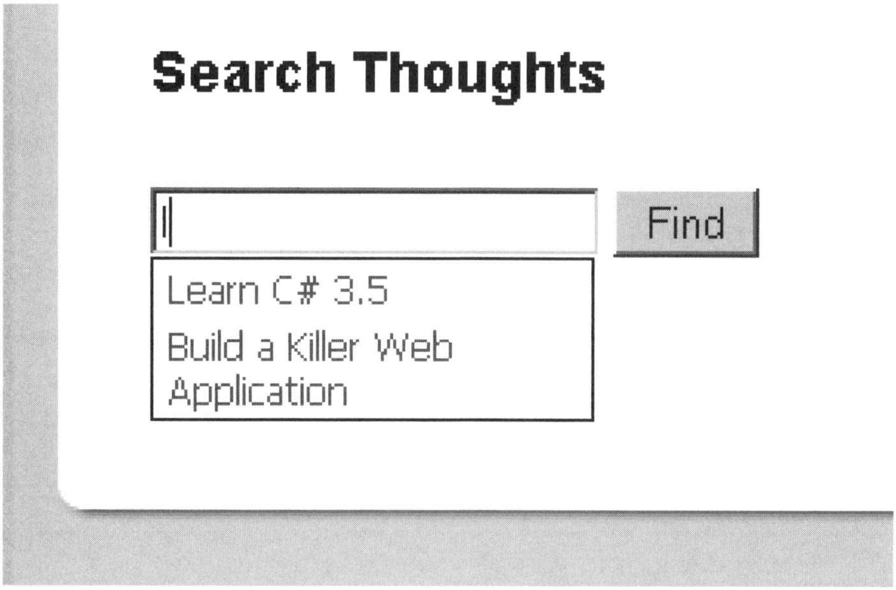

Search Thoughts

| |
| Learn C# 3.5 |
| Build a Killer Web |
| Application |

Figure 7.1: AUTOCOMPLETE MAKES SEARCHING MORE INTERACTIVE.

Other Useful jQuery Plug-Ins

Autocomplete, jQuery-UI, and Color Picker (Section 4.3, *Adding a Little Color with jQuery*, on page 68) are just three of hundreds of useful jQuery plug-ins. You can use plug-ins to do everything from creating Ajax requests to creating visually impressive effects (see Figure 7.2, on the next page).

Plug-ins are nice, but there are even more features of MVC that will also save us time and duplication. Welcome to the world of MVC partials.

7.3 Using Partials to Reduce Duplication

Because of the concept of graceful degradation, we will eventually have view code that is exactly the same on two different pages. Partials help solve this problem that using Ajax introduces.

Partials are like view fragments. For developers who come from a traditional ASP.NET background, partials are comparable to user controls. They allow us to write out a bit of view once and reuse it across multiple views. There is one partial that we are using already, and that is the

Function	Plug-in Name	URL
Multiple file upload	Uploadify	http://www.uploadify.com/
Editing fields without clicking Submit	In-Line Text Edit	http://www.codenothing.com/archives/jquery/inline-text-edit/
Drag and drop	$.event.special.drag	http://blog.threedubmedia.com/2008/08/eventspecialdrag.html
Client-side validation	jQuery Validation	http://bassistance.de/jquery-plugins/jquery-plugin-validation/

Figure 7.2: JQUERY PLUG-INS BY FUNCTION

LogOnUserControl.ascx in the View/Shared directory. The partial renders either the user's name or the signup and login links, and since it is used on every page, it is referenced in the Site.Master. All of this reduces duplication and makes maintaining our code a lot easier.

Let's take a look at partials in action. Our next feature for GetOrganized is to actually create the Todos without leaving the main /View/Todo/ Index.aspx page. We'd better create a new partial from a section of the /View/Todo/Create.aspx if we don't want to repeat ourselves (remember the DRY principle!).

Refactoring to Use a Partial

To perform this refactoring, we're going to move most of the view code from the Create.aspx view to a new partial view. We'll then render this partial inside the Create.aspx view, and everything will look and work as it did before.

We create a partial with the Add View Wizard (Figure 7.3, on page 152). In the wizard, you'll select the first check box indicating that you want to create a partial. It's worth noting that you can make strongly typed partials as well, but in this case we're just going to copy and paste them from Create.aspx into our newly created CreateElements.ascx.

More Robust Text Searches

Searching text is arguably one of the most important features of a business to consumer (B2C) website. Imagine how much Amazon invests in making books easier to find for end users. Although we may never have the resources of Amazon or Google when it comes to text search, we can use several tools that will get us closer.

The first, and more traditionally used, is a free-text index that most relational databases, including Microsoft SQL Server, have. Although fairly good in results, this can put a lot of demand on your database to manage these indexes. A popular alternative is to use the open source project Lucene.* Lucene manages text searching as a stand-alone server, so from an infrastructure perspective, this allows you to scale out more Lucene servers as your text-based searching increases. Oren Eini wrote an article on how to integrate NHibernate with Lucene, giving us the power of both the database and an excellent text search engine. †

*. http://lucene.apache.org/java/docs/index.html
†. http://ayende.com/Blog/archive/2007/03/18/Googlize-your-entities-NHibernate--Lucene.NET-Integration.aspx

ajax/CreateElements.ascx

```
<%@ Control Language="C#" Inherits="System.Web.Mvc.ViewUserControl" %>
<% using (Html.BeginForm()) {%>
<fieldset>
  <legend>Fields</legend>
  <div class="editor-label">
    <%= Html.LabelFor(model => model.Title) %>
  </div>
  <div class="editor-field">
    <%= Html.TextBoxFor(model => model.Title) %>
    <%= Html.ValidationMessageFor(model => model.Title) %>
  </div>
  <p>
    <input type="submit" value="Create" />
  </p>
</fieldset>
<% } %>
```

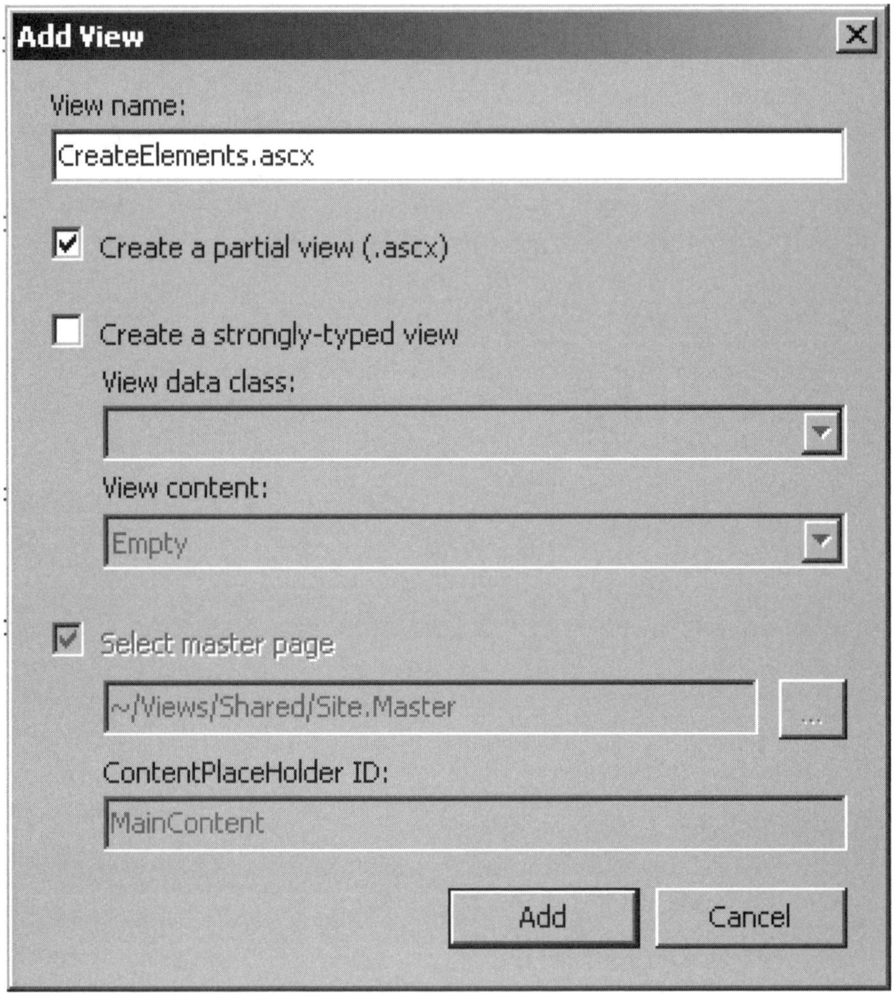

Figure 7.3: Creating partials helps you reduce duplicate markup.

Here we move the entire HTML form tag into the partial including all the textboxes, validations, and submit button. Line 1 of the partial indicates that it inherits from System.Web.Mvc.ViewUserControl. This is the base class for all partials. We didn't change any other code here except to extend the HTML form tag to give it the **id** of CreateTodo. This allows us to use jQuery to intercept the submit button click event and instead do an Ajax call. Right now, however, we're going to want to restore the Create.aspx to its former glory.

`ajax/Create.aspx`

```
Line 1   <asp:Content ID="Content2"
    -        ContentPlaceHolderID="MainContent" runat="server">
    -
    -      <h2>Create Todo</h2>
    5      <%= Html.ValidationSummary() %>
    -
    -      <% Html.RenderPartial("CreateElements"); %>
    -
    -      <div>
   10          <%=Html.ActionLink("Back to List", "Index") %>
    -      </div>
    -    </asp:Content>
```

Rendering a partial is done through the HTML helper method RenderPartial(string partialName) on line 7. Notice that we don't specify a directory of the partial, like /View/Todo/CreateElements.ascx. Instead, we rely on the MVC framework's view engine to perform this search on our behalf. The default WebFormViewEngine looks inside two virtual directories. The first is the location of the calling view, in this case /View/Todo, and the other is the /View/Shared. View engines are another key extensibility point in the MVC framework (the *Joe Asks...* on the next page).

Partials can also take model or other view data as a parameter, which we didn't need to do here. This is useful if you're rendering the details of part of a model such as a customer's address, for example. That's all we need to do to get our partial working. You can hit F5 and verify that the original Create.aspx is still working. Up next, let's add some Ajax.

Creating New Models with Ajax

Because we have extracted the CreateElements.ascx partial, we can now improve the user's experience by adding a new Todo straight from /View/Todo/Index.aspx. You can accomplish this by adding the partial to the /View/Todo/Index.aspx in a hidden **div** tag.

> ### ＼// Joe Asks. . .
> ### ２ｆ When to Use a Different View Engine?
>
> Sometimes it's a personal preference to move to something like NHamel* or StringTemplate;† however, there are some clear advantages to going with them. First, they can be a lot more succinct in the number of lines of code. The same view in NHamel might take up less space by providing conventions like autoterminating the end of your tags. The other is to enforce less logic in the view. For StringTemplate, there is no **if** or **else** syntax available to you, so this forces you to place all conditional logic into view helpers.
>
> The big downside to using one of these alternative view engines or extending them to create your own is support. Most mainstream ASP.NET developers will be much more familiar with the Web Forms view engine instead of the more exotic NHaml or StringTemplate. If your team is more experienced and you have the confidence that you can provide supporting documentation to the people who will eventually support your application, then using a custom view engine can be a really good idea.
>
> ─────────────
> *. http://code.google.com/p/nhaml/
> †. http://code.google.com/p/string-template-view-engine-mvc/

We're going to use some more jQuery to reveal and hide the partial as the user sees fit:

`ajax/Index.aspx`

```
Line 1   <asp:Content ID="Content1"
    -       ContentPlaceHolderID="head" runat="server">
    -    <script type="text/javascript" language="javascript">
    -      $(document).ready(function() {
    5      // omitted jQuery code from previous step
    -
    -        $("#Create_Link").click(function() {
    -            $("#Create_Div").slideToggle("slow");
    -        });
   10        $("#Create_Link")[0].href = "#";
    -      });
    -    </script>
    -    </asp:Content>
    -    <asp:Content ID="Content2"
   15      ContentPlaceHolderID="MainContent" runat="server">
```

```
     <!-- omitted grid code -->
     <p>
       <%= Html.ActionLink("Create New", "Create",
         null, new { id="Create_Link"}) %>
20   </p>
     <div id="Create_Div" style="display:none">
       <% Html.RenderPartial("CreateElements"); %>
     </div>
     </asp:Content>
```

We add the partial on line 22 and hide it by setting the **display** attribute to none. This way when the screen loads for the first time, our form doesn't take up all the real estate. We then add a link on line 19 that users can click to reveal or hide the **div**. We put an **id** attribute on the link and the **div** so that we can manipulate them with jQuery.

The first select on line 8 wires up the click event to the link on the page. This invokes the slideToggle(var speed) to hide or show the **div** with an animation slide effect. What's helpful about this method is it handles both show and hide scenarios. The other selector, on line 10, takes care of graceful degradation by setting the link to reference itself. This way users who don't have JavaScript will still be able to use the old Create.aspx view. In Figure 7.4, on the following page, we can see how the finished slider saves us space on the View/Todo/Index.aspx view.

Adding without leaving the screen works well, but you'll notice it's still refreshing the page every time we add a new Todo. Before you can add a jQuery post(), you'll need to modify the TodoController to return some JSON.

ajax/TodoController.cs

```
Line 1  // POST: /Todo/Create
        [AcceptVerbs(HttpVerbs.Post)]
        public ActionResult Create(Todo todo)
        {
5         todo.Validate(ModelState);

          if (ModelState.IsValid)
          {
            CreateTodo(todo);
10          if (Request.IsAjaxRequest())
              return Json(todo);
            return RedirectToAction("Index");
          }
          else
15        {
            return View();
          }
        }
```

Figure 7.4: JQUERY TOGGLING CAN HELP FREE UP PAGE REAL ESTATE.

On line 10, we check whether the request is sent by Ajax using the IsA-jaxRequest() method. We talked about this method before in Section 7.1, *Working with Ajax*, on page 140 but didn't explain how it performs its magic. When a web request is sent via Ajax, it adds the HTTP header X-Requested-With: XMLHttpRequest to let the web server know this is a different kind of request. IsAjaxRequest() is checking for the presence of that header and returns true if it is there. In our case, the Ajax request needs to return our Todo as JSON.

The last thing we have to do is add some jQuery to the Index.aspx page, and we'll have a newly created Todo without a screen refresh.

`ajax/Index.aspx`

```
Line 1  <asp:Content ID="Content1"
          ContentPlaceHolderID="head" runat="server">
        <script type="text/javascript" language="javascript">
        $(document).ready(function() {
     5    $("#CreateTodo").submit(function() {
            $.post(
              $(this).attr('action'),
              $("#CreateTodo").serialize(),
```

```
10    function(data, textStatus) {
        var html =
        "<tr><td><a id=\"" + data.Title + "\"" +
        "class=\"deleteTodoLink\" href=\"#\">" +
        "Delete</a></td>" +
15      "<td><a href=\"/Todo/Edit?Title="
        + data.Title + "\">Edit</a></td>" +
        "<td>" + data.Title + "</td></tr>";

        $(html).appendTo($("#main table")).
20        effect("highlight", {}, 3000);
      },
      // Return type
      "json"
    );
25    return false;
    });
  }
```

We want to create a new Todo but also dynamically add it to the HTML
Document Object Model (DOM) so the page doesn't have to be refreshed.

First we have to intercept the submit button click on line 5. We use
the usual jQuery post() command and grab the URL from the HTML
form's **action** attribute. There is a special method called serialize() that
turns your form **input** tags into a querystring. We do this on line 8 as
the second parameter to the POST.

The usage of this post() is slightly different from when we deleted a Todo.
Here we want a callback from the server on line 11. This method takes
the JSONified Todo and inserts it into a new row. The row is attached
to the DOM on line 20 with a little jQuery UI effect that highlights the
new row. Because we're expecting JSON, we also specify that as the
last parameter to the post() on line 23.

We can now add without a page refresh. Highlighting the new row
clearly shows the user what they created. However, there is one problem. When you click delete on any of the newly created Todos, nothing
happens. This is because the jQuery we wrote to handle delete events
only wired up ones that existed when the document loaded. Luckily,
jQuery has a very popular plug-in called Live Query that can solve this
for us without a fuss.

ajax/Index.aspx

```
Line 1   <script type="text/javascript" language="javascript">
    -    $(document).ready(function() {
    -        $(".deleteTodoLink").livequery('click', function() {
    -            var element = $(this);
    5            var todoTitle = element.attr("id");

    -            $.post(
    -              "Todo/Delete",
    -              { title: todoTitle },
    10             function() {
    -                element.closest("tr").
    -                fadeOut("slow", function()
    -                { $(this).remove(); });
    -              }
    15           );
    -        });
    -    });
    -    </script>
    -    </asp:Content>
```

On line 3, we replaced the click(function()) with livequery('click', function(). Live Query works by observing the jQuery DOM manipulation methods like append() and addClass() to detect changes to the DOM and rewire events as necessary. So long as the DOM is modified through valid jQuery methods or plug-ins, Live Query is your savior.

With that change at hand, our create and delete with Ajax is complete and functional. Long live Web 2.0!

Up Next

In this chapter, we learned to use the jQuery Ajax method $.post(). We also saw how jQuery plug-ins save us valuable development time for common features like autocomplete. We saw how using partials reduces code duplication when adding Ajax. Keep in mind that partials are similar to traditional ASP.NET user controls, except they do not have any state or application logic in them.

Next up, you'll find out about the ORM that we'll use to replace these ugly static lists we've been using. No need to dust off those SQL skills, because we're about to learn to use NHibernate.

Part III

Integrating with Other Frameworks

It is a common experience that a problem difficult at night is resolved in the morning after the committee of sleep has worked on it.

▶ John Steinbeck

Chapter 8

Persisting Your Models

Up until now we've been working mostly with MVC on its own. However, no framework is an island, and MVC is no exception. To complete an MVC application from end to end, we'll need to make it work with other frameworks. This part of the book will introduce how to do this with a few frameworks, specifically NHibernate and Castle Windsor. In this part, we'll also work on setting up web services to integrate with other applications.

Although we will work through these particular frameworks, the approach to integration is similar for other frameworks. So, even if you choose to use a different persistence framework, these chapters will provide a reference for how to integrate.

This chapter introduces NHibernate. We've gotten by with using static lists to store our models long enough. It's time to replace them with the NHibernate persistence framework, which saves us valuable time by handling the chore of persisting and retrieving objects from the database. It abstracts Structured Query Language (SQL) and allows us to keep our focus on objects instead. NHibernate translates between our models and the columns and rows in the database.

We'll be covering a lot of ground with NHibernate, so we're going to split the information into the next two chapters. This chapter deals with setting up NHibernate and getting CRUD operations going for the Todo model. You'll see how to use the repository pattern to map your MVC models to be persistable objects by creating a TodoRepository class. You will also see how to configure NHibernate with the help of FluentNHibernate.

In Chapter 9, *Integrating Repositories with Controllers*, on page 177, we'll join the TodoRepository back into the MVC framework. By the end of these two chapters, GetOrganized will be saving and retrieving all the information in the database. You'll have a solid foundation for using NHibernate when working on your own MVC projects.

Before we dive into setting up NHibernate, it is important to understand the different approaches to using an ORM with MVC. The approach we use in this book will cover a large number of cases, but it's good to know the alternative design patterns and frameworks that fit the other circumstances.

8.1 MVC's Next Top Model: NHibernate

MVC lets you choose the best way for your project to store and retrieve model data. We're using NHibernate because it's the most mature ORM in .NET, and it's based on an even more mature Java project: Hibernate. There is a ton of free online documentation associated with NHibernate, and its performance and reliability are second to none.

NHibernate isn't your only option. LINQ to SQL is also popularly paired with MVC. It is a quick and easy framework to get you started and is bundled as part of the .NET Framework 3.5. Although starting out with NHibernate is a little more demanding initially, the trade-offs of learning a more robust ORM will quickly outweigh that initial investment.

NHibernate is very flexible, but we'll be using only a small fraction of its power in this book. For more in-depth coverage, I suggest reading *NHibernate in Action* [KBKH09], because it discusses caching, batching, and advanced queries using Hibernate Query Language (HQL). Another project to watch is the LINQ provider to NHibernate, which will give you the query syntax of LINQ instead of string-based HQL.[1] Because NHiberate is so flexible, we'll need to choose one way to use it in GetOrganized.

When to Use Active Record, Query Object, or the Repository Pattern

There are many ways that applications implement persistence. Active Record, Query Object, and Repository are among the most common design patterns used in enterprise software development.

---

1. http://sourceforge.net/projects/nhibernate/files

All these patterns are described in more detail in *Patterns of Enterprise Application Architecture* [Fow03] by Martin Fowler. The Repository pattern insulates the data access code by creating a layer of classes to translate back to application code. The advantage to Repository is it has a clear separation of concerns between application logic and ORM/database access code. Active Record has been popularized more recently by Ruby on Rails. Instead of using Repository classes to encapsulate the ORM code, it uses the model classes themselves to manage data access. NHibernate can also be configured to use the Active Record pattern.[2] Query Object is a pattern that propagates a number of small lightweight classes that contain a complex query. This can prevent your Repository or Active Record objects from becoming too large but more importantly can encourage query reuse.

For GetOrganized, we're going to use the Repository pattern because it's the easiest to understand and get started with. It's also the most frequently seen in .NET web applications. The Repository pattern insulates the data access code by creating a layer of classes to translate back to application code. It gives you a place to put code that deals with any data access optimizations or quirks that can come up while using an ORM. In ASP.NET MVC, the repository class manipulates data access, and the controller class coordinates a user's request.

There is no straightforward answer to the question of which one is the best to use. Although not as religiously debated as "angle brackets on their own line," it is the source of a lot of discussion in developer communities. Remember that any design pattern implemented poorly will make a bad name for itself.

8.2 Using the Repository Pattern

This pattern keeps our data access code in a discrete set of objects. This lets us test our ORM code independently of our controller code. Since GetOrganized already has a number of model objects, we're only going to convert the Todo static lists into a TodoRepository. The rest of the object code will be converted and available for download with the rest of the solution. Before we can test-drive new repositories in GetOrganized, we need to configure NHibernate to work against our database. For this

---

2. http://www.castleproject.org/ActiveRecord

we'll use Fluent NHibernate, a project that helps simplify configuration and class mapping for NHibernate.

Configuring NHibernate Fluently

First we'll create a second database instance to run our repository tests against. This protects the other instance from being overwritten as we run repository tests. If you don't recall how to do this, take a look back at Section 5.2, *Set Up SQL Server for the Membership Provider*, on page 89. We'll call this database instance test_GetOrganized. The next thing to do is create a new test project to hold our persistence test called Test.Persistence just like we created Test.Unit. Having separate projects for persistence tests allows us to monitor more easily if tests living in Test.Unit are wrongly accessing the database. You'll need to download and add references to the latest copy of Fluent NHibernate binaries. For this book, we're using Build #636.[3] Place these files in your Library folder, the same place you've stored NUnit and Rhino Mocks. Don't forget to add a reference to the Web project because that is where the repositories and configuration code will live.

Inside our Web project, we're going to need to add a directory called Persistence. This is where we'll store classes related to the connection and configuration for NHibernate. We'll also create the subdirectory Repositories to hold the repository classes for our project. We'll add one more subdirectory called ClassMaps to hold our database-to-class mapping files, Section 8.3, *Mapping with Fluent NHibernate*, on page 166. That will be our basic housekeeping for new directories. Let's create the **class** NHibernateConfiguration to hold configuration information:

`persistingmodels/NHibernateConfiguration.cs`

```
Line 1  using System;
        using FluentNHibernate.Cfg;
        using FluentNHibernate.Cfg.Db;
        using NHibernate;
     5  using NHibernate.Cfg;
        using NHibernate.Dialect;
        using NHibernate.Tool.hbm2ddl;

        namespace GetOrganized.Persistence
    10  {
          public class NHibernateConfiguration
          {
            public static ISessionFactory SessionFactory { get; private set; }
```

---

3. http://fluentnhibernate.org/downloads/fluentnhibernate-binary-1.0.0.636.zip

```
15    public static void Init(IPersistenceConfigurer databaseConfig,
         Action<Configuration> schemaConfiguration)
      {
        SessionFactory = Fluently.Configure()
          .Database(
20          databaseConfig)
          .Mappings(m => m.FluentMappings.
            AddFromAssemblyOf<NHibernateConfiguration>())
          .ExposeConfiguration(schemaConfiguration)
          .BuildSessionFactory();
25    }

      public static ISession CreateAndOpenSession()
      {
        return SessionFactory.OpenSession();
30    }
    }
  }
```

On line 13, we declare the NHibernate SessionFactory, which acts as our connection manager to the database. It also supports data caching and other NHibernate features. The factory provides an ISession that the **class** used to make calls to the database. An ISession is expensive to create, because it is obtaining connections to the database. You only want to use one per request. We'll use the method CreateAndOpenSession() on line 29 to wrap the SessionFactory and provide an open and ready ISession that our repositories can access.

Configuring NHibernate is done through the Init(IPersistenceConfigurer databaseConfig, Action<Configuration> schemaConfiguration) on line 16. The first parameter is the database configuration; for example, MsSql-Configuration.MsSql2005 specifies a connection to SQL Server 2005. The second parameter allows us to pass in some particularly useful NHibernate objects, SchemaUpdate or SchemaExport. SchemaUpdate compares the current database schema to one that you've defined in your NHibernate mappings. SchemaExport just wipes out the existing schema with whatever NHibernate mappings you've defined. This is useful from a testing perspective; however, you'd never do this for a production database! The second parameter is in use on line 23 where the NHibernate configuration is exposed, allowing the schema update or export to be performed.

The meat of the Init() is to configure the SessionFactory. This is done based on database information on line 19 as well as model class mapping information. We're going to cover class mappings in Section 8.3, *Mapping with Fluent NHibernate*, on the next page, but on line 21, we tell NHibernate that our mapping files are all in the same assembly as NHibernateConfiguration. Fluent NHibernate will load all the class maps into the configuration, instead of manually adding a line to a configuration file each time we create a new mapping. This is a similar technique to what we'll use when we introduce how to register controllers and repositories with Windsor Container in Section 9.2, *Using Inversion of Control with the IControllerFactory*, on page 181.

NHibernateConfiguration will be used by both test and production code, but before we can initialize a useful SessionFactory, we'll need to map some classes to the database.

8.3 Mapping with Fluent NHibernate

For an ORM to do its job, it needs instructions on how your objects map to database tables. The simplest way to do this is automapping. Automapping can be configured to look for specific namespaces so that only your actual model classes are mapped. This prevents controller classes, for example, from being mapped to the database. Automapping works by matching .NET data types to the equivalent data type for the database. For example, the .NET Integer **Int32** would translate to the **int** data type in SQL Server. Adding automapping to your Fluent NHibernate configuration is as simple as appending the following code to our Fluently.Configure() in NHibernateConfiguration:

```
persistingmodels/NHibernateConfiguration.cs
var model = AutoMap.AddFromAssemblyOf<NHibernateConfiguration>()
  .Where(t => t.Namespace == "GetOrganized.Models");

var configuration = Fluently.Configure()
  .Database(databaseConfig)
  .Mappings(m => m.AutoMappings.Add(model));

configuration.BuildSessionFactory();
```

However, automapping will take you only so far, such as when you need to specify specific relationships and data types. That is why we'll be working with class maps. Traditionally these maps exist as XML files, one for each class. Our Todo class would have an embedded XML file called Todo-mapping.xml. Fluent NHibernate lets us map classes using C# classes by inheriting the class ClassMap. Using C# classes to map makes it easier to check for syntax errors and also makes navigating the class map files easier.

We're going to store all our maps in the directory Persistence/ClassMaps. Let's map Todo using Fluent NHibernate:

persistingmodels/TodoMap.cs

```
Line 1   using FluentNHibernate.Mapping;
    -    using GetOrganized.Models;
    -
    -    namespace GetOrganized.Persistence.ClassMaps
    5    {
    -      public class TodoMap : ClassMap<Todo>
    -      {
    -        public TodoMap()
    -        {
   10          Id(x => x.Title);
    -          Map(x => x.Completed);
    -          Map(x => x.Outcome);
    -          References(x => x.Topic).ForeignKey().Not.LazyLoad();
    -        }
   15      }
    -    }
```

The class inherits from ClassMap and uses Todo as the generic type. The object to database mapping happens in the constructor of TodoMap. On line 10, we map the Title as the primary key using the Id(). The other fields are mapped on line 11 using the Map() method. We can also specify how long we want that string to be in the database by adding Map(x => x.Outcome).Length(250), where Outcome will now be an **nvarchar(250)** column in the database.

When it comes to referencing another type like Topic where we have a *many-to-one* relationship, we use the method References() on line 13. We also add the method ForeignKey() to ensure that our database schema generates an actual foreign key constraint.

The Not.LazyLoad() lets NHibernate know that it should completely load the Topic associated with each Todo. The default behavior of NHibernate, like most ORMs, is to load objects lazily—that is, to only bring back the first layer of information. Details of objects like Topic are only fetched as needed. This prevents performance problems with the underlying database pulling too much information when it's not required. This will come in handy in Section 10.2, *Listing Models as XML*, on page 205 when we need to serialize this object as XML.

Now it's your turn. To finish this project, we need a TopicMap; go ahead and create one. If you get stuck, the complete solution is in the downloadable code in the GetOrganizedFinal/ folder when you unzip it.

As you've seen, Fluent NHibernate makes mapping easy. You'll learn about other relationships such as many-to-one and many-to-many in Section 8.7, *Additional ORM Data Relationships*, on page 175. For now, we can move onto test-driving our first repository.

8.4 Creating and Reading Records

We want GetOrganized's create, read, update, and delete functions to now work with the database. This means test-driving the TodoRepository. The first test will be to read a Todo out of the database. However, if there is nothing in there to begin with, what are we going to read? If we start by testing the create function, how can we verify that our creation worked without reading that data back out again? Because we can't test one without the other, we'll have to test the read and create together.

Since we'll be creating a repository for each model, it would be a good idea to put the configuration and setup of the NHibernate's ISession in one place. We'll create a base class test fixture, RepositoryTestBase, that all of our repository test fixtures inherit from:

persistingmodels/RepositoryTestBase.cs

```
Line 1  public class RepositoryTestBase
     -  {
     -    protected ISession session;
     -
     5    [SetUp]
     -    public void setup()
     -    {
     -      NHibernateConfiguration.Init(
     -        MsSqlConfiguration.MsSql2005.ConnectionString(
    10          builder =>
     -          builder.Server("localhost").
     -            Database("test_GetOrganized").
     -            TrustedConnection()),
     -        RebuildDatabase());
    15
     -      session = NHibernateConfiguration.CreateAndOpenSession();
     -    }
     -
     -    [TearDown]
    20    public void teardown()
     -    {
     -      if (session != null) session.Dispose();
     -    }
     -
    25    private Action<Configuration> RebuildDatabase()
     -    {
     -      return config => new SchemaExport(config).Create(false, true);
     -    }
     -  }
```

On line 8, we specify the test database we created back in Section 8.2, *Configuring NHibernate Fluently*, on page 164. If you have a lot of persistence tests and are finding things are running too slow, you might consider connecting to an in-memory database like SQLite. To connect to SQLite, just use the following code instead in your database section:

```
SQLiteConfiguration.Standard.InMemory()
```

To get SQLite to work, you'll need to download the .NET drivers,[4] but note that the SchemaExport is currently not working properly. On line 16, we make sure that a new ISession is available for each test. In the configuration, we also specify that we want to wipe out the database and use the latest schema (based on our class maps) on line 27. The method Create(bool createScript, bool dropExistingSchema) on the Schema-Export performs this for us. If you wanted the Data Definition Language (DDL) from NHibernate, you can specify the first parameter, bool create-Script, to be **true**.

We need to take care to clean up the session on line 22 by calling Dispose() if it hasn't been called already. We do this explicitly to free up connections to the database. Whenever external resources such as database connections are being used, practice good housekeeping, and ensure they are being recycled.

Now we'll move onto our TodoRepositoryTest, which inherits from our RepositoryTestBase.

persistingmodels/TodoRepositoryTest.cs

```
Line 1  [TestFixture]
    -   public class TodoRepositoryTest : RepositoryTestBase
    -   {
    -     private TodoRepository repository;
    5
    -     [SetUp]
    -     public void Setup()
    -     {
    -       //remove this call to setup once ReSharper
    10      //unit test runner supports NUnit 2.5
    -       setup();
    -       repository = new TodoRepository(session);
    -     }
    -
    15    [Test]
    -     public void Should_Create_And_Read()
    -     {
    -       Todo todo = CreateTodo();
```

---

4. http://sqlite.phxsoftware.com

```
         var actual = (IList) repository.GetAll();
20       Assert.Contains(todo, actual);
         Assert.AreEqual(1, actual.Count);
     }

     private Todo CreateTodo()
25   {
         var todo = new Todo {Title = "Build Repositories",
           Outcome = "Database is working"};
         repository.SaveOrUpdate(todo);

30       session.Flush();
         return todo;
     }
}
```

On line 12, we create our TodoRepository with an NHibernate ISession in the setup portion of the test fixture. This ensures we'll get a new repository to test against in every test. When it comes to our create and read test, the first thing we do is perform the create Todo on line 28. We've extracted this into a private method called CreateTodo() because every one of our tests, including edit and delete, will need some data to validate that these operations work. Notice how the name of the method is SaveOrUpdate(), because NHibernate will determine this for us based on the mapping we've set up already.

Once the Todo is created, we need to force a connection to the database with the Flush() method on the session. NHibernate knows that it's costly to connect to the database and so tries to minimize the number of times it does this. One way to guarantee that a call is made to the database is to invoke Flush() in our code. For tests this is OK because we're simulating multiple requests, but for most cases of our production code, we can leave this up to NHibernate to decide when to call out to the database.

With the Todo created, we can now perform our read operation on line 19. This is the second method, GetAll(), that we'll need to work on to get this test to pass. We'll assert that the actual Todo is in the collection and that there is only one item in the collection. To get this test passing, we're going to need to create a base repository class as well as the actual TodoRepository because we don't want to repeat the same CRUD over and over again. Let's get part of the test passing by creating the BaseRepository inside Persistence/Repositories in our Web project.

Specifying Additional Criteria

You can add other criteria by specifying the Expression class along with one or more of its various methods. For example, if you wanted to return all the Todos with the Topic of "Work," you can do that with Expression.Eq(x => x.Topic.Title == "Work"). Alternatively, NHibernate has its own full-blown query language called Hibernate Query Language. HQL gives you a more powerful query syntax. For more complicated queries and longer-running projects, it is the recommended approach. CreateCriteria( ) is much more suited for some dynamic queries.*
The LINQ provider for NHibernate is yet another way to express criteria for queries and will allow you to use LINQ syntax to query NHibernate.

---

*.   http://avende.com/Blog/archieve/2009/06/01/nhiberate-queries-ndash-should-i-use-hql-or-criteria.aspx

persistingmodels/BaseRepository.cs

```
Line 1   public abstract class BaseRepository<T>
         {
           protected readonly ISession session;

5          protected BaseRepository(ISession session)
           {
             this.session = session;
           }

10         public virtual void SaveOrUpdate(T model)
           {
             session.SaveOrUpdate(model);
           }
         }
```

First, we'll need to handle the constructor on line 5. This simplifies the constructors for each repository because all repositories use the ISession. By declaring it as a **protected** member, we let repositories that inherit the base access it. Next, we'll implement our create method by delegating to NHibernate's method of handling the create or update on line 10. Using generics with the T prevents us from having cast from one type to another. Having this inside the RepositoryBase makes its children more concise. All **public** methods need to also use the keyword

virtual. This is because eventually we'll use Rhino Mocks to mock out the repositories, and it requires methods to be **virtual**. Similarly, when we have a class, such as Todo, its methods and properties must also be **virtual**. Both Rhino Mocks and NHibernate use a technology called *dynamic proxy*, which allows a C# **class** to be generated at runtime that has different behavior than the real class. Let's now move onto the TodoRepository, which will inherit from BaseRepository.

persistingmodels/TodoRepository.cs

```
Line 1  public class TodoRepository : BaseRepository<Todo>
     2  {
     3    public TodoRepository(ISession session) : base(session) { }
     4
     5    public virtual IList<Todo> GetAll()
     6    {
     7      return session.CreateCriteria(typeof (Todo)).List<Todo>();
     8    }
     9  }
```

Because so much is abstracted into the base class, there is only one method we need to implement in TodoRepository. On line 7, we use the NHibernate method CreateCriteria(Type typeOfModel) to specify a constraint on the kinds of Todos we want back. In this case, we are interested in all of the Todos, so we don't add any other restrictions. Calling List<Todo>() turns the results into a list of Todos. This code makes both conditions of the test pass. With this working, let's move on to editing an existing Todo to persist.

8.5 Editing Models

Since our TodoRepository already handles editing with the SaveOrUpdate(), we just need to make sure that it works based on our mappings.

persistingmodels/TodoRepositoryTest.cs

```
Line 1  [Test]
     -  public void Should_Edit()
     -  {
     -    var originalTodo = CreateTodo();
     5
     -    session.Clear();
     -
     -    var toModify = repository.Get(originalTodo.Title);
     -    toModify.Outcome = "Get Update working";
    10    repository.SaveOrUpdate(toModify);
     -
     -    session.Flush();
     -    session.Clear();
     -
```

```
15   var actual = (IList)repository.GetAll();
-    Assert.Contains(toModify, actual);
-    Assert.IsFalse(actual.Contains(originalTodo));
- }
```

To test that editing works, we need to create a new Todo. We then reload it from the database, make some changes to it, and save it back again. We'll verify those changes were committed to the database. On line 4, we create our test Todo. After creating our model, we need to clear the NHibernate ISession cache on line 6. The method Clear() removes all items in the cache, allowing us to simulate that our changes are getting persisted to the database. After we load back the Todo from the database, we modify its Outcome and save our changes on line 10. We explicitly flush and clear the session to ensure that the edits get back to the database. We then load them back and assert that the change we made happened. We also check that the original Todo is no longer there in order to rule out the case of creating two Todos instead of updating the existing one. The test requires a new method, GetAll(), on line 8, which we'll need to implement in the BaseRepository to get this test to compile.

persistingmodels/BaseRepository.cs

```
public virtual T Get(object primaryKey)
{
  return (T) session.Get(typeof (T), primaryKey);
}
```

Similar to how we implemented SaveOrUpdate(), the Get() delegates its work to the NHibernate ISession's method to retrieve a single object based on primary key. With that method working, our test is now passing. Our last operation is to handle deleting a Todo.

8.6 Deleting Records

We test deleting the same way we tested editing. We'll need to create a new Todo but this time delete it and verify that it is no longer there.

persistingmodels/TodoRepositoryTest.cs

```
Line 1   [Test]
2        public void Should_Delete()
3        {
4          var originalTodo = CreateTodo();
5          repository.Delete(originalTodo);
6          session.Flush();
7          session.Clear();
8          Assert.IsEmpty((ICollection) repository.GetAll());
9        }
```

> ### ⋎⋏ Joe Asks...
> #### Where Are Your Interfaces?
>
> Most of the time when you see the Repository pattern imple-
> mented, you're going to see a lot of matching interfaces. For
> example, the TodoRepository will implement ITodoRepository. This
> leads to code navigation hell, because when you are following
> code in the IDE, you are brought to the interface, not the con-
> crete implementation. Having all these interfaces also violates
> the true reason we have an interface as a language feature.
> Interfaces are for when you have more than one implementa-
> tion to a common problem. When it comes to the Repository
> pattern, most applications use a single ORM.
>
> The reason you'll see an interface for each repository stems
> from a limitation of older mocking frameworks. A mocking
> framework like NMock* is only able to mock out interfaces.
> Luckily, we're using Rhino Mocks, which lets you mock out any-
> thing with **virtual** methods. That's why for GetOrganized we're
> not going to carry on this proliferation of useless interfaces.
>
> ---
> *. http://www.nmock.org

On line 5, we try to delete the newly created Todo. After a quick session
flush and clear, we call the Repository's GetAll() and check to see that
there are no items in the database. To get this test to pass, we'll need
to implement the Delete() method in the BaseRepository.

`persistingmodels/BaseRepository.cs`

```
public virtual void Delete(T model)
{
  session.Delete(model);
}
```

Because this is a candidate for a generic operation, we put it in the
base class. The method passes the responsibility of the delete onto the
ISession to the real work of removing the item for the database. With
these couple lines of code, we now have a fully functional repository
that we can use in Chapter 9, *Integrating Repositories with Controllers*,
on page 177.

Before we move onto integrating NHibernate into MVC, let's cover a few more types of relationships that will likely come up when mapping your classes, like one-to-many and many-to-many.

8.7 Additional ORM Data Relationships

We've already demonstrated a many-to-one when we said that there are many Todos to each Topic. We'll touch on two other important types of relationships that are often modeled in web applications.

One-to-Many

This is where one model has a collection of another. For example, if we said that a Todo can have more than one Topic, that would make it a *one-to-many* relationship. To express this in Fluent NHibernate, we use the method HasMany() in a class map constructor. So, our hypothetical class map of a Todo with multiple Topics would look like HasMany(x => x.Topics). We'll also need to add the collection itself to the Todo for this to work.

Many-to-Many

Every so often, we need to express a two-way relationship where two models each hold a collection of one another. A classic example of this is with users and roles. There are many users in a system, each with one or more roles. Similarly, roles have many different users. Mapping this in Fluent NHibernate gives us the HasManyToMany() method. The code for the user-to-roles relationships would look like HasManyToMany(x => x.Roles). A *many-to-many* relationship requires the creation of a separate intermediate database table. Fluent NHibernate lets us name that table explicitly if we want by adding .WithTableName("UserRoles").

There is a lot more to cover in NHibernate than we can do here without taking us too far away from MVC. I highly recommend the Fluent NHibernate website for other examples and how-tos on common database setups and advanced mapping support.[5]

Up Next

With NHibernate set up and our repositories crafted, it's time to get these working with the rest of our solution. The next chapter is all about

---

5. http://fluentnhibernate.org

integrating our repository with a controller. This will make GetOrganized remember all of our Todos whenever we shut down our web server.
Away with static lists!

Chapter 9

Integrating Repositories with Controllers

In the previous chapter, we built our first repository to access and modify the database. A repository on its own won't do anything unless it's tied back into MVC, though. This means getting the repository working with a controller. For GetOrganized, we'll take the TodoController and have it retrieve information directly from the TodoRepository. This will finally rid us of the static list Todo.ThingsToBeDone.

To do that, we'll use an open source product called the Castle Windsor container that will help create controllers with their respective repositories. That will leave us in a good place to begin test-driving controllers by mocking out the repositories.

Once we have repositories integrated with controllers, we can simplify the way we validate models. We'll apply NHibernate's built-in validation framework to our MVC models. This makes validations easier to read and implement.

Finally, we'll take a look at NHProfiler, a commercial NHibernate profiler that can help you easily identify performance problems with your usage of NHibernate. It's worth knowing the basics of a profiler like NHProfiler to help spot performance problems early on.

Some of the code in this chapter was adapted from the open source project Sharp-Architecture.[1] Sharp-Architecture provides a highly testable architecture for an ASP.NET MVC application. Here it has helped with setting up the NHibernate session and handling the database transactions.

---

1. http://www.sharparchitecture.net/

The first thing we need to do to integrate NHibernate into MVC is to get the NHibernate session going.

9.1 Fixing the NHibernate Session Inside MVC

For NHibernate to work with MVC, we'll need a place to store the NHibernate ISession. For this job, we'll create a class called NHibernate-SessionStorage located in the Persistence in the Web project right next to the NHibernateConfiguration class. It will be responsible for retrieving and opening the NHibernate ISession in the HttpContext for every web request that comes in.

repositoriesAndControllers/NHibernateSessionStorage.cs

```
public class NHibernateSessionStorage
{
  private const string CURRENT_SESSION_KEY =
    "nhibernate.current_session";

  public static ISession RetrieveSession()
  {
    HttpContext context = HttpContext.Current;
    if (!context.Items.Contains(CURRENT_SESSION_KEY)) OpenCurrent();
    var session = context.Items[CURRENT_SESSION_KEY] as ISession;
    return session;
  }

  private static void OpenCurrent()
  {
    ISession session = NHibernateConfiguration.CreateAndOpenSession();
    HttpContext context = HttpContext.Current;
    context.Items[CURRENT_SESSION_KEY] = session;
  }

  public static void DisposeCurrent()
  {
    if (!HttpContext.Current.Items.Contains(CURRENT_SESSION_KEY))
      return;
    ISession session = RetrieveSession();
    if (session != null && session.IsOpen)
      session.Close();
    HttpContext context = HttpContext.Current;
    context.Items.Remove(CURRENT_SESSION_KEY);
  }
}
```

The public method RetrieveSession() returns an NHibernate ISession. On line 8, we obtain the current HttpContext, which is used as the storage device. We then check to see whether an ISession exists in the collection of Items under the key CURRENT_SESSION_KEY. This makes the method RetrieveSession() safe to call multiple times by either opening a new ISession on line 14 or returning the one that has already been opened for this web request. If the request has no ISession, then OpenSession() is called and asks NHibernateConfiguration to create a new one. It then stores the ISession back into the HttpContext.

The other public method, DisposeCurrent(), closes and releases the NHibernate ISession from the HttpContext. On line 24, we make sure that an ISession exists in the HttpContext, because only requests that use NHibernate will have one. If there is no ISession, then we don't want to call RetrieveSession(), because that opens a new one.

Now we'll put the NHibernateSessionStorage and NHibernateConfiguration to work. We'll need to modify Global.asax.cs to initialize NHibernate and make sure every web request has an ISession. Also, Global.asax.cs will be responsible for safely disposing of the NHibernate ISession once the web request is finished.

`repositoriesAndControllers/Global.asax.cs`

```
public class MvcApplication : HttpApplication
{
  private readonly object lockObject = new object();
  private bool wasNHibernateInitialized;

  private void Application_BeginRequest(object sender, EventArgs e)
  {
    InitializeNHibernate();
  }

  private void Application_EndRequest(object sender, EventArgs e)
  {
    NHibernateSessionStorage.DisposeCurrent();
  }

  private void InitializeNHibernate()
  {
    if (!wasNHibernateInitialized)
    {
      lock (lockObject)
      {
        if (!wasNHibernateInitialized)
        {
          NHibernateConfiguration.Init(
            MsSqlConfiguration.MsSql2005.
```

```
  -            ConnectionString(builder => builder.
  -            FromConnectionStringWithKey("ApplicationServices")),
  -            UpdateDatabase());

30           wasNHibernateInitialized = true;
  -        }
  -      }
  -    }
  -  }

35
  -  private Action<Configuration> UpdateDatabase()
  -  {
  -      return config => new SchemaUpdate(config).Execute(false, true);
  -  }
40  }
```

Every web request that comes into MVC triggers the method Application_BeginRequest(). Alternatively, you can create an HttpModule that runs the same code and wire it up in Web.config. Here we'll just modify the ASP.NET life-cycle events directly in Global.asax.cs for ease of readability.

Application_BeginRequest() checks to see whether NHibernate has been initialized. It *never* calls RetrieveSession() as you might expect. This is because there might be some controllers that don't require database connectivity and therefore never use a session. Instead, an ISession is retrieved only when a repository needs one. This will be covered a little later in Section 9.2, *Using Factory Methods in Castle Windsor to Retrieve Sessions*, on page 185.

The private method InitializeNHibernate() calls NHibernateConfiguration in a thread-safe way. It uses the two private members, lockObject and wasNHibernateInitialized, to ensure thread safety. On line 18, we quickly check to see whether NHibernate has been initialized already, since we want to do this only once. Next on line 20, we use the keyword **lock** to instruct the program to get an exclusive lock on lockObject. This prevents any other thread (incoming web request) from running the rest of this code while the current thread does. To be extra safe, we'll do a second check on the wasNHibernateInitialized on line 22 to make sure that milliseconds before we got the lock another thread didn't already initialize the NHibernate.

Once we're sure about the first thread to initialize NHibernate, we call NHibernateConfiguration to do the job. We pass it the connection string from the Web.Config on line 27. This is the same connection string we set in Section 5.2, *Set Up SQL Server for the Membership Provider*, on page 89. Also, the database schema is set to be upgraded on line 28 by calling Execute(bool generateSQLscript, bool performUpgradeOnDatabase).

Just as we want to ensure we create only one NHibernate session per web request, we also want to safely dispose them once the request is complete. The method Application_EndRequest() is called by ASP.NET after the request is completed. This is where we call NHibernateSession-Storage's DisposeCurrent() method to clean up this resource.

This is all the setup we need to have one NHibernate ISession per request. We can now move on to initializing our repositories and ISessions using an Inversion of Control (IoC) container.

9.2 Using Inversion of Control with the IControllerFactory

As your web application gets larger and more complex, there tends to be a lot more duplication of code. This can happen when you have a team of developers who aren't on the same page about how you do something like creating a repository. For example, the easiest way to create a new repository is to directly invoke the **new** keyword. Easiest isn't always the smartest. After a while, you'll catch yourself repeating this line of code over and over again.

One way to avoid this repetition is to create a RepositoryFactory class. The factory will give you a particular repository in a state that is configured and ready to use. Now all the configuration of the particular repository is in one place. So, the RepositoryFactory helps reduce the duplication and allows developers on teams to create objects in a consistent manner. They do have a downside, however. If repositories start to have their own dependencies on other objects, then you'll end up making the RepositoryFactory more complicated than it needs to be.

Luckily, these headaches of dependency and object creation can be solved by using an Inversion of Control container. An IoC container manages and resolves dependencies between objects. They also centralize object creation, similar to the RepositoryFactory, except they do this for all classes of objects in your application.

For our IoC container, we'll be using the open source Castle Windsor container. There are many IoC containers in the .NET space, other than

Castle Windsor. StructureMap,[2] Ninject,[3] Unity,[4] and Spring.NET,[5] all perform the same job in roughly the same way. We're going to use the Castle Windsor container because it is among the most popular and has a lot of documentation for working with both MVC and NHibernate.

Now let's hook the Castle Windsor container into MVC.

Treat Your Objects like Royalty at Castle Windsor

Back in Section 5.1, *IControllerFactory: Where Controllers Are Born*, on page 86, you saw that the IControllerFactory is the entry interface for the creation of all controllers. Naturally, this is the most logical place to create and inject the repositories into the controllers.

First, download Castle Windsor 2.0,[6] and add the following DLLs to your Lib folder:

- Castle.Core.dll

- Castle.DynamicProxy2.dll

- Castle.MicroKernel.dll

- Castle.Windsor.dll

Creating objects in Castle Windsor is fairly straightforward. You first need to register the type of classes with the Castle Windsor container and then ask the container for an object of that type:

```
repositoriesAndControllers/WindsorSample.cs

IWindsorContainer container = new WindsorContainer();
container.Register<Foo>();
Foo newFoo = container.Resolve<Foo>();
```

Here we create a **new** Castle Windsor container, register a Foo, and then obtain a new Foo. You use the Register() method to register a type and call Resolve() to get a new object. The default behavior of Castle Windsor is to return the exact object that was registered. In Castle Windsor terminology, this is known as having a LifestyleType of Singleton, meaning we only ever have one of these objects in the system. Most of the time

---

2. http://structuremap.sourceforge.net/Default.htm
3. http://ninject.org
4. http://www.microsoft.com/downloads/details.aspx?displaylang=en\&FamilyID=ab3f2168-fea1-4fc2-b40c-7867d99d4b6a
5. http://www.springframework.net
6. http://sourceforge.net/projects/castleproject/files/InversionOfControl/2.0/Castle-Windsor-2.0.zip/download

we want a new object, so we'll set the LifestyleType to Transient. You can register an object with a specific lifestyle like this:

`repositoriesAndControllers/WindsorSample.cs`

```
container.Register<Foo>(LifestyleType.Trasient);
```

That's how to use Castle Windsor in its simplest way. Now it's time to use Castle Windsor to register both controllers and repositories. To get those controllers out, we're going to need to change the DefaultController-Factory to do that. Luckily, MVCContrib already has written the code to take care of this for us.

MVCContrib has two classes related to this function: WindsorController-Factory and WindsorExtensions. Extensions adds the method RegisterControllers() to the IWindsorContainer, allowing us to register all the controllers in our Web project. To demonstrate how the factory code works, we'll include a snippet of it here. It's good to know in case you ever end up building your own controller factory one day:

`repositoriesAndControllers/WindsorControllerFactory.cs`

```
public class WindsorControllerFactory : DefaultControllerFactory
{
  private IWindsorContainer _container;

  protected override IController GetControllerInstance(
    RequestContext context, Type controllerType)
  {
    if(controllerType == null)
    {
      throw new HttpException(404,
        string.Format("The controller for path '{0}' " +
        "could not be found or it does not implement IController.",
        context.HttpContext.Request.Path));
    }

    return (IController)_container.Resolve(controllerType);
  }
}
```

WindsorControllerFactory extends the DefaultControllerFactory and overrides the GetControllerInstance(). This checks for a **null** type and then uses an overload of the Resolve(Type typeToReturn) method to return the appropriate controller.

This will take care of the controller creation, but we need to replace the DefaultControllerFactory with the new WindsorControllerFactory in the Global.asax.cs.

repositoriesAndControllers/Global.asax.cs

```
Line 1   public class MvcApplication : HttpApplication
    -    {
    -      //omit NHibernateConfiguration code...

    5      protected void Application_Start()
    -      {
    -        SetupWindsorContainer();
    -        RegisterRoutes(RouteTable.Routes);
    -      }
   10
    -      private void SetupWindsorContainer()
    -      {
    -        IWindsorContainer container = new WindsorContainer();

   15        RegisterControllers(container);
    -        RegisterNHibernateSessionFactory(container);
    -        RegisterRepositories(container);
    -      }
    -
   20      private void RegisterControllers(IWindsorContainer container)
    -      {
    -        ControllerBuilder.Current.
    -          SetControllerFactory(new WindsorControllerFactory(container));
    -        container.RegisterControllers(typeof (HomeController).Assembly);
   25      }
    -    }
```

We only want to register Castle Windsor once, so the Application_Start() method is the right place for the job. It is called once when the application starts up when the first web request arrives. In this method, we'll call SetupWindsorContainer(), which contains three **private** methods that will set up the container.

We are registering the WindsorControllerFactory in the RegisterControllers(I-WindsorContainer container) method. We'll talk about the RegisterNHibernateSessionFactory() and RegisterRepositories() later in Section 9.2, *Using Factory Methods in Castle Windsor to Retrieve Sessions*, on the facing page. To register the controllers, we access the ControllerBuilder on line 22. This object lets us assign the WindsorControllerFactory with the Castle Windsor container as the new IControllerFactory. On line 24, we use the WindsorExtension class's extension method to register all the controllers in the same assembly as the HomeController.

This takes care of registering controllers with Castle Windsor, but we also need to register other components like our repositories and the NHibernate ISessions.

Using Factory Methods in Castle Windsor to Retrieve Sessions

A **static** method that returns a newly created object is called a *factory method.* NHibernateSessionStorage has a nontraditional factory method called RetrieveSession(). It is nontraditional in the sense that the method returns the same object every time it is created, whereas a true factory will produce new objects every time. In this case, we want the same ISession to be used for the lifetime of a single web request. This is because NHibernate ISessions are expensive to create.

Castle Windsor has a special way to register factory methods. This will provide a way for the repositories we register to obtain an ISession.

`repositoriesAndControllers/Global.asax.cs`

```
Line 1  private void RegisterNHibernateSessionFactory(
     2    IWindsorContainer container)
     3  {
     4    container.AddFacility<FactorySupportFacility>();
     5    container.Register(Component.For<ISession>().
     6      UsingFactoryMethod(() =>
     7      NHibernateSessionStorage.RetrieveSession()).
     8      LifeStyle.Is(LifestyleType.Transient));
     9  }
```

A *facility* is an extension point of the Castle Windsor framework. Here we are using the FactorySupportFacility on line 4. The facility gives providers a way to register factory methods, which we do on line 5, for the ISession type. We call the method UsingFactoryMethod() and pass it a lambda expression on line 6 to specify that the source of the ISession is on the factory method RetrieveSession(). Finally, we instruct Castle Windsor that the ISession is Transient on line 8 so that we get a new one every time one is requested.

With ISessions registered with the factory method, the last step is to register the repositories themselves:

`repositoriesAndControllers/Global.asax.cs`

```
Line 1  private void RegisterRepositories(IWindsorContainer container)
     -  {
     -    IEnumerable<Type> repositories = Assembly.GetExecutingAssembly().
     -      GetTypes().Where(IsRepository);
     5
     -    foreach (Type repository in repositories)
     -    {
     -      container.AddComponentLifeStyle(repository.Name, repository,
     -        LifestyleType.Transient);
    10    }
     -  }
     -
```

```
    private bool IsRepository(Type type)
    {
15    return type.Namespace != null && type.IsClass && !type.IsAbstract &&
        type.Namespace.Contains("GetOrganized.Persistence.Repositories");
    }
```

On line 4, we obtain a list of repositories from the executing assembly (GetOrganized.dll). We restrict the types of classes we get back using the LINQ method Where() with the expression IsRepository() on line 15. This method filters back classes that are concrete (not **abstract** or an **interface**) and in the **namespace** GetOrganized.Persistence.Repositories. For each repository, we register it as transient on line 9 so every request has its own copy.

We have completed registration of the controllers, the repositories, and the NHibernate ISession. Our Castle Windsor container is now ready to serve a web request near you. We can now test-drive our controllers using our newly registered repositories.

9.3 Injecting Repositories into Controllers

All of this registration is the background work to replacing **static** lists with repositories. We learned how to test-drive the repository back in Section 8.4, *Creating and Reading Records*, on page 168. It's time now to test-drive controllers that contain one or more repositories. We do this by mocking out the repository using Rhino Mocks.

Once you become comfortable with mocking the repository, this will become the preferred order for test-driving your code. By starting with controller tests, you get a better idea of what data you will need based on the action it performs.

For example, while test-driving the controller action ProcessOrder(), you uncover that you need to modify both Order and Customer models. If you had started test-driving the OrderRepository first, you might not have seen the need to modify Customer until later. By understanding your coding requirements earlier, you will reduce this kind of rework.

Let's put this into practice. We're going modify the TodoController, which we last left off in Section 5.4, *Test-Driving Authorization*, on page 98. For this test, we're going to work on the Index() action. Let's test-drive this by mocking the TodoRepository.

repositoriesAndControllers/TodoControllerTest.cs

```
Line 1   [TestFixture]
         public class TodoControllerTest
         {
           private TestControllerBuilder builder;
5          private TodoController todoController;
           private MockRepository mocks;
           private ISession session;
           private TodoRepository todoRepository;

10         [SetUp]
           public void setup()
           {
             mocks = new MockRepository();
             builder = new TestControllerBuilder();
15             session = mocks.DynamicMock<ISession>();
             todoRepository = mocks.StrictMock<TodoRepository>(session);
             todoController = new TodoController(todoRepository);
             builder.InitializeController(todoController);
           }
20
           [Test]
           public void Should_Display_Todo_List_And_Logged_In_Users_Name()
           {
             const string userName = "Jonathan";
25           var todoList = new List<Todo>
               { new Todo { Title = "Refactor to NHibernate" } };

             builder.HttpContext.User =
               new GenericPrincipal(new GenericIdentity(userName), null);
30
             Expect.Call(todoRepository.GetAll()).Return(todoList);
             mocks.ReplayAll();

             var viewData = todoController.Index().
35             AssertViewRendered().ViewData;

             Assert.AreEqual(todoList, viewData.Model);

             Assert.AreEqual(userName, viewData["UserName"]);
40           mocks.VerifyAll();
           }
         }
```

To add a mock object, we set it up in the Setup() portion so that it is available to all tests in the fixture. On line 16, we use StrictMock<Todo-Repository>() to create the mock object. We then inject that mock into the TodoController constructor on line 17.

The test itself will use the Expect object, which is part of Rhino Mocks, which we already downloaded and installed in Section 5.4, *Using MVC-*

Contrib's TestControllerBuilder to Test Controllers, on page 99. This object is used to add expected behavior to the mock repository. On line 31, we set the expectation that TodoRepository's method GetAll() will be called and will return the todoList. The expectation needs to be replayed in the mocks collection itself, so on line 32 we use the method ReplayAll(). Alternatively, you can call the mock object explicitly using Replay(object mockObject).

Rhino Mocks objects need to be replayed for them to emulate the desired behavior. Other mock frameworks, like NMock,[7] inherently do this for you but at the cost of having to hard-code the names of the methods you want to mock in a string.

Mock objects will cause the test to fail only if they are improperly or never called. For this to happen, we need a verification step. All mock frameworks (including Rhino Mocks and NMock) have this built into them. After our normal assertions, we call VerifyAll() at the end of the test on line 40. Again, there is a second flavor of Verify(object mockObject) that verifies only a single mockObject. This test won't compile until we create a new constructor for TodoController that accepts a TodoRepository. Let's get this test to pass:

repositoriesAndControllers/TodoController.cs

```
Line 1   [Authorize]
         public class TodoController : Controller
    -    {
    -      private readonly TodoRepository repository;
    5
    -      public TodoController(TodoRepository repository)
    -      {
    -        this.repository = repository;
    -      }
   10
    -      //
    -      // GET: /Todo/
    -
    -      public ActionResult Index()
   15      {
    -        ViewData["UserName"] = User.Identity.Name;
    -
    -        ViewData.Model = repository.GetAll();
    -
   20        return View();
    -      }
    -    }
```

---

7. http://nmock.org

First we add the new constructor on line 6. The repository is set to a **private readonly** member to ensure that it is never modified after construction. In the Index() action itself, we simple remove the call to the **static** list. Instead of using Todo.ThingsToBeDone, we now call todoRepository's GetAll() method on line 18. This makes the test pass. We've finally removed our **static** list and replaced it with a more testable repository.

The rest of the GetOrganized solution needs to be converted in a similar way. Any time you have a call to the static list, it will be replaced with a call to the repository. The full conversion is available in the downloadable code, available in the GetOrganizedFinal/ folder.

Another important aspect to ensuring our controllers work with repositories is to have them manage NHibernate transactions.

9.4 Creating a Custom Action Filter: The (Transaction) Attribute

Transactions are a programmatic boundary that marks the start and end of one or more database operations. They are an "all or none" guarantee that commits all the operations or rolls them all back if something goes wrong.

Most operations that update or save models ought be transactional, such as if there are multiple models being modified but one of those updates goes wrong and we don't want any of those changes saved. Otherwise, it'd be hard to know which models were modified and which failed. Let's say it's because of invalid information in only one of the models. In this case, you don't want the system to have updated and saved half or three quarters of the models.

This is where a transaction can save you from worrying about these scenarios. They save you from the nightmare of inconsistent data brought about by the application. Trust me, you don't want to explain to your boss that it was your code that created database soup.

What transactions don't do is ensure against stale data. For example, if one person is on the edit screen and another person clicks the save button first, then transactions will not save you from this headache. One technique is to perform a checksum on the data and before saving the data check to see whether the data is consistent with what it was before you are making the change. Alternatively, you can compare the timestamps on the records.

Those who know transactions from ADO.NET will be familiar with creating a **using** block around a System.Transactions.Transaction object. This object wraps your database operations and then commits them if everything went well. Otherwise, it rolls those operations back. This code becomes repetitive, so for MVC and NHibernate we'll create a custom action filter to handle it. First, we need to build the capability of accessing the NHibernate ITransaction object, which is available off the ISession:

repositoriesAndControllers/NHibernateSessionStorage.cs

```
public class NHibernateSessionStorage
{
  //omit start of class...

  public static ITransaction Transaction
  {
    get { return RetrieveSession().Transaction;}
  }
}
```

We create a new getter property called Transaction, which exposes the current web request's ISession. With that now available to us, we can create our TransactionAttribute action filter:

repositoriesAndControllers/TransactionAttribute.cs

```
Line 1  public class TransactionAttribute : ActionFilterAttribute
   -    {
   -      public override void OnActionExecuting(
   -        ActionExecutingContext filterContext)
   5      {
   -        NHibernateSessionStorage.Transaction.Begin();
   -      }
   -
   -      public override void OnActionExecuted(
  10        ActionExecutedContext filterContext)
   -      {
   -        ITransaction currentTransaction =
   -            NHibernateSessionStorage.Transaction;
   -
  15        if (currentTransaction.IsActive)
   -        {
   -          if (filterContext.Exception == null)
   -          {
   -            currentTransaction.Commit();
  20          }
   -          else
   -          {
   -            currentTransaction.Rollback();
   -          }
  25        }
   -      }
   -    }
```

This code is a modified version of the one available in Sharp Architecture.[8] During the OnActionExecuting(), which happens at the start of the controller's action, we begin the NHibernate transaction on line 6. At the end of the action, the action filter method OnActionExecuted() is called to check whether to commit or roll back the ITransaction.

If an ITransaction has already been committed or rolled back (explicitly by the program), we don't want to do this again. On line 15, we check the property IsActive to guard against this scenario. For a transaction to be eligible for a commit, it must contain no Exceptions. We check for that on line 17.

To show off the [Transaction] attribute in action, we'll create a contrived example. Say we want to open 1,000 database records and update the timestamp:

repositoriesAndControllers/MassModificationController.cs

```
public class MassModificationController : Controller
{
  [Transaction]
  public ActionResult UpdateTimeStamp()
  {
    for (int i = 1; i < 1001; i++)
    {
      var model = repository.Get(i);
      model.LastUpdated = DateTime.Now;
      repository.SaveOrUpdate(model);
    }
  }
}
```

This example illustrates one way of using a transaction in MVC. If something fails during one of the updates to the models, you don't want only *some* of the records being left modified. Since we apply the [Transaction] attribute, we are safe from this scenario.

The code inside UpdateTimeStamp() is all wrapped up in one NHibernate ITransaction so that if an exception is thrown, then the TransactionAttribute class will detect it and call Rollback(). This will revert all the changes, preserving the integrity of the data and allowing the operation to be tried again later.

We now have repositories integrated into the controllers and the tests to support it. We also have the ability to wrap controller actions with

---

8.   http://github.com/codai/Sharp-Architecture/blob/master/src/SharpArch/SharpArch.Web/ NHibernate/TransactionAttribute.cs

transactions. Now we'll leverage NHibernate's model validation framework to save us time when performing validations.

9.5 Linking NHibernate and MVC Validations

Earlier, in Section 6.4, *Adding Validations Using ModelStateDictionary*, on page 131, we used ModelStateDictionary to make sure a Todo had a Title of no more than twenty-five characters long. NHibernate has its own validation framework that is very similar to the new ASP.NET one (discussion on page xviii). Based on the way we implemented validation, adding NHibernate support is only a few steps away.

Instead of implementing the IValidatable interface on every model, we can instead use an extension method. Extension methods allow us to add new methods to classes without modifying the class code. We've already used them before, because all HTML helpers are extension methods of the Html class.

This approach to NHibernate validations and MVC was inspired from a blog post by David Hayden.[9] We'll modify the existing IValidatable interface and add an extension method in a new ValidationExtension class. Both of these classes will live in the Models/Validation directory. First let's modify the existing interface:

repositoriesAndControllers/IValidatable.cs

```
using System.Web.Mvc;

namespace GetOrganized.Models.Validator
{
    /// <summary>
    ///  Marker for Models that can run
    ///  ValidationExtension.Validatable(ModelState state)
    /// </summary>
    public interface IValidatable { }
}
```

We removed the method Validate(ModelStateDictionary state) and used this interface as a marker for models that can be validated.

---

9. http://www.pnpguidance.net/post/NHibernateValidatorTutorialValidateBusinessObjectsMVC.aspx

Now we'll add a new extension method:

repositoriesAndControllers/ValidationExtension.cs

```
public static class ValidationExtension
{
  public static void Validate(this IValidatable model,
    ModelStateDictionary state)
  {
    InvalidValue[] invalidValues =
      new ValidatorEngine().Validate(model);

    foreach (var error in invalidValues)
    {
      var errorMessage = error.PropertyName + " " + error.Message;
      state.AddModelError(errorMessage, errorMessage);
    }
  }
}
```

To get NHibernate validations to work, you will need to download the NHibernate Contrib Validator package; for this book, we're using 1.2.0.CR1.[10] You'll add NHibernate.Validator.dll (contained within the NHibernate Contrib download) to your Lib directory. Also, add this reference to your Web project. Iterate through InvalidArgs collection, and add to ModelStateDictionary as errors come up.

Notice how we created the variable errorMessage by concatenating the PropertyName and the Message. This is done to make the keys in the ModelStateDictionary unique for multiple validations of the same field. For example, if we added a restriction on the length and on the kinds of characters allowed in the Name property, we'd want to display both error messages if both rules were triggered.

Before the code can work, we need to modify the Todo class to support NHibernate validations:

repositoriesAndControllers/Todo.cs

```
public class Todo : IValidatable
{
  [Length(0,25)]
  public string Title { get; set; }

  //... omitted rest of class ...
}
```

---

10. http://sourceforge.net/projects/nhcontrib/files/NHibernate.Validator/1.2.0%20CR1/NHibernate.
Validator-1.2.0.CR1-bin.zip/download

\\\//
ɔˀ **Joe Asks. . .**
˿

What About Ajax Validations?

Since we introduced Ajax functions in Chapter 7, *Composing Views with Ajax and Partials*, on page 139, we broke the Todo/Index.aspx screen. Right now the validation logic works only on the Todo/Create.aspx page because our jQuery does not handle errors. One way to preserve the Ajax as well as the validation logic is to use an open source tool called xVal.*

xVal bridges NHibernate validations back to any client-side validation technology including jQuery validation (Figure 7.2, on page 150) and ASP.NET JavaScript validations. It is authored by Steve Sanderson, and he provides an easy-to-follow tutorial on his blog. †

∗.   http://xval.codeplex.com
†.   http://blog.codeville.net/2009/02/27/xval-08-beta-now-released/

We replaced the method Validate() with the NHibernate validation attribute [Length(0,25)]. There are many other validation attributes like [Email] for email or [Pattern("regularExpression")] for regular expressions. You can also extend and create your own validators. Apply the [ValidatorClass] attribute, and point it to a class that implements NHibernate.Validator. Engine.IValidator. This makes reusing validation logic easy and, of course, testable.

With our Todo modified, we can now let the controller perform the actual validation. The code will work without modification. Because we replaced the interface method with an extension method, we didn't have to change the TodoController code at all. The code for that controller is described in Section 6.4, *Adding Validations Using ModelState-Dictionary*, on page 131. However, these validations don't provide nice messages back when Ajax is being used (see the *Joe Asks. . .* on the current page).

With NHibernate validations all wired up, we can quickly touch on how to help deal with performance problems by profiling NHibernate.

9.6 Preventing Performance Problems with Profiling

The good thing about the architecture presented in this chapter is that there is only one NHibernate ISession per web request. This means you won't run into a common performance problem of having more than one ISession. However, you can still write NHibernate code to load large amounts of data, such as your whole customer database. Or perhaps you might end up modifying and saving hundreds of models within the same controller.

Such scenarios can grind your application to a halt. Sometimes finding the performance killer is easy. Other times it can be hair-pulling experience. Thankfully, there are tools like NHProf that can help you pinpoint where your NHibernate code is going down the wrong path.

Download the latest build from NHProf's website.[11] You'll need to register by email to get a thirty-day trial. After you've activated the trial, you need to copy HibernatingRhinos.NHibernate.Profiler.Appender.dll to your lib directory. Also, add it as a reference to the GetOrganized Web project, and add the following code to your Global.asax.cs:

repositoriesAndControllers/Global.asax.cs

```
Line 1  protected void Application_Start()
2       {
3         SetupWindsorContainer();
4         RegisterRoutes(RouteTable.Routes);
5
6         HibernatingRhinos.NHibernate.Profiler.
7           Appender.NHibernateProfiler.Initialize();
8       }
```

Activating profiling in your application is done on line 7. You don't want this line to go into production code, because it will slow down the system. You can now launch the NHProf client HibernatingRhinos.NHibernate.Profiler.Client.exe, and presto! You're profiling! When you hit the http://localhost/Todo/Index URL, you'll see the following output on the NHProfiler screen in Figure 9.1, on the following page.

NHProfiler will give you detailed information about what is going on with your database and NHibernate code. It will point out the time it takes to run particular queries as well as provide statistics on your NHibernate session factory.

---

11. http://nhprof.com

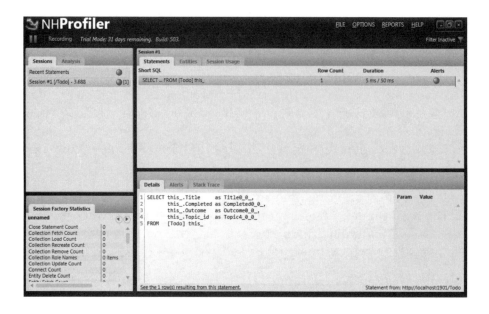

Figure 9.1: NHPROF REVEALS BOTH THE EXACT SQL THAT IS OCCUR-
ING AS WELL AS NHIBERNATE STATISTICS SUCH AS THE NUMBER OF SES-
SIONS.

For example, when writing this chapter and profiling a page in GetOrganized, NHProfiler picked up a big problem. The method DisposeCur-
rent() in the NHibernateSessionStorage was opening multiple NHibernate
ISessions for every request. It was creating an ISession for each HTTP GET
call, including every CSS, image, and JavaScript file. By adding a check
in the HttpContext for an existing ISession, the code started to behave as
it was intended. It creates a single ISession for every request that uses a
repository. It would have been difficult to spot that problem without a
profiler.

Profiling often reveals other problems, such as when large amounts of
data are being read repeatedly. One solution to this is to use second-
level caching. In this book we won't cover how to use second-level
caching in NHibernate, but there are many useful articles online that
do.[12] A popular option for a second-level cache is to use a Memcached[13]
server. Memcached is an open source in-memory caching server that

12. http://ayende.com/Blog/archive/2009/04/24/nhibernate-2nd-level-cache.aspx
13. http://www.cnblogs.com/RicCC/archive/2007/10/13/NHibernate-Memcached.html

temporarily stores data for faster retrieval. This is one of many solutions that can address a performance problem.

Having the profiler running on a daily basis will help you catch performance problems. It will help you understand how to best use NHibernate. NHProfiler also gives you tips and warnings about your NHibernate code that can also save you time.

In case you don't want to shell out the cash for NHProfiler, there are also free options available.

A Free Alternative: NHibernate Interceptors

One alternative to using this commercial product is to create your own NHibernate Interceptor. Interceptors are an architectural extension point of NHibernate similar in principle to MVC action filters. They hook into NHibernate events before, during, and after a call to the database is made. I attended a presentation where Oren Eni, a contributor to NHibernate, showed off a rather novel usage of an NHibernate Interceptor. Let's call the Interceptor LocalMachineProdSimulatorInterceptor and have it add a one-second delay to every NHibernate database call:

repositoriesAndControllers/LocalMachineProdSimulatorInterceptor.cs

```
public class LocalMachineProdSimulatorInterceptor : IInterceptor
{
  public void PreFlush(ICollection entities)
  {
    Thread.Sleep(1000);
  }
}
```

The class implements NHibernate.IInterceptor, which has all the events that you can hook into. In our case, we're interested in PreFlush() because this is the event that happens prior to a database connection. We tell the application to Sleep(int miliseconds) for 1,000 milliseconds to simulate the network call.

This forces developers working on their local machine to feel the pain of a production situation. In production, web servers and database servers are separate physical machines. Every database call requires a round-trip on the network, which adds up to pages loading slower than they do on a local developer machine. Oren's interceptor provides an easy way to simulate this on your machine. Another good use of

NHibernate interceptors is to help with creating an audit trail for all your models.[14]

That completes our introduction to NHibernate and how it's an essential tie-in to MVC. NHibernate gives you a way to store and retrieve models in a relational database without having to use SQL.

The other repositories and controllers in GetOrganized have been converted to use NHibernate and are available for download with the source code for this book. You can find the complete solution in the GetOrganizedFinal/ folder when you unzip it.

Up Next

The marriage of repository and controller was made possible by MVC's IControllerFactory interface and the Castle Windsor container. We also know how to better leverage NHibernate's validation framework within MVC. If we run into trouble with performance, we can use NHProfiler to help highlight the problem.

To put the finishing touches on MVC applications in general, we're going to cover how to consume and publish web services. Next up, we'll create our own web service to allow Todos to be added by other applications and published to Blogger's web services.

---

14. http://stackoverflow.com/questions/892220/nhibernate-interceptor-auditing-inserted-object-id

I have made this letter longer than usual, only because I have not had the time to make it shorter.
  ► Blaise Pascal

Chapter 10

Building RESTful Web Services

Take it from Pascal; it's more effort to make a point in fewer words. Web services have become the de facto standard for communication among applications, but they have traditionally been verbose and require generated code to get the communication set up properly. MVC itself does not come prepackaged with any web services framework. However, by using a few objects within MVCContrib and relying on a REST-style syntax, we can publish web services that even Pascal will be proud of.

We're going to build a couple of web services from the Todo model. You'll see how you can expose models for other programmers to use. We'll return lists of Todo as plain old XML (POX) and expose a web service that adds new models. A lot of enterprise development effort these days involves integrating systems. Setting up web services like this will make it easier for you to integrate with other applications.

Of course, the communication needs to flow both ways. We'll also learn about how to communicate with other people's web services. For GetOrganized, this means publishing a Todo as a blog entry on Blogger.[1]

Let's start with a little context about web services themselves and where the technology is at across the industry.

10.1 Use SOAP or Take a REST Instead?

Web services—programmable interfaces over HTTP—are a way for web applications to communicate with each other. Microsoft introduced Simple Object Access Protocol (SOAP) in 1998, and it quickly became

---

1. http://www.blogger.com

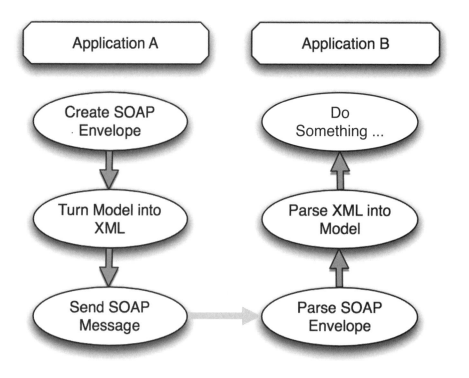

Figure 10.1: SENDING SOAP MESSAGES TAKES EXTRA PROCESSING.

the standard enabling applications written in different languages to talk to each other.

The idea was all well and good, but the industry started to realize that SOAP is bulky and difficult to work with (see Figure 10.1). For example, when coding up a .NET ASMX web service using SOAP, it was difficult to generate a Java client to work with it automatically. The promise of interoperability was not truly delivered, and so a simpler solution was created.

Representational State Transfer (REST) was introduced as a simpler way for web applications to talk (see Figure 10.2, on the facing page). REST relies on the basic verbs built into HTTP such as GET, POST, DELETE, and PUT to describe the kinds of operations being performed. Also, REST relies on well-named URLs to describe the resource that is being operated on. ASP.NET MVC, by default, uses RESTful URLs such

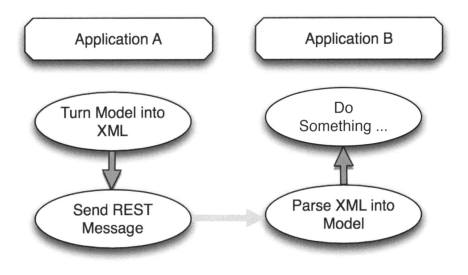

Figure 10.2: REST IS SIMPLER THAN SOAP.

as http://localhost/Todo/Create to create a new Todo. This is in contrast to a SOAP definition that uses a lot of XML to describe the same thing.

Most web service vendors are now moving to support both SOAP and REST, but for this chapter we'll focus exclusively on REST because it is simpler to use. Microsoft's standard web services package, Windows Communication Foundation (WCF), now supports both SOAP and REST. The MVC team is also working on better integration with WCF in a future version (see the *Joe Asks...* on the next page).

Although WCF seems like the most common choice for most .NET developers when it comes to building web services, we won't be using it here. This is mainly because it is unnecessarily complicated for most real-world scenarios. Just like REST is simpler than SOAP, we can leverage what's already in MVC to produce simpler services than WCF gives us. For more information, MSDN has decent resources on WCF to get you started.[2]

With this background on RESTful web services, let's dig into creating our first one.

---

2. http://msdn.microsoft.com/en-ca/netframework/aa663324.aspx

> \\/ **Joe Asks...**
> <u>**How About the MVC REST Extension?**</u>
>
> This extension relies on replacing the ControllerFactory with one that recognizes different formats. It is a bit too early to adopt, but it's worth keeping an eye on as it matures. Some form of this will probably make it into MVC 3.0. You can download a preview of the code on CodePlex.*
>
> ---
>
> *. http://aspnet.codeplex.com/Release/ProjectReleases.aspx?ReleaseId=24471#DownloadId=79561

10.2 Creating a Web Service

Test-driving web services requires that we create a third test project, Test.Integration, so named because the classes we are testing require external resources. In our case, we'll be relying on both our Web project and the Google's Blogger web services to be running.

Creating a web services is a three-step process. First, we authenticate against the service. This is similar to what we do when we log on to a site. Second, we prepare the parameters in the request and send it. Lastly, we receive the response and translate it into usable objects.

Let's get started with the first step: authentication.

Using Forms Authentication with HttpWebRequest

Production web services generally use basic authentication over SSL. This means each request sends the username and password along for the ride. Unfortunately, this means that the credentials you give out to other developers who will use your services need to be part of Windows authentication, and in most cases that means being in Active Directory.

GetOrganized, like many of the applications you will write, uses Forms authentication, which we covered in the sidebar on page 99. This means that users of the system are stored elsewhere—or in our case, the database. The simplest way around this is to have consumers of your web services authenticate like everyone else by using Forms authentication.

To make a web request in .NET, we use the System.Net.HttpWebRequest object. On it, we set the URL and parameters we need to complete our request. On a successful connection, it returns a System.Net.HttpWebResponse, which we'll use to extract the received data.

To start, we'll create a new test fixture called TodoWebServiceTest, which will handle this section's tests. The first test will verify authentication is working:

`webServices/TodoWebServiceTest.cs`

```
[TestFixture]
public class TodoWebServiceTest
{
  [Test]
  public void Should_Authenticate_Against_Form()
  {
    HttpWebResponse response =
      WebServiceUtil.AuthenticateWithForms("jonathan", "password",
      "http://localhost:1901/Account/LogOn");

    Assert.AreEqual(1, response.Cookies.Count);
    Assert.AreEqual(".ASPXAUTH", response.Cookies[0].Name);
  }
}
```

Here we create a web request that returns the HttpWebResponse from a new class we'll create called WebServiceUtil. The method AuthenticateWithForms() takes the username, the password, and the URL of the Account-Controller's action LogOn().

If we authenticate successfully, the response will have exactly one Cookie. The Cookie will have the default name *.AUTH* and contain the authentication token for future requests. You can change the name that ASP.NET gives this cookie in the Web.config file's authentication section, but for our purposes here, the default will do.

To make the test pass, we'll need to create WebServiceUtil in a new Common directory in the Web project.

`webServices/WebServiceUtil.cs`

```
Line 1   public class WebServiceUtil
   -     {
   -       public static HttpWebResponse AuthenticateWithForms(string username,
   -         string password, string url)
   5       {
   -         string parameters = "&userName=" + username +
   -         "&password=" + password + "&rememberMe=true";
   -
```

```
 10      return SendWebRequest(url, parameters,
           "application/x-www-urlencoded");
       }

       public static HttpWebResponse SendWebRequest(string uri,
         string parameters, string contentType, params Cookie[] cookies)
 15    {
         var request = (HttpWebRequest) WebRequest.Create(uri);

         request.CookieContainer = new CookieContainer();
         if (cookies !=null)
 20        cookies.ToList().ForEach(cookie =>
             request.CookieContainer.Add(cookie));

         request.AllowAutoRedirect = false;
         request.Method = "POST";
 25      request.ContentType = contentType;
         request.ContentLength = parameters.Length;

         using (var requestWriter = new StreamWriter(
           request.GetRequestStream(), System.Text.Encoding.ASCII))
 30      {
           requestWriter.Write(parameters);
         }

         return (HttpWebResponse) request.GetResponse();
 35    }
       }
```

On line 7, we convert the incoming parameters into a querystring that
the web service will accept. We then specify that the content type of the
request is application/x-www-form-urlencoded. This lets the service know
this is a form request.

The call to the method SendWebRequest(string uri, string parameters, string
contentType, params Cookie() cookies) creates the HttpWebRequest. The
new request is created via the WebRequest's static method Create(string
url). We also have built the method to accept a Cookie on line 21. This
is so we can reuse this method for authenticated requests. Also, it can
be used for both GET and POST requests. We've hard-coded it for POST
on line 24 since all the requests we're sending will accept this.

To get the parameters into the request stream, we use a StreamWriter
on the HttpWebRequest's GetRequestStream() on line 31. This example
encodes the parameters to the ASCII format. Our method then returns
an HttpWebResponse by calling the method GetResponse().

You'll need to launch your web browser and then run the test, which will now pass. Alternatively, if relaunching the site gets to be annoying, you can deploy the site to Internet Information Services (IIS) locally. This is covered in Section 12.2, *Deploying Locally to IIS*, on page 246.

Now that authentication is working, we can work on getting a list of Todos back in the form of XML.

Listing Models as XML

In the next test, we'll need to create two requests, one for authentication and one to call a list of Todos via the Index() action. The goal is to return an XML document instead of an HTML representation of the Todos. Although this is written as a test, this code will look similar to what other developers (if using .NET) will use to access this service.

```
webServices/TodoWebServiceTest.cs
```

```
Line 1   [Test]
         public void Should_Get_List_Of_Todos_As_XML()
         {
           var authenticateResponse =
    5        WebServiceUtil.AuthenticateWithForms("jonathan", "password",
             "http://localhost:1901/Account/LogOn");

           var responseWithXML =
             WebServiceUtil.SendWebRequest("http://localhost:1901/Todo/",
   10        string.Empty, "text/xml", authenticateResponse.Cookies[0]);

           var xmlReader = XmlReader.Create(
             responseWithXML.GetResponseStream());

   15      XDocument todoDoc = XDocument.Load(xmlReader);

           Assert.AreEqual("ArrayOfTodo", todoDoc.Root.Name.ToString());
           Assert.AreEqual("Todo",
             todoDoc.Root.Elements("Todo").First().Name.ToString());
   20      Assert.AreEqual("Title", todoDoc.Root.Elements("Todo").
             Elements("Title").First().Name.ToString());
           Assert.AreEqual("Id", todoDoc.Root.Elements("Todo").
             Elements("Id").First().Name.ToString());
         }
```

First we obtain a cookie by authenticating on line 6. Then, once we have the token, we can pass it along to the second request on line 10. We then have to set the request header to be text/xml so our controller's action realizes this is a web service request.

From this request, we'll expect an XML document that has a root node of list-todo and contains two todo elements. Each of these elements will have a Title and Id.

To get this XML out of the response, we use an XmlReader, which provides an easy way to parse out elements that we want to assert against. Now we'll get this test to pass:

```
webServices/TodoController.cs

public ActionResult Index()
{
    ViewData["UserName"] = User.Identity.Name;

    ViewData.Model = repository.GetAll();

    if (Request.Headers["Content-Type"] == "text/xml")
        return new XmlResult(ViewData.Model);
    else
      return View();
}
```

We modified very little in this action. We just add a check to see whether the Request.Header["Content-Type"] is of the type text/xml. If it is, we return an XmlResult. This class comes from MVC Contrib and will automatically serialize your model as XML.

You can use a similar pattern to return the result as JSON. Simply have the HTTP's accept header be set to text/json, and inspect for that header in the controller's action.

So, we now know how to return XML from a web service, but we'll also need to send XML to the service. Next, we'll take XML as part of the request to create a Todo.

Sending XML in the Request Using Model Binding

Some developers might not be comfortable sending in a querystring of parameters to your web service. This is because if you change the name of any of the members of your model, it will break their code. For example, if we changed the Todo's Title property to Name, it would force other developers to have to modify their code. Breaking your own unit test is acceptable; breaking someone else's code by changing the interface is just asking for trouble.

Luckily, MVC has yet another extension point called *model binding*, which lets us create a less volatile interface that programmers can rely on.

We're going to create a custom model binder for our Todo class. We'll call it TopicXmlBinder. MVC lets us apply a model binder next to the action's parameter with the ModelBinderAttribute. This overrides the DefaultModelBinder, which translates form requests into models.

This means we can safely change the Todo model and map it back to the XML using this custom binder class. Let's write our test to drive the code for the binder:

webServices/TodoWebServiceTest.cs

```
Line 1  [Test]
        public void Should_Send_Xml_To_Create_Todo()
        {
          var xdoc = new XDocument(
5             new XDeclaration("1.0", "utf-8", "yes"),
              new XElement("todo", new XElement("title", "foo")));

          string xml = xdoc.Declaration + xdoc.ToString(SaveOptions.None);

10        var authRequest =
            WebServiceUtil.AuthenticateWithForms("jonathan", "password",
            "http://localhost:1901/Account/LogOn");

          var xmlRequest =
15          WebServiceUtil.SendWebRequest(
            "http://localhost:1901/Todo/CreateWithXml",
            xml, "text/xml", authRequest.Cookies[0]);

            var xmlReader =
20            XmlReader.Create(xmlRequest.GetResponseStream());
            XDocument todoDoc = XDocument.Load(xmlReader);

          Assert.AreEqual("Todo", todoDoc.Root.Name.ToString());
          Assert.AreEqual("foo" ,
25          todoDoc.Root.Element(XName.Get("Title" )).Value);
        }
```

We're using a new LINQ class called XDocument, which makes constructing XML documents easier than using the older Microsoft System.Xml namespace. With XDocument, we'll build up a well-formed Todo as XML. For the XML declaration and the contents of the document to both be sent, we concatenate them together on line 8.

Similar to the previous test, we make an authentication request so we can get a cookie back.

We use a RESTful name to indicate that we're creating using XML, so the action is called CreateWithXML(). However, if you are publishing an interface that might have multiple versions, it's a good idea to reflect that in the URL. The simplest way to do this would be to deploy a separate website for any supported version of the web service. You'll learn more about creating automated deployments in Chapter 12, *Build and Deployment*, on page 237. Otherwise, when you make a change to the service, you might break other developers' code.

Finally, we get our response back and use an XmlReader to parse the XML. We can then assert against the different elements and validate that the information is correct. Now let's get the test to pass.

Create a new binder in the directory Models/Binders:

```
webServices/TodoXmlBinder.cs
Line 1  public class TodoXmlBinder : IModelBinder
   -    {
   -      public object BindModel(ControllerContext controllerContext,
   -        ModelBindingContext bindingContext)
   5      {
   -        using (var reader= new StreamReader(
   -          controllerContext.RequestContext.
   -          HttpContext.Request.InputStream))
   -        {
  10          var rawXml = XmlReader.Create(reader);
   -          XDocument doc = XDocument.Load(rawXml);
   -          var todoTitle = doc.Root.Element(XName.Get("title")).Value;

   -          var todo = new Todo();
  15          todo.Title = todoTitle;
   -          return todo;
   -        }
   -      }
   -    }
```

Model binders all implement the IModelBinder interface. This exposes the method BindModel(), which has both the ControllerContext and a ModelBindingContext. The ControllerContext gives us access to the HttpContext. We use this to get the raw InputStream on line 8.

Out of the stream we create an XmlReader, which allows us to parse the XML document. On line 14, we create the new Todo and assign it values from the request. To complete the binding, we assign the bindingContext.Model the new Todo and also return the model on line 16.

The test isn't passing yet, because we need to create the new action on the controller:

```
webServices/TodoController.cs
[Authorize]
[AcceptVerbs(HttpVerbs.Post)]
public ActionResult CreateWithXml(
  [ModelBinder(typeof(TodoXmlBinder))] Todo todo)
{
  Create(todo);
  return new XmlResult(todo);
}
```

The action delegates to the existing Create() to do work. Since the model binder already mapped the XML to the model, there isn't much to do here. We simply call the XmlResult so that an XML version of the newly created Todo can be returned to the application that submitted the request. The test is now passing, and we can take a REST.

Now we have a fully published RESTful web service! By exposing services in this fashion, not only did we enable simple integration with other applications, but we also applied the DRY principle by reusing the Create() action.

Now that we've learned how to publish our own web services, we can tackle consuming others' services.

10.3 Publishing to Blogger

Let's assume that you're going to start a blog by creating an account at http://www.blogger.com. Blogger is a free site that lets you post your thoughts and ideas to anyone who wants to read them.

Writing a decent blog post takes time and effort. Adding a feature to GetOrganized that transforms a Todo into a draft blog article can save precious time in the publishing process.

We'll walk through how to do it with Blogger; then you can use the same knowledge to integrate with other services. For Blogger, it is a two-step process, as illustrated in Figure 10.3, on the next page.

Google has been pretty good about making its services accessible to developers. Its *GData* interface allows for authorization and publication

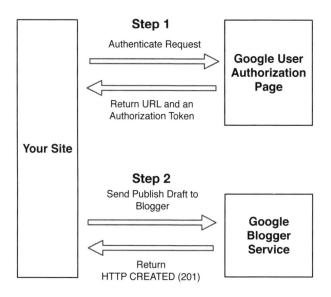

Step 1

Authenticate Request

Return URL and an
Authorization Token

**Google User
Authorization
Page**

Your Site

Step 2

Send Publish Draft to
Blogger

Return
HTTP CREATED (201)

**Google
Blogger
Service**

Figure 10.3: First you authenticate, and then you publish your
blog post.

to most of its services, including Blogger. To access its services, we'll
first need to authenticate using the AuthSub interface.[3]

```
webServices/BloggerGatewayTest.cs

[TestFixture]
public class BloggerGatewayTest
{
  [Test]
  public void Should_Authenticate_With_Blogger()
  {
    var gateway = new BloggerGateway();
    var googleURL = gateway.AuthenticateURL("foo");

    Assert.AreEqual(
      "https://www.google.com/accounts/AuthSubRequest?" +
      "next=http://10.1.10.12:1901/Todo/BloggerAuthorized" +
      "?title=foo&scope=" +
      "http://www.blogger.com/feeds/2580952471083668495/" +
      "posts/default", googleURL);
  }
}
```

---

3. http://code.google.com/apis/accounts/docs/AuthSub.html#AuthSubRequest

We create an instance of BloggerGateway to encapsulate the logic necessary to communicate with Blogger. Google's web services require a human interaction to allow our site to access its Google account (see the sidebar on the following page). Therefore, we need to send along other information like the Todo's Title because Google will redirect us to the URL we give it.

To verify that all this occurred, we simply check the response URL for the presence of *google* and check that our parameter is there. Let's get this test green:

```
webServices/BloggerGateway.cs
public class BloggerGateway
{
  const string ipAddressOfSite = "10.1.10.12";
  const long blogId = 2580952471083668495;

  public string AuthenticateURL(string todoTitle)
  {
    return string.Format(
      "https://www.google.com/accounts/AuthSubRequest" +
      "?next=http://{0}/Todo/BloggerAuthorized?title={1}" +
      "&scope=http://www.blogger.com/feeds/{2}/posts/default"
      , ipAddressOfSite, todoTitle, blogId);
  }
}
```

We'll use my blog as a test case.[4] Let's hard-code both the ipAddress of our site as well as the unique identifier for the blog we want to modify. We also pass in the title of the Todo. Google requires that two parameters be passed to its service for authorization. The first is next, which instructs Google to redirect to our site's URL on successful authorization. In this case, we're setting this to the ipAddress of our computer. Next is the scope parameter, which specifies the URL of the Google service from which we are requesting information. Here we want to put in the unique blog address that we want to access.

Again, since authentication requires human interaction, we cannot automate beyond this without registering our site with Google. So for now, we'll switch to manual testing to verify the rest of the gateway. After the user types in their Google account credentials, they'll be redirected to the controller's action BloggerAuthorized().

---

4. http://jonathanmccracken.blogspot.com

> ### Stubbing + Web Services = Fewer Headaches
>
> Another effective use of a mocking framework is to create stubs
> for web services that you talk to. It removes the need to have
> those services available when you're developing on your local
> machine. To do so, simply register a stub with Castle Windsor
> instead of the class that makes a network call to the real web
> service.

Before we can work on that controller action, we'll first need to inject a
BloggerGateway into the constructor:

webServices/TodoController.cs
```
private readonly TodoRepository repository;
private readonly BloggerGateway gateway;

public TodoController(TodoRepository repository,
  BloggerGateway gateway)
{
  this.repository = repository;
  this.gateway = gateway;
}
```

This is exactly what we did for the Repository pattern; we pass in the
BloggerGateway at the time we construct the object. This allows us to
mock out the gateway for testing purposes. With the constructor fixed
up, we can now work on the BloggerAuthorized() action:

webServices/TodoController.cs
```
public ActionResult BloggerAuthorized(string title, string token)
{
  var todo = repository.GetAll().Where(x => x.Title == title);

  gateway.PublishAsDraft(todo, token);

  return Redirect("http://jonathanmccracken.blogspot.com");
}
```

This is the action that would be called by Google's web service. It will
have a unique security token, generated by Google, and also contain
our Todo title. At this point we're authorized to make a single request to
the Google API.

Next, we'll look up the proper model using our repository and then call the next method on BloggerGateway's PublishAsDraft(). On a successful publish, we're also going to redirect the user to the blog itself to start authoring. In a real application, the blog address wouldn't be hard-coded.

With the controller ready, we need to finish the gateway code:

`webServices/BloggerGateway.cs`

```
public void PublishAsDraft(Todo todo, string token)
{
  string xml = string.Format(
  @"<entry xmlns='http://www.w3.org/2005/Atom'>
  <title type='text'>{0}</title>
  <content type='xhtml'>
  <p>Empty</p>
  </content>
  <app:control xmlns:app='http://purl.org/atom/app#'>
  <app:draft>yes</app:draft>
  </app:control>
  </entry>", todo.Title);

  string blogFeedUri = "http://www.blogger.com/feeds/" +
    blogId + "/posts/default";

  var response =
    WebServiceUtil.SendWebRequestWithAuthToken(blogFeedUri, xml,
    "application/atom+xml", token);

  if (response.StatusCode != HttpStatusCode.Created)
    throw new WebException(response.StatusCode.ToString());
}
```

Publishing to the Google service is similar to how we constructed an XML document for our own service in the previous section. In this case, Google is expecting an XML document with the root element *entry*. The entire Blogger specification for this XML is documented online.[5]

To make the XML more readable, it's been included in a formatted **string**. We substitute in the title of the blog entry with the Todo Title. We then pass in the unique URL for the blog feed, along with the security token Google gave us. Finally, we'll check that the response we received was *CREATED* (HTTP 201), or else we throw a WebException along with the HttpStatusCode to indicate something went wrong.

---

5. http://code.google.com/apis/blogger/docs/2.0/developers_guide_protocol.html

Because we're sending a different kind of web request, we need a new method on WebServiceUtil that will send the token we received from Google along with the request:

`webServices/WebServiceUtil.cs`

```
Line 1  public static HttpWebResponse SendWebRequestWithAuthToken(
          string uri, string parameters, string contentType, string token,
          params Cookie[] cookies)
        {
     5    HttpWebRequest request =
            CreateRequest(uri, cookies, contentType, parameters);
          if (token != null)
            request.Headers.Add("Authorization",
              "AuthSub token=\"" + token + "\"");
    10    WriteRequest(parameters, request);
          return (HttpWebResponse)request.GetResponse();
        }
```

Here we added a few lines to append an HTTP header with the authorization token on line 8. We also refactored the class to support both web request methods. On line 6 we make sure the secure request does not encode the parameters since Google's service is expecting content in XML format. Similarly, on line 10 we make sure that both utility methods share the same logic to write the output of the requests. For the complete refactored class, check out GetOrganizedFinal in the downloadable code.

Now that our gateway will publish a draft, we need to hook the View/Todo/Index.aspx page up so users can blog their Todo:

`webServices/TodoController.cs`

```
public ActionResult PublishToBlogger(string title)
{
  Todo todo = repository.GetAll().Where(x => x.Title == title).First();

  return Redirect(gateway.AuthenticateURL(todo.Title));
}
```

This action calls the BloggerGateway to authenticate with Google. We obtain the proper URL that includes both the Title and the blog we're trying to publish to. It's simply a matter of using the Redirect() to send the user to the authentication page (see Figure 10.4, on the next page).

Before this controller will run, we'll need to add a definition for the BloggerGateway with the Castle Windsor container.

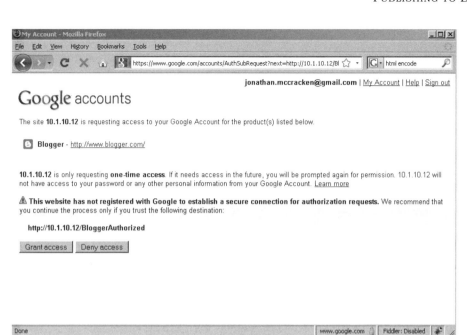

Figure 10.4: GOOGLE'S DATA AUTHSUB IN ACTION

```
webServices/Global.ascx.cs
private void SetupWindsorContainer()
{
  IWindsorContainer container = new WindsorContainer();

  //register other components

  RegisterGateways(container);
}

private void RegisterGateways(IWindsorContainer container)
{
  container.AddComponentLifeStyle("bloggerGateway",
    typeof(BloggerGateway), LifestyleType.Transient);
}
```

Since we have only one gateway, we can just wire it up manually.
Because the gateway has some state (blogId and ipAddress), we need
to ensure that its lifestyle is Transient.

Now that the component is registered with Castle Windsor, we need to perform one final step. We'll add another column to the grid in the Index.aspx view:

```
<%= Html.Grid(Model).Columns(column => {
        column.For(
          x =>
          Html.ActionLink("Blog it!","PublishToBlogger",
            new { x.Title }))
        .DoNotEncode();

//omitted rest of Grid
```

The Grid view helper lets us add columns with ease. We add a new link using the ActionLink() method and make sure to pass it the Title of the Todo.

That completes our integration with Blogger. We can now publish a common Todo into the start of an award-winning blog post! Just remember that Google will need to have access to your web server for this to work, so make sure the proper firewall ports are open.

Working through these examples gives you an approach for exposing your own web services as well as publishing to other web services. Whether you're talking to public sites like Google or a private intracompany portal, you now know how to talk to someone else's web service and have them talk back to you.

Up Next

We've completed GetOrganized by publishing our own web services for models. We've also successfully integrated with Blogger's public web service. You'll find publishing and consuming RESTful web services saves you and the developers you need to integrate with a lot of time.

Now it's time to add more security, logging, and error handling to the application.

Part IV

Security and Deployment

Chapter 11

Security, Error Handling, and Logging

We have our MVC application to a point that it's almost ready to publish. In this part, we'll focus on essential concepts that will help make our applications bullet-proof. Deploying the application, and deploying it often, is one of the keys to successful software development. In Chapter 12, *Build and Deployment*, on page 237, we'll learn how to do set this up automatically. We'll also learn about building security, error handling, and logging into our MVC applications. This will make sure, like Benjamin Franklin reminds us, that we fix or are able to detect any leaks in our web application.

When developing code, we're often focused on getting the most critical features out as quickly as possible. With the pressure of deadlines and launch dates, we sometimes neglect the less obvious parts of the system, more commonly called *nonfunctional requirements*. Nonfunctional requirements include things such as security, logging, and error handling. The repercussions of putting code into production without these elements can be disastrous.

It's important to address nonfunctional requirements in tandem with new features. Don't leave these until the end of your project; otherwise, you'll end up with security holes and unhandled exceptions all over your code. On top of that, if you don't have logging throughout your codebase, you'll have little visibility into the code when a production problem occurs.

This chapter is all about learning how to reduce the risk of that happening. We'll see how to secure our applications by preventing scripting attacks. Then we'll implement some robust error-handling solutions to

deal with unhandled exceptions. Finally, we'll set up a logging framework to help us diagnose production problems when they happen.

11.1 Applying Additional Security

So far in this book we've covered how to handle both authorization
and authentication (see Section 5.2, *Logging In*, on page 88). Although
these form the basics of security, there is more to securing a site than
just logging in and assigning roles to users. To protect a site, we're
also going to have to handle encryption of sensitive information and
plugging up security vulnerabilities.

Although not comprehensive, because .NET security could comprise a
whole book, these next few sections cover the major areas of vulnerability and how you can fix them using MVC. We'll work through adding
site encryption and a variety of client-side scripting attacks. We'll also
touch on how to implement a custom ASP.NET Membership provider,
which gives more control over user information and authentication.

Let's start by protecting the transport layer using HTTPS.

Encrypting Traffic Using SSL

The first way to secure sensitive information is to force the user's browser to use Secure Sockets Layer (SSL). SSL is a communication protocol
that encrypts all the traffic between the web server and browser. This
protects the information from outside viewing or tampering. You can
tell whether a website is using SSL to protect your information if the
web address starts with an *https://* instead of *http://*. This is why SSL
is often referred to as HTTPS.

Switching the user over to HTTPS automatically is easy in MVC. The
action filter RequireHttpsAttribute does the job. This filter detects whether
the incoming request is using SSL and, if not, forces a redirect with
HTTPS enabled.

securityErrorHandlingAndLogging/SecuredController.cs

```
public class SecuredController : Controller
{
  [RequireHttps]
  public ActionResult Secured()
  {
    return View();
  }
}
```

You can apply the filter to the controller level or for an individual action like we did here. Adding SSL incurs a performance overhead, so use it wisely. Most commercial ecommerce sites use SSL only for login and account management pages, while the rest of the site remains unsecured. However, if you're handling sensitive information, then there is no other choice but to use SSL for the entire site.

When testing this locally, the web server that comes with Visual Studio does not support SSL, so you'll have to switch to IIS to accomplish this. You can change this setting in Project Properties on the Web tab.

Also, you will need to generate a self-signed SSL certificate for your machine. There are several ways to do this depending on which version of IIS you're using. If you're using IIS 5.1, which comes with Windows XP, the best way is to download OpenSSL and follow the steps detailed on Dylan Beattie's blog.[1] If you're using IIS 6.0, which comes with Windows 2003, then using the IIS Resource Kit is the easiest way. You can find instructions for IIS 6.0 on Jonathan Maltz's site.[2] If you're using Vista or Windows 7, then you have IIS 7 or 7.5, and Scott Guthrie's blog has a tutorial on how to set up an SSL certificate.[3]

Just adding SSL to secure pages is not a silver bullet. There are other kinds of attacks that we need to guard against, and cross-site scripting (XSS) is one of them.

Preventing Cross-Site Scripting

One of the more dangerous kinds of attacks is broadly known as XSS. It is the injection of malicious client-side scripts into your web application to compromise or manipulate other users. Most XSS vulnerabilities occur because web application authors fail to sanitize the HTML that is displayed to the user. This results in JavaScript being executed on a user's browser that was never supposed to be executed.

At first glance, XSS vulnerabilities might appear to be harmless. This is especially apparent if your site does not post content that other users can view, unlike a social networking site. In that case, who cares if someone submits JavaScript back to their own browser, since it will only compromise the person who sent it. However, attackers have been

---

1. http://www.dylanbeattie.net/docs/openssl_iis_ssl_howto.html
2. http://www.visualwin.com/SelfSSL/
3. http://weblogs.asp.net/scottgu/archive/2007/04/06/tip-trick-enabling-ssl-on-iis7-using-self-signed-certificates.aspx

using phony emails that exploit sites vulnerable to XSS to compromise other people's information.

For example, let's say you were sent an email from your favorite hobby website. Unfortunately, that site has an XSS vulnerability, and the email's link also contains scripts that visit all the popular banking websites and sends your session information to the attacker. In the case that you've logged into your banking site in the past fifteen minutes prior to clicking the phony email link, you could risk someone having full access to your accounts!

XSS attacks are also a problem when users are allowed to publish information that other users can see. With these kinds of attacks, no phony emails are required. Users simply visiting a page will be vulnerable to injected scripts. For example, let's say an attacker posts a similar script that visits your banking sites to a message board. Another user is looking through message posts and comes across the message with the hidden malicious script. All of a sudden you're in the same boat as with the email attack, because your browser will execute the script as soon as you read the message post.

The best way to prevent against XSS attacks is to encode all the information you display to the user. In MVC, we can use the HTML helper method Encode(), which cancels out any scripting an attacker would have submitted.

securityErrorHandlingAndLogging/EncodeHtml.aspx

```
<%= Html.Encode("<SCRIPT>alert(\"attacked!\")</SCRIPT>") %>
```

Here we're using the Encode() to render harmless a potential XSS attack. The method converts special characters such as quotes and angle brackets to HTML-safe representations. If you were to load the page from the following code and view the source code, it would look quotes and angle brackets to HTML-safe representations. If you were to load the page from the following code and view the source code, it would look like this:

```
&lt;SCRIPT&gt;alert(\&quot;attacked!\&quot;)&lt;/SCRIPT&gt;
```

Although this might not be pretty, it's effectively harmless to the user's browser. It's a good practice to encode all information that is being displayed to the user. For more information on the different types of attacks, the public hacker's site[4] contains hundreds of attacks you can test against your site to make sure it is safe.

With the release of ASP.NET 4.0 (included with Visual Studio 2010), you can also use a special syntax in your views:

```
<%: //do stuff here :%>
```

These angle brackets will automatically HTML-encode all the output, and you'll also notice if you are using Visual Studio 2010 that the generated templates for views use these angle brackets by default.

Another attack that we need to worry about is called *cross-site request forgery* (CSRF).

Guarding Against Cross-Site Request Forgery Attacks

Unlike XSS attacks that rely on the user trusting the site to be safe, CSRF attacks result from a site being sent commands on behalf of trusted users who have not authorized these commands. Popular attacks have used email schemes to access people's bank accounts by creating clickable links or links disguised as image tags that execute commands that the victims never intended.

These attacks rely on authentication cookies being active and so are difficult to prevent without additional measures.

Lucky for us, MVC has a way to protect against this kind of forgery. By adding a antiforgery token to a view and checking for that token using a action filter, you can prevent a CSRF attack. Start by applying the antiforgery token to the page that will submit a sensitive command or transaction:

securityErrorHandlingAndLogging/WireMoney.aspx

```
Line 1    <form action="Wire" method="post">
2
3         <%= Html.AntiForgeryToken() %>
4
5         Wire Money: <%= Html.TextBox("money") %>
6
7         <input type="submit" value="Wire" />
8         </form>
```

On line 3, we use the HTML helper method AntiForgeryToken() to generate a hidden field on the form. Also, it generates a cookie that is specific to

---

4. http://ha.ckers.org/xss.html

the next request. The next step is to check for that token when the user submits the action:

securityErrorHandlingAndLogging/MoneyController.cs

```
public class MoneyController : Controller
{
  [ValidateAntiForgeryToken]
  public ActionResult Wire(decimal money)
  {
    //transfer money
  }
}
```

We apply the action filter ValidateAntiForgeryToken to the Wire() action to check for the presence of the cookie and hidden field. Without knowing this additional token, the wire transfer attack will not work, because MVC will throw an error if it is not there.

It seems like a pain to add this logic to all of your views and actions, but for now it is the only way to ensure key transactions are protected. In the future, the MVC team is looking at ways to incorporate this into every request, but for now you should think about applying it to every command that attackers might target.

On a last note for security, we'll also want to know how to customize authentication and authorization by touching on the ASP.NET Membership API.

Customizing the ASP.NET Membership Provider

Back in Section 5.2, *Logging In*, on page 88, we worked through how to use the default ASP.NET Membership provider. That provider used stored procedures to achieve all its functionality. Because this is different from how the rest of our architecture works using NHibernate, it makes sense to replace it with our own provider.

Another advantage to customizing the Membership API is it gives you more control to integrate with third-party authentication services like Google and Microsoft (see the sidebar on the next page).

Implementing a custom membership provider means inheriting the System.Web.MembershipProvider class and overriding its methods and properties. We'll also need to implement a role provider from System.Web.RoleProvider. The role provider handles creating, deleting, and adding user to roles, while the Membership provider creates and manages user accounts.

Facebook, Google, and Microsoft Live Authentication

Asking a user who visits your site to create a new username and password is one of those annoying steps you often force first-time visitors into. Luckily, a software company called RPXNow is making it easier for you. It allows you to register new users on your site using one of their existing accounts at a major provider like Google, Facebook, and Microsoft Live. Best of all, RPXNow provides this for free, along with commercial support if you need it.

To get started, download the open source rpxlib project from Google Code.* It's a simple set of steps to add a custom provider to your IoC container. In no time you'll have people registering using their Facebook accounts. RPXNow also supports Google, Microsoft Live, Twitter, Yahoo, MySpaceID, OpenID, AOL, VeriSign, and myOpenID.

---

*. http://code.google.com/p/rpxlib/wiki/GettingStartedWithMVC

See Section 8.4, *Creating and Reading Records*, on page 168 to refresh your memory on how to build a UserRepository class and a UserMap class. When you've done so, you can jump right into your own NHibernateMembershipProvider, which will delegate to the UserRepository for any database work.

securityErrorHandlingAndLogging/NHibernateMembershipProvider.cs

```
public class NHibernateMembershipProvider : MembershipProvider
{
    private UserRepository userRepository;

    public NHibernateMembershipProvider()
    {
     userRepository = new UserRepository();
    }

    public NHibernateMembershipProvider(UserRepository userRepository)
    {
     this.userRepository = userRepository;
    }

  public override MembershipUser CreateUser(
    string username, string password,
    string email, string passwordQuestion,
    string passwordAnswer, bool isApproved,
```

```
      Object providerUserKey,
      out MembershipCreateStatus status)

      {
        userRepository.Create(username, password, email);
        status = status.Success;

      }

  //omit rest of the implementation of the class
}
```

Because the provider is going to be created much earlier in the ASP.NET life cycle than when the Castle Windsor container exists (Section 9.2, *Treat Your Objects like Royalty at Castle Windsor*, on page 182), we need to add the UserRepository ourselves. This means that when coding the UserRepository, we cannot inject an NHibernate ISession and instead grab it from the HttpContext manually for every method call.

For testing purposes, we also support a constructor with a dependency injection of UserRepository. The implementation of the overridden methods in the provider is delegated to the UserRepository.

When implementing methods such as CreateUser() and handling parameters like password, it is *critical* that you do not store this information in clear text. The best way to store passwords is using a one-way hash. Specifically, we will use the SHA-256 algorithm found in System.Security.Cryptography. This algorithm prevents administrators or potential intruders from learning passwords if they have access to your database. Also, adding what is known as a *salt phrase* further obfuscates the encrypted password. Salt phrases are random bits of information to help further improve encryption. For example, if you hash the password *foo*, it will result in 32 bytes of data. By adding a salt to the password, like *salty*, you now hash the two strings together to give you a completely different result. Salting improves security by further obscuring passwords from people nosing around your database.

It is not necessary to implement all the provider methods if your application does not need them all. However, you must override Validate-User(string userName, string password) in order for login to work.

We'll follow the same pattern of delegating to the RoleRepository for the NHibernateRoleProvider.

securityErrorHandlingAndLogging/NHibernateRoleProvider.cs

```
public class NHibernateRoleProvider : RoleProvider
{
  private RoleRepository roleRepository;

  public NHibernateRoleProvider()
  {
    roleRepository = new RoleRepository();
  }

  public NHibernateRoleProvider(RoleRepository roleRepository)
  {
    this.roleRepository = roleRepository;
  }

  public override void AddUsersToRoles(
    string[] usernames, string[] roleNames)
  {
    roleRepository.AddUsersToRoles(usernames, roleNames);
  }

  //omit rest of class implementation
}
```

This provider manages the roles of the users. We've implemented Add-UsersToRoles(), which takes a list of users and roles as arguments. You'll also need to make sure you implement GetRolesForUser(string userName) for your user's roles to be populated.

Finally, you'll need to change your Web.config to include the provider using the following code:

securityErrorHandlingAndLogging/Web.Config

```
Line 1  <system.web>
     -  <membership defaultProvider="NHibernateMembershipProvider" >
     -  <providers>
     -    <clear/>
     5    <add
     -      name="NHibernateMembershipProvider"
     -      type="GetOrganized.Membership.NHibernateMembershipProvider"
     -      enablePasswordRetrieval="false"
     -      enablePasswordReset="false" />
    10  </providers>
     -  </membership>
```

```
    <roleManager defaultProvider="NHibernateRoleProvider"
      <providers>
        <clear />
15      <add
          name="NHibernateRoleProvider"
          type="GetOrganized.Membership.NHibernateRoleProvider"/>
      </providers>
    </roleManager>
20  </system.web>
```

On line 2, we specify the default provider for membership to be NHibernateMembershipProvider. Defining that provider follows by adding the name and fully qualified namespace of the class. You can also turn on or off features of the provider here. Since we've implemented the bare minimum, we'll turn off the password reset and retrieval features for now.

On line 12, we define the role provider in a similar fashion. In both cases, we start with a clear element that removes any of the default providers that are installed.

Your application is now free from stored procedures, and you can begin to add third-party authentication schemes as you want.

So, your application is now super secure. But just because you've implemented security doesn't mean that you'll be free of production problems. Unhandled exceptions can mar even the most secure site.

11.2 Using an Action Filter to Handle Errors

Most of the time, we'll try to catch exceptions that happen in our code by surrounding them with a **try** and **catch** block. Not all of our code is surrounded by these blocks, so unhandled exceptions pass through. MVC provides a handy action filter to help us catch these unhandled exceptions called HandleErrorAttribute. By capturing unhandled exceptions, you are in essence *handling* them and not letting them be seen in their raw form by users of the system. When combined with effective logging techniques, handling exceptions gives you insight into production issues before your users can report it.

Here is a simple demonstration of applying it to an entire controller:

securityErrorHandlingAndLogging/ErrorHandlingController.cs

```
[HandleError]
public class ErrorHandlingController : Controller
{
}
```

Applying this action filter will catch all unhandled exceptions thrown in this controller. When one of the controller's actions throw an unhandled exception, this filter will redirect the user to the /View/Shared/Error.aspx view. However, if you create your own Error.aspx in the controller's view folder, it will use that one instead. This lets you write customized error pages for controllers when you need to do so.

Handling Custom HTTP Error Codes with MVC

There are other errors that are generated *outside* the web application. For example, when you try to access a page or resource that is not there, the web server generates a 404 Page Not Found error. By default IIS will send you to a generic Page Not Found page, but this can confuse your users because it does not comply with the style of your site. Customizing how to handle HTTP errors like these is tied into how do the setup, and we use the [HandleError] action filter, which we'll work through now.

To handle these error codes and to enable the [HandleError] action filter to work, you'll need to enable a setting in the Web.config file:

securityErrorHandlingAndLogging/Web.Config

```
<system.web>
  <customErrors mode="On">
  </customErrors>
</system.web>
```

By turning on custom logging, the HandleError filter will now work. When modifying this section of the Web.config file, we can also direct the user to specific web pages depending on the HTTP status error code.

securityErrorHandlingAndLogging/Web.Config

```
<customErrors mode="On" defaultRedirect="DefaultErrorPage.html">
  <error statusCode="404" redirect="PageNotFound.html"/>
  <error statusCode="500" redirect="InternalError.html"/>
</customErrors>
```

For example, here we send all 404 Page Not Found errors to the Page-NotFound.html page. Similarly, if there is an internal server error for the request, a 500 error, we redirect the browser to the InternalError.html page. Otherwise, the default page that will be displayed is DefaultError-Page.html. For a complete list of HTTP status codes, check out Wikipedia.[5]

---

5. http://en.wikipedia.org/wiki/List_of_HTTP_status_codes

If you want your error pages to be generated by MVC to comply with the style of the rest of your site instead of the previous plain HTML, you can change the URLs to go to a custom ErrorController. Just create a standard controller with all the error codes you'd like to support:

securityErrorHandlingAndLogging/ErrorController.cs

```
public class ErrorController : Controller
{
  public ActionResult Index()
  {
    return View();
  }
  public ActionResult PageNotFound()
  {
    Response.StatusCode = (int)HttpStatusCode.NotFound;
    return View();
  }
  public ActionResult InternalError()
  {
    Response.StatusCode = (int)HttpStatusCode.InternalServerError;
    return View();
  }
}
```

We had to specify the return codes to the response in each of the actions so that the user's browser registers the kind of error that was returned. Also, we'll need to create views in the /View/Error/ directory to correspond to each action, like /View/Error/NotFound.aspx. Now instead of using the DefaultErrorPage.html, PageNotFound.html, and InternalError.html pages in Web.config, we'll specify the URL routes for the ErrorController like so:

securityErrorHandlingAndLogging/Web.Config

```
<customErrors mode="On" defaultRedirect="~/Error">
  <error statusCode="404" redirect="~/Error/PageNotFound"/>
  <error statusCode="500" redirect="~/Error/InternalError"/>
</customErrors>
```

Most exceptions that we throw are not HTTP status code errors. For instance, a SqlException will not trigger a 500 error when it is thrown. This is where MVC's [HandleError] catches those exceptions for us. You can also apply [HandleError] to a single action:

securityErrorHandlingAndLogging/ErrorHandlingController.cs

```
[HandleError]
public ActionResult HandleError()
{
  throw new Exeception();
}
```

The sample action HandleError() will always throw a new general exception. It will then redirect it to the shared error view. You can also specify a type of exception that you want to catch and a corresponding view you want to direct them to.

securityErrorHandlingAndLogging/ErrorHandlingController.cs

```
[HandleError(ExceptionType = typeof(SqlException),
  View = "DatabaseError")]]
public ActionResult CallDatabase()
{
  throw new SqlExeception();
}
```

In this example, we apply the HandleError with additional parameters. We want to catch all SqlExceptions that are thrown and redirect them to the view /Shared/DatabaseError.aspx. This will give your users more information about what went wrong. For example, if you're integrating with someone else's web service, you might want to let people know that the service is currently unavailable.

Error handling can also be dealt with more generically inside Global. asax.cs. This is done by catching the event in the method Application_ Error(). The following is an example:

securityErrorHandlingAndLogging/Global.asax.cs

```
protected void Application_Error()
{
  Exception error = Server.GetLastError();

  // log something using this exception
}
```

Using the object Server's method GetLastError(), it retrieves the last exception that was thrown. With the exception available to you, the next step is to log it so that you'll be able to see the errors that users are experiencing.

11.3 Using Logging to See What Went Wrong

Error handling without logging is like having glass frames without lenses. Without it, you'll never be able to see what's going on with your application when things go wrong.

Logging and monitoring help report production issues and trends before you're overwhelmed with user requests. Since they say that only 50 percent of customers who have a negative experience actually report it, having robust logging in place will help address that.[6]

In this section, we're going to cover the basics of logging. We'll cover two open source logging frameworks for .NET logging that make writing to error logs easy. We'll also briefly touch on the application monitoring provided as part of ASP.NET to help you keep track of the site's general health.

Logging in .NET

Many logging frameworks exist in .NET, but since NHibernate uses Log4Net and it's one of the best supported open source .NET logging frameworks, we are going to use it. Simply download the Log4Net's libraries to your Lib folder, and add log4net.dll to your project references.[7]

Using Log4Net

Log4Net can have simple or more complex configurations based on your needs. For our purposes, we're going to use a basic configuration.

Log4Net has a concept called an *appender* that can be configured to publish logs to separate mediums, such as email or RSS. You can add a FileAppender to write the messages to the web server's file system. Adding an appender requires that you create a Log4Net configuration section in your Web.config file or add it pragmatically when the web application starts up:

securityErrorHandlingAndLogging/Global.asax.cs

```
public void Application_Start()
{
  //omitted other code
  FileAppender appender = new FileAppender();
  appender.File = "GetOrganized.log";
  log4net.Config.BasicConfigurator.Configure(appender);
}
```

Here we add the FileAppender along with the name of the log file, GetOrganized.log. Using the BasicConfigurator simplifies the configuration of Log4Net. As your logging requirements become more complex, it's probably best to resort to a separate configuration file.

To make logging available to all our controllers and repositories, we'll need to add it to the Windsor container.

---

6. http://www.newtoncomputing.com/zips/basicfacts.pdf
7. http://logging.apache.org/log4net/

Adding Log4Net to Windsor

Back in Section 9.2, *Using Factory Methods in Castle Windsor to Retrieve Sessions*, on page 185 we used a Windsor facility to supply us with NHibernate ISession objects. Here, we're going to use the Log4Net integration facility Castle.Services.Logging.Log4netIntegration.dll that comes with Windsor to hook in Log4Net. The facility will then provide ILoggers to classes that require them, such as repositories and controllers.

First let's create a sample controller that will take an ILogger:

`securityErrorHandlingAndLogging/LoggingController.cs`

```
public class LoggingController : Controller
{
  private ILogger logger;

  public LoggingController(ILogger logger)
  {
    this.logger = logger;
  }
}
```

The interface needs to be ILogger for the facility to work correctly. With Log4Net injected, we can create an action that performs different kinds of logging:

`securityErrorHandlingAndLogging/LoggingController.cs`

```
public ActionResult LoggingTest()
{
  logger.Debug("debugging");
  logger.Info("application started up");
  logger.Warn("something bad may happen");
  logger.Error("something bad happened");
  logger.Fatal("something really bad happened");
}
```

We're using all five levels of logging available to us. The severity and the frequency of these messages should be the indicator for which one to use for the situation. For example, if the server's memory resources are nearly out, you might choose to log a Fatal(). If you're logging that someone failed a login attempt, you might use Info() instead.

Based on how you've configured Log4Net to work, the message will be directed to the appropriate destination. In our case, all messages will be logged to the file GetOrganized. However, you could have all Error() and Fatal() logs be sent by email or to the Windows event log. All of that can be done by changing the configuration of Log4Net, without having to touch our logging code.

Logging All Unhandled Errors

Revisiting our catchall error handler in Global.asax.cs, we now have the means to log it using Log4Net:

securityErrorHandlingAndLogging/Global.asax.cs

```
protected void Application_Error()
{
  Exception error = Server.GetLastError();
  container.Get<ILogger>().Fatal(error);
}
```

First you need to move the IWindsorContainer to a member variable for you to be able to reference it here. After that, just use the Get() to get your ILogger to perform the logging.

Alternatively, you can use a more pluggable option to display unhandled errors called ELMAH.

ELMAH: A Logging Alternative

There is an open source pluggable logging framework called Error Logging Modules and Handlers (ELMAH)[8] that works easily with both ASP.NET and MVC. What makes ELMAH such a good alternative is that it provides a nice web interface for viewing messages. Another advantage is that it is able to include an additional dump of form and session data that were in memory at the time of the error. Finally, it supports notifications to Twitter and RSS out of the box. If you need Twitter or RSS support, you're probably best to go with ELMAH; otherwise, you can stick to the more popular Log4Net.

Once you've downloaded and included the DLL reference, you'll need to add the following code to your Web.config file to set it up:

securityErrorHandlingAndLogging/Web.Config

```
Line 1  <sectionGroup name="elmah">
   -      <section name="security" requirePermission="false"
   -        type="Elmah.SecuritySectionHandler, Elmah" />
   -      <section name="errorLog" requirePermission="false"
   5        type="Elmah.ErrorLogSectionHandler, Elmah" />
   -      <section name="errorMail" requirePermission="false"
   -        type="Elmah.ErrorMailSectionHandler, Elmah" />
   -      <section name="errorFilter" requirePermission="false"
   -        type="Elmah.ErrorFilterSectionHandler, Elmah" />
   10 </sectionGroup>
   -
```

---

8. http://code.google.com/p/elmah/wiki/MVC

```
    <elmah>
      <errorLog type="Elmah.XmlFileErrorLog, Elmah"
        logPath="~/App_Data" />
15  </elmah>

    <system.web>
      <httpModules>
      <add verb="POST,GET,HEAD" path="elmah.axd"
20      type="Elmah.ErrorLogPageFactory, Elmah" />
      </httpModules>
    </system.web>

    <location path="elmah.axd">
25    <system.web>
        <authorization>
          <deny users="jonathan" />
        </authorization>
      </system.web>
30  </location>
```

On line 13, we configure everything to a set of XML files in the App_Data of your web application. ELMAH works through an ASP.NET feature called *HttpModules*, which works as part of the ASP.NET request life cycle. We add the ELMAH module to our request pipeline on line 19. The great thing about ELMAH is that you can view all the errors via the web address http://yourapplication/elmah.axd.

Because we don't want just anyone to view these logs, we add a Location element to secure the URL on line 24.

With basic logging covered, we're next going to delve into application health monitoring. This will round out our understanding of how to keep ahead of production problems.

11.4 Checking for a Pulse with ASP.NET Health Monitoring

Health monitoring differs slightly from logging because it refers to the overall availability of an application. This definition can differ based on how you implement logging. For example, if you end up creating logging events in your code that check whether the connection to the database works every five minutes, you've implemented your own health monitoring using the logging framework. This isn't a bad thing to do necessarily, but there are separate frameworks and products that do the same job already. Think of application health monitoring like a heart rate monitor, constantly displaying data on how the application is doing. Monitoring that your website is up and running is important so that you can respond quickly if it does go down.

ASP.NET has a built-in health monitoring solution that covers certain events such as start-up and shutdown. These types of events are useful to monitor because when you're supporting your application, it's important to know how many servers are available. Similar to logging frameworks, monitoring can also be configured to be sent to many different sources. The good thing about ASP.NET's application health monitoring is that it takes only a single line to configure:

securityErrorHandlingAndLogging/Web.Config

```
<system.web>
  <healthMonitoring Enabled="true" />
</system.web>
```

Inside the Web.config file, add the health monitoring config section. This will by default direct ASP.NET errors to the Windows event logs. It can also be set up to send email notifications or write to a database. If you want to send these events to another source, like Twitter, for example, you can always implement your own System.Web.Management. WebEventProvider.

Up Next

We've learned to apply additional security to our applications and protect against malicious users. We've also worked through setting up more robust error handling and logging so that our application is easier to monitor.

We've built our ASP.NET MVC application from start to finish. There's just one thing left to do: deploy it into production.

People in their handlings of affairs often fail when they are
about to succeed. If one remains as careful at the end as he
was at the beginning, there will be no failure.
  ► Lao Tzu

Chapter 12

Build and Deployment

Getting software into production is the most common point of failure. At least that's Roy Singham's point of view in his essay "Solving the Business Software Last Mile" from *The ThoughtWorks Anthology* [Tho08]. Singham suggests the only way to reduce this risk of failure is to develop a discipline of continuous deployment. That's exactly what we're going to work on in this chapter—getting disciplined about deploying our ASP.NET MVC applications often.

In this chapter, we're going to learn about how to automate the process of deployment. First, we'll create an automated build that is portable across all machines. Next, we'll extend that build to remotely manage deployment to other servers.

12.1 Automating Builds

Think about your daily developer activities. You write a test, watch it fail, get the test to pass, and then check in the code to version control. At every step you need to compile your code. You'll also find yourself deploying to your local web server to simulate a more production-like environment. You might also be checking your application's code coverage by running a report.

Doing all this manually becomes boring quickly. Also, mistakes can happen when steps in the process are forgotten or incorrectly performed. We've all run into the situation where we're sure we fixed a bug, but there it is on the customer's machine. At that point, we make the useless excuse, "But it works on my machine."

Fixing these kinds of problems requires an approach that is called *build automation*. It is a way to delegate these tasks to something that

---

Version Control and Automated Builds

Adding version control to your automated build helps ensure you have the right version for the right environment. Most build systems can be configured to interact with the version control system. Common tasks include automatically tagging successful builds with the version number or retrieving and building a specific version of the application.

Having your build version control aware helps keep your team on the same page about what needs to be promoted to which environment and reduces the risks of human error. For more information on integrating MSBuild with common version control systems like Team System and Subversion, you can read more about the Tigris MSBuild tasks.*

---

*. http://msbuildtasks.tigris.org

---

doesn't mind repetition: your computer. Mike Clark explains in *Pragmatic Project Automation* [Cla04] that effective automated builds are CRISP: Complete, Repeatable, Informative, Scheduleable, and Portable.

Complete builds have a list of everything that is required to deploy the software. *Repeatable* means the build can be reproduced on another machine, usually in conjunction with version control. Informative builds broadcast relevant information, such as if tests are failing, to multiple formats like the console and XML. It makes the system more reliable if you schedule frequent deployments. To schedule a build, it needs to be complete and repeatable. Complete builds start from a blank slate and then compile and deploy the code. Repeatable builds reply on completeness; otherwise, you won't be able to repeat the process. Finally, if a build is portable, it can run on different machines. In this chapter, we're going to focus on creating a build that covers all these criteria except for version control (see the sidebar on the current page).

Lucky for us there are plenty of tools to help with build automation in .NET, such as NAnt, MSBuild, and more recently Psake (which uses PowerShell). There are other tools, such as continuous integration servers, that we won't cover here but that can augment your automation (see the sidebar on the facing page). We're going to use MSBuild because

---

Continuous Integration

Another advantage to having an automated build is it allows you to take advantage of continuous integration (CI) servers. These servers will run your build after every check-in to version control. One of the most popular CI servers is Cruise Control .NET.* We won't be covering CI here, but once you have an automated build going, it is a fairly simple process (and rewarding). You can read more about CI by reading Martin Fowler's blog post about it.[†]

---

*. http://sourceforge.net/projects/ccnet/
†. http://martinfowler.com/articles/continuousIntegration.html

---

it comes with the rest of the .NET Framework and is already installed both locally and on production machines.

12.2 Using MSBuild to Automate the Build

The simplest way to introduce MSBuild is to use it against a Visual Studio project file. All Visual Studio project files (.sln, .proj, or .targets) are all MSBuild files. Executing MSBuild against the GetOrganized solution file will compile the entire project, as we can see here:

```
C:\Development\GetOrganized>
  C:\Windows\Microsoft.NET\Framework\v3.5\MSBuild.exe GetOrganized.sln
...
compilation output omitted
...
Build succeeded.
0 Error(s)

Time Elapsed 00:00:36.51
```

A copy of MSBuild.exe is located for each version of the .NET Framework under Windows\Microsoft.NET\Framework\vX.XX. To run MSBuild, we pass it the build file as the argument. MSBuild will execute the default instructions, known as a *target*, which in this case is to compile the whole solution.

The output of the build is fairly informative and has been truncated here to save pages. It will let you know about compiler warnings or errors and the time it takes to perform the whole build.

Let's go ahead and create our own build file. To start with, we'll make our build file compile the solution. This is the same thing the GetOrganized.sln file does already, but it will serve as an introduction to how MSBuild and build files work. The filename of the MSBuild file will be Build.msbuild, and we'll keep it in the root directory of our solution, right next to the solution file GetOrganized.sln.

`buildAndDeploy/Build.msbuild`

```
Line 1  <Project DefaultTargets="All"
     2    xmlns="http://schemas.microsoft.com/developer/msbuild/2003">
     3
     4    <Target Name="All" DependsOnTargets="Compile" />
     5
     6    <Target Name="Compile" >
     7
     8    </Target>
     9
    10  </Project>
```

This is our first look at an MSBuild file. Build files are XML with the root node *Project*. The XML namespace also needs to be referenced, as we do on line 2. There also needs to be a default target, which we define as All. Targets define stages in the build process. Build files have numerous targets such as Compile, Clean, Documentation, and Deploy.

Our first target, All, is defined on line 4. This target is completely empty but uses the attribute DependsOnTarget, which instructs MSBuild to call those targets before it runs. The attribute lets you chain targets together. In this case, we're adding Compile as the first step in the default build process.

Targets are composed of individual tasks. Tasks perform some sort of work, such as copying files, connecting to a remote computer, or compiling source code. On line 7, we add the Compile target. We've left it empty for now, but the next step is to add a compile task.

`buildAndDeploy/Build.msbuild`

```
Line 1  <Target Name="Compile" >
     2    <MSBuild Projects="GetOrganized.sln" Targets="Build" />
     3  </Target>
```

Here we're using the MSBuild task to compile the solution on line 2. This task is doing the same thing we would have done on the command line to run MSBuild against the GetOrganized.sln solution file.

Now let's execute against our build file:

```
C:\Development\GetOrganized>
  C:\Windows\Microsoft.NET\Framework\v3.5\MSBuild.exe
  Build.msbuild /t:Compile
...
compilation output omitted
...
Build succeeded.
0 Error(s)

Time Elapsed 00:00:30.43
```

MSBuild is now doing all our compiling. We passed in an optional argument called /t:Compile to instruct MSBuild to execute only that target. Since we specified the default target All in our build file, this is redundant in this case. However, it is important to know how to specifically call a build target. This is because as your project grows, each target will take longer to run. If you can skip targets by calling only the specific ones you need, you'll save yourself time. Next, we need to add the database to our build.

Incrementally Deploying Your Database

Setting up your database to the latest version of the schema is a useful thing to automate in the build. It saves manually re-creating databases to reflect the current codebase.

There are several ways of doing this. You can generate a SQL script and store it in a specific folder like DatabaseDeltaScripts using a tool like db.deploy.NET (see the sidebar on page 243). However, there is a trend toward building database migrations using a modern language, such as C# instead of SQL. This method has become popular because it takes advantage of object-oriented language features to reduce duplication and make migrations easier to read. This is the method we'll use. To help us with build C# migrations, we'll use Migrator.NET, an open source database migration framework.

Introducing Migrator.NET

Migrator.NET lets you create C# migration files to upgrade your database. It also has NAnt and MSBuild tasks you add to your build to execute those migrations.

To get started, you'll want to download the DLLs (Migrator.Framework.dll, Migrator.Providers.dll, Migrator.dll, and Migrator.MSBuild.dll) and put them in your Lib folder.[1] There is also a Migrator.Targets file that you'll need to copy to Lib for the MSBuild task. Next, add a reference to Migrator.Framework.dll in your Web project, and you'll be able to create your first migration file. To keep your code organized, it's best to create a separate folder in your project called Migrations.

To show how migrations work, we'll add a migration that adds our Todo and Topic tables:

buildAndDeploy/AddTopicAndTodoTables.cs

```
Line 1    [Migration(20100101081010)]
    -     public class AddTopicAndTodoTables : Migration
    -     {
    -       public override void Up()
    5       {
    -         Database.AddTable("Topic",
    -           new Column("Id", DbType.Int32, ColumnProperty.PrimaryKey),
    -           new Column("Name", DbType.String, 100),
    -           new Column("ColorHtml", DbType.String, 255)
    10          );
    -
    -         Database.AddTable("Todo",
    -           new Column("Id", DbType.Int32, ColumnProperty.PrimaryKey),
    -           new Column("Title", DbType.String, 25),
    15          new Column("Outcome", DbType.String, 100),
    -           new Column("Complete", DbType.Boolean),
    -           new Column("Topic_Id", DbType.Int32)
    -           );
    -
    20        Database.AddForeignKey("FK_Todo_Topic",
    -           "Todo", "Topic_Id", "Topic", "Id");
    -       }
    -
    -       public override void Down()
    25      {
    -         Database.RemoveForeignKey("Todo", "FK_Todo_Topic");
    -         Database.RemoveTable("Todo");
    -         Database.RemoveTable("Topic");
    -       }
    30    }
```

All migration classes have two things in common. First they all inherit the Migration class, which forces the class to **override** the Up() and Down() methods. The migration class also has the attribute [Migration], which represents the sequence the migration falls into. This can be done by starting with 1 and incrementing every migration; however, a better

---

1. http://code.google.com/p/migratordotnet/

An Alternative: dbDeploy .NET

db.deploy.NET takes SQL scripts and runs them in sequence against the database to bring them up to the current version. Using NHibernate's SchemaUpdate object to produce a SQL script is one way to generate the delta scripts. Alternative, they can be created by hand.

Using db.deploy.NET lets you avoid having to write classes to do migrations. However, this is becoming less popular with developers. Modern development efforts are focusing more time in object-oriented languages such as C# as opposed to SQL.

practice is to use a timestamp. This ensures uniqueness if multiple developers are writing migrations at the same time.

The Up() method is the database logic for upgrading the database. Its complement is the Down() method, which downgrades the database to the previous version. Both methods use the key object Database to perform operations against the database.

Within Up(), we start by adding a table on line 6. This AddTable() takes multiple Column objects that represent columns in the database table. We add the Topic table first and then the Todo after because one of its columns references Topic. On line 17, we add this column, which is known as a *foreign key*. A foreign key is a way to reference information that is listed in another table. To enforce the integrity of a foreign key, we add a constraint to the database on line 21. This constraint makes sure that rows in the Todo table reference a valid TopicId.

When it comes to the Down() method, we remove things in reverse order. We start by removing the foreign key constraint on line 26. We do this before we start dropping the tables because the database will complain if you don't remove the foreign key constraint first. Next, we remove the two tables using the method RemoveTable(string nameOfTable).

With both methods implemented, this completes this migration. As you can see, reading the migrations is a lot easier than dropping into SQL to see what a table does. They also are reversible, which is useful if you need to downgrade a database.

Let's run the migration against our database.

Using the Migrator.NET Task

Migrator has an MSBuild task to do the migration for us. So, let's create a new target in our build file to upgrade the database to the latest version:

```
buildAndDeploy/Build.msbuild
```

```
Line 1    <UsingTask AssemblyFile="lib\Migrator.MSBuild.dll"
            TaskName="Migrator.MSBuild.Migrate" />


          ...omit other targets...
    5
          <Target Name="Migrate" DependsOnTargets="Compile">
            <Migrate Provider="SqlServer"
              Connectionstring="Database=GetOrganized;Data Source=localhost;
                User Id=user;Password=password;"
    10          Migrations="GetOrganized\bin\GetOrganized.dll"/>
          </Target>
```

To include other MSBuild files in your build, use the *UsingTask* element. On line 2, we include the Migrator .NET DLL in the Lib directory. This enables the migrate task, which we then use on line 7. The task takes a Connectionstring to the database as one of its attributes. Also, you need to specify a Provider for the database type. Finally, you need to provide the assembly that the migrations are in by using the Migrations attribute.

Executing this target will upgrade your database to the latest version. With the most current database ready, we can now run our persistence and unit tests against it.

Adding Unit Tests to the Build

Making tests part of the build is an important step for continuous integration. It's also makes it easier to run the full suite of tests before checking your code in. Since MSBuild does not have a task for running NUnit tests, we need to get that from somewhere else.

As we saw in the previous section, we can extend MSBuild with custom tasks. Tigris, an open source consortium, provides an MSBuild project extension with more than 85 useful tasks, one of which is an NUnit task. To use it in our build file, you'll need to download the MSBuild tasks from Tigris.[2] There are two files that need to be added to the Lib folder in your solution, the MSBuild.Community.Tasks.dll and the

---

2. http://msbuildtasks.tigris.org/

MSBuild.Community.Tasks.Targets. The latter is an MSBuild file that imports all custom tasks.

The NUnit task uses the nunit-console.exe. We covered how to use this command-line utility in Section 2.2, *Watching the Test Fail*, on page 25. Getting this MSBuild task working means you'll also need to add the following files to your Lib folder from NUnit: nunit-console.exe, nunit.core.dll, nunit-console-runner.dll, nunit.util.dll, and nunit.core.interfaces.dll.

With those files in place, we can reference the custom tasks in our build file:

buildAndDeploy/Build.msbuild

```
<PropertyGroup>
  <MSBuildCommunityTasksPath>.</MSBuildCommunityTasksPath>
</PropertyGroup>
<Import Project="Lib\MSBuild.Community.Tasks.Targets" />
```

Here we use the import element to reference the MSBuild.Community.Tasks. Targets for the additional tasks. We also had to add a property to point those target tasks to the right directory. The directory we specify here is . because the file we're importing, MSBuild.Community.Tasks.Targets, is in the same directory as all the community task DLLs and the NUnit binaries. Now we'll add the Nunit target and task.

buildAndDeploy/Build.msbuild

```
<Target Name="Test" DependsOnTargets="Compile;Migrate">
  <NUnit Assemblies="Test.Unit\bin\Debug\Test.Unit.dll;
    Test.Persistence\bin\Debug\Test.Persistence.dll"
    ToolPath="lib" />
</Target>
```

The Nunit task takes the Assemblies where your unit tests are. In this case, we're using two projects and separating them by a semicolon. This will run all the NUnit tests and output the results to the screen. There are other options with this task that will allow you to output the result as XML, which is useful for continuous integration servers to report on. Note that we need to add the property ToolPath to point the task to the Lib directory where nunit-console.exe and the other NUnit files are located.

With both database migrations and tests running, it's time to deploy the site to our local IIS to see how it to bring it one step closer to production.

Deploying Locally to IIS

With the site compiled, tested, and database ready, it's time to deploy it to IIS. Deploying to IIS instead of the Visual Studio Cassini web server is important because that is what it will use in production.

We've already installed the Tigris Community MSBuild tasks, which have all the tasks we need. Let's add those tasks to a deploy target:

buildAndDeploy/Build.msbuild

```
Line 1   <Target Name="LocalDeploy" DependsOnTargets="Compile;Migrate">

    -    <PropertyGroup>
    -            <VirtualDirectory>C:\inetpub\GetOrganized</VirtualDirectory>
    5            <VirtualDirectoryName>GetOrganized</VirtualDirectoryName>
    -    </PropertyGroup>

    -    <WebDirectoryDelete VirtualDirectoryName="$(VirtualDirectoryName)"
    -      ContinueOnError="true" />
   10    <RemoveDir Directories="$(VirtualDirectory)" />

    -    <ItemGroup>
    -      <WebFiles Include="GetOrganized\**\*.*" Exclude="**\.svn\**"/>
    -    </ItemGroup>
   15    <Copy SourceFiles="@(WebFiles)"
    -      DestinationFolder="$(VirtualDirectory)\%(RecursiveDir)"/>

    -    <WebDirectoryCreate VirtualDirectoryName="$(VirtualDirectoryName)"
    -                  VirtualDirectoryPhysicalPath="$(VirtualDirectory)" />
   20    </Target>
```

Here we define a couple of properties using the PropertyGroup element. Properties are like member variables. The first we create is VirtualDirectory, which is for the physical directory where the website is located. VirtualDirectoryName is the name of the virtual directory we access through IIS. In this example, we'd be accessing the URL http://localhost/GetOrganized.

Targets should be repeatable, so we need to begin by removing the website if it exists. On line 9, we use the WebDirectoryDelete task. We also use the RemoveDir task to delete the contents of the physical directory. We also set the property ContinueOnError to true, because the first time this task runs, there will be no directory to delete, and we don't want it to fail during the rest of the task.

Finally, we use the Copy task to move the new site over on line 15. This also re-creates the directory structure. We need to add an ItemGroup with the wildcard **/*.* to recursively copy all the files. We also will want to exclude special files like source control—in this case Subversion—by adding the **\\.*svn*** to the Exclude attribute. This is referenced as @(WebFiles) in the copy command. Note the use of /%(RecursiveDir) to the Copy task. This lets the Copy task know that you want to preserve the directory structure from the source it is copied from. We then use the WebDirectoryCreate task to build a virtual directory.

This deploys the site locally. However, you might get the error message *Login failed for user '{MACHINE NAME}\ASPNET'.* because some versions of IIS will try to run as the user ASPNET, which won't have access to the database. To correct this, add ASPNET as a database user through SQL Server Management Studio. Simply add the *db_owner* under *User Mappings* tab.

Now we'll fix up the All target to complete all the targets we've created so far:

buildAndDeploy/Build.msbuild

```
<Target Name="All"
  DependsOnTargets="Compile;Migrate;Test;LocalDeploy" />
```

Specifying the default targets in this order allows us to invoke MSBuild without specifying any parameters. It's important to note how we migrate the database before running tests. This is because we want to make sure the database is in the correct state for the persistence tests.

To make it one step easier to run your command-line build, you might find it useful to wrap your MSBuild in a .bat file. For example, you could have a filename build.bat that looks like this:

buildAndDeploy/build.bat

```
C:\Windows\Microsoft.NET\Framework\v3.5\MSBuild.exe Build.msbuild /t:%1
```

This way, you can avoid the path to MSBuild and your build file itself. The *%1* is the batch file notation for the first parameter you pass to build.bat. This allows you to pass any target to run, like Deploy, if you didn't want to run the full test suite.

Now that we have a fully functional build file, there are some nuances of getting deployments working depending on which version of IIS you're using. The next few sections address each version of the Windows operating system and its corresponding version of IIS.

> **Microsoft's Web Deployment Tool**
>
> This tool is another way to deploy your site to multiple servers. It is downloadable from Microsoft's site or using the Web Installer Platform.* Although it cannot be automated via MSBuild, it does make the process simpler than doing it manually via the command prompt. A useful thing about this tool in that the 1.1 version supports running a SQL script against a remote database.
>
> *. http://www.iis.net/expand/WebDeploymentTool

IIS 5.1 on Windows XP Pro

If you have IIS 5.1, you'll need to add a wildcard mapping within IIS. This will make sure the URLs are captured by the aspnet_isapi.dll ISAPI filter. To add the mapping, you need to open the IIS control panel. Next right-click Default Website, and click the Configuration button. With the new window open, click the Add a New Mapping button. Set the extension .* and the executable to aspnet_isapi.dll, which is normally installed in C:\Windows\Microsoft.NET\Framework\v2.0.50727. Do not check the box "Verify that file exists," since the URLs for MVC do not reference physical files.

IIS 6.0 on Windows Server 2003 or XP Pro x64

You can do the same for IIS 6.0 by using a wildcard, but for a production environment, this will incur a performance hit. Essentially all requests, including image, CSS, and JavaScript files, are directed through the ASP.NET filter. A process was refined by Steve Sanderson to use Helicon's rewrite engine.[3]

Once you install this rewriter,[4] you want to add a rewrite rule. This rule will add an *.aspx* extension to most requests so that the aspnet_isapi.dll will catch it. Here's a look at the rewrite rule:

buildAndDeploy/httpd.ini

```
Line 1   # Add extensions to this rule to avoid them being processed by ASP.NET
     2   RewriteRule (.*)\.(css|gif|png|jpeg|jpg|js|zip) $1.$2 [I,L]
     3
```

---

3. http://blog.codeville.net/2008/07/04/options-for-deploying-aspnet-mvc-to-iis-6/

4. http://www.isapirewrite.com/

```
4  # Prefixes URLs with "rewritten.aspx/", so that ASP.NET handles them
5  RewriteRule /(.*) /rewritten.aspx/$1 [I]
```

On line 2, we exclude all files that we don't want processed by ASP.NET. We've listed CSS, images files, and ZIP files. For every other request, we want to append *.aspx* on line 5.

Before the request is processed, we append some logic to the Application_BeginRequest() in the Global.asax.cs to strip the *.aspx* from the URL.

buildAndDeploy/Global.asax.cs

```csharp
protected void Application_BeginRequest(Object sender, EventArgs e)
{
  HttpApplication app = sender as HttpApplication;
  if (app != null)
    if (app.Request.
        AppRelativeCurrentExecutionFilePath == "~/rewritten.aspx")
      app.Context.RewritePath(
          app.Request.Url.PathAndQuery.Replace("/rewritten.aspx", "")
      );
}
```

The code checks the request for the rewritten.aspx file in the Request.App-RelativeCurrentExecutionFilePath and uses String.Replace() to remove it. Now you have IIS 6.0 working with ASP.NET MVC without the performance restrictions.

IIS 7.0 or 7.5 on Windows Server 2008 R2, Windows 7, and Vista

This is the simplest configuration of them all. Run the Turn Windows Features On or Off program, and ensure that ASP.NET, ISAPI Extensions, and ISAPI Filters are all selected. All that you need to do is make sure your website's Application Pool option is set to Integrated Mode, and you're done!

With all the local deployment steps complete, we can leverage all this automation and get production deployment going.

12.3 Deploying to Production

There are a couple of steps involved in getting our code into production. First we need to upload the site via FTP, and then we deploy the site to IIS. There are multiple ways to do this (see the sidebar on the preceding page), but we're going to set up an automated deployment. By automating these steps, we'll avoid having to manually do this for every deployment. This will make deployments much more enjoyable.

Uploading the Site Using FTP

Remote file upload can be done through the FTP task as part of Tigris's community tasks. To make it easier to upload the entire solution, we'll also compress the files into a zip file.

buildAndDeploy/Build.msbuild

```
<Target Name="Ftp" DependsOnTargets="Compile">

<ItemGroup>
  <WebFiles Include="GetOrganized\**\*.*"/>
</ItemGroup>

<Zip Files="@(WebFiles)" ZipFileName="GetOrganized.zip" />
<FtpUpload LocalFile="GetOrganized.zip"
  RemoteUri="ftp://localhost/" RemoteFiles="GetOrganized.zip" />

</Target>
```

The Zip task takes a list of Files or a pattern to match the files to compress. Also, it specifies a ZipFileName as the name of the archive to create. After the archive is created, we then proceed to upload it using the FtpUpload task. It uploads a single file using the LocalFile property. The FTP site to connect to is specified using the RemoteUri attribute. This example is connecting to an unsecured site, since no credentials are provided.

To connect to a secure site, you can add the properties UserName and Password.

Running this task will upload the site to the remote computer. If you don't have MVC installed on the remote server, you'll need to complete an extra step to the Web project file (see the sidebar on the facing page).

With the site uploaded, we'll need to execute some MSBuild tasks remotely to complete the deployment. For that we'll use a handy command-line utility provided by Microsoft.

Performing Remote Management at the Command Line

We are going to use a package called PSTools that contains the executable psexec.exe, a free utility provided by Microsoft's TechNet.[5] This command-line utility allows you to execute remote commands. psexec.exe works off the remote computer's $Admin share to remove the need to manually install the server-side program.

---

5. http://technet.microsoft.com/en-us/sysinternals/bb897553.aspx

Using MVC Without Installing MVC

It's possible to have your MVC application run on a machine that does not have it installed. This might be the case if you're running in a hosted environment. In those cases, you'll need to take some additional steps. Add all the MVC libraries—System.Web.Mvc.dll, System.Web.Routing.dll, and System.Web.Abstractions.dll—to the Lib directory. Next copy these files either using MSBuild or using Visual Studio's Solution Explorer to the bin directory. This will make sure that you don't need MVC to be installed for your application to run.

To begin with, try to connect to your local machine to make sure everything is working prior to connecting to a remote machine. So in the examples below, just specify your computer's IP address to start.

After you download the zip file, place the psexec.exe executable in your Lib folder.

First it's important to test that the connection works between your local machine and the remote server. To do this, we'll use the Windows net command. The following is an example of connecting to a remote file share:

```
C:\Development\GetOrganized\Lib>
  net use Z: \\192.168.0.100/$Admin /user:Administrator password
...
Drive Mounted Successfully.
```

Here we use the command net to mount the *$Admin* file share on the remote computer with the IP address of *192.168.0.100*. To pass credentials, we specify the username *Administrator* and the password *password*. The drive successfully mounts, so we're clear to use psexec.exe.

Sometimes problems occur because of firewall restrictions. In these cases, make sure file sharing ports are open and there are no intermediary firewalls preventing file sharing from occurring. Generally, this works best if you're on the same domain or network, but it is possible to do this over the Internet.

Next, we can invoke psexec.exe to run a simple command like hostname, which outputs the friendly name of the computer.

```
C:\Development\GetOrganized\Lib>
  psexec \\192.168.0.100 -u Administrator -p password hostname
...
hostname
production_server_A
```

We instruct psexec to connect to *192.168.0.100* and pass it the proper credentials. The last argument is the command we want to specify on the remote machine. The output is an echo of the command we sent and the output of the remote machine's host name, which is *production_server_A*.

Now let's get practical and start remotely executing MSBuild. We're going to get the remote server to execute MSBuild against the FTP folder that was uploaded in the previous section:

```
C:\Development\GetOrganized\Lib>
  psexec \\192.168.0.100 -u Administrator -p password
    C:\Windows\Microsoft.NET\Framework\v3.5\MSBuild.exe
            C:\ftp\upload\Build.msbuild /t:Compile
...
Error: C:\ftp\upload\Build.msbuild file not found
```

This example uses psexec.exe to execute the MSBuild target Compile on the remote server. Similar to the way we executed hostname, here we execute our MSBuild.exe and pass it both our build file *Build.msbuild* and the target Compile.

Although MSBuild executes, it can't find our build file. This is because it is still in a zip file. To uncompress it, we're going to upload our build files separately, which is part of what we will do in the next section. We have MSBuild being called remotely now, but we had to execute the command manually. Next we'll make this command work with our own MSBuild custom task.

Building a Custom MSBuild Task to Remote In

Custom MSBuild tasks are easy to create for whatever automation task you require. In this case, we're going to use one to wrap psexec.exe and allow us to include its usage in our build file.

The interface to wrap MSBuild tasks is Microsoft.Build.Framework.ITask. To make life easier from a logging perspective, Microsoft also provides a concrete class called Microsoft.Build.Utilities.Task.

You'll need to add the references to both Microsoft.Build.Framework.dll and Microsoft.Build.Utilities.dll to the project to use them.

There is only one method to **override**, and that is Execute(). Let's code up our custom task:

`buildAndDeploy/RemoteTask.cs`

```
Line 1   public class RemoteTask : Task
    -    {
    -      public string ExecutableLocation {get;set;}
    -      public string RemoteIP {get;set;}
    5      public string UserName {get;set;}
    -      public string Password {get;set;}
    -      public string WorkingDirectory {get;set;}
    -      public string RemoteCommand {get;set;}
    -      public string Parameters {get;set;}
   10
    -      public override bool Execute()
    -      {
    -        string psExecCommand = ExecutableLocation + "\\"
    -          + "psexec.exe";
   15
    -        string psExecArguements = "\\\\" + RemoteIP
    -          + " -u " + UserName + " -p " + Password;
    -
    -        string remoteCommand = "-w \"" + WorkingDirectory +
   20        "\" \"" + RemoteCommand + "\" " + Parameters;
    -        try
    -        {
    -          Process p = Process.Start(
    -            psExecCommand, psExecArguments + " " + remoteCommand);
   25
    -          p.WaitForExit();
    -          return true;
    -        }
    -        catch (Exception e)
   30        {
    -          Log.LogError(e.Message);
    -          return false;
    -        }
    -      }
   35   }
```

Whichever properties you make public in your class can be accessed via the XML markup. RemoteIP, for example, is set as follows:

```
<RemoteTask RemoteIP="192.168.0.100" />
```

We set up six properties in our RemoteTask here to correspond to all the things that will vary, such as credentials, locations of the program to execute, and its parameters.

When building up the remote commands, we need to specify what the working directory on the remote machine is. We use the switch -w for this on line 19. This will make sure that your paths work when you execute remote commands.

Next, we use Process.Start() to execute the command-line tool. In the happy path, all things go well, and we return **true** on line 27. If something exceptional happens, we use the MSBuild logger to record the error on line 31. This code is fairly brittle because it does not validate all the properties. For your tasks, you could craft something more robust.

Once you've compiled the task into a DLL, you need to reference it in your build file like so:

buildAndDeploy/Build.msbuild

```
<UsingTask TaskName="RemoteTask"
  AssemblyFile="GetOrganized\bin\GetOrganized.dll" />
```

The UsingTask element imports your custom task into the build file. If we compiled the custom task as part of the sample project, GetOrganized, then the assembly would be GetOrganized.dll.

With the remote task available, we need to add to the *Ftp* target in our build file. This will fix the problem we had in the previous section of psexec.exe not being able to find our build file.

After the target is finished uploading the zip file to the remote location, we'll want it to execute a yet to be created MSBuild target called *Publish*.

buildAndDeploy/Build.msbuild

```
Line 1  <Target Name="Ftp" DependsOnTargets="Compile">
    -   //omit previous code
    -
    -   <FtpUpload LocalFile="Build.bat"
    5     RemoteUri="ftp://192.168.0.1/" RemoteFiles="Build.bat" />
    -
    -   <FtpUpload LocalFile="Build.msbuild"
    -     RemoteUri="ftp://192.168.0.1/" RemoteFiles="Build.msbuild"/>
    -
   10   <FtpUpload LocalFile="Lib\MSBuild.Community.Tasks.dll"
    -     RemoteUri="ftp://192.168.0.1/"
    -     RemoteFiles="MSBuild.Community.Tasks.dll"/>
    -
    -   <FtpUpload LocalFile="Lib\MSBuild.Community.Tasks.targets"
   15     RemoteUri="ftp://192.168.0.1/"
    -     RemoteFiles="MSBuild.Community.Tasks.targets"/>
    -
    -   <RemoteTask RemoteIP="192.168.0.1"
    -     UserName="Administrator"
   20     Password="Password"
```

```
      ExecutableLocation="Lib"
      RemoteCommand="C:\Development\GetOrganized\Build.bat"
      WorkingDirectory="C:\Development\GetOrganized"
      Parameters="Publish" />

  </Target>
```

The first time this runs, no build file will exist on the remote machine. We need to upload four additional files. This includes the Build.bat, our abbreviation for running our project's custom build file. Build.msbuild is the build file itself. Finally, we need to include the MSBuild community tasks, MSBuild.Community.Tasks.dll, along with the build file, MSBuild.Community.Targets.targets, from the Lib folder.

On line 18, we invoke RemoteTask. We set each of the parameters to connect with our remote server and execute the Publish target on the remote machine.

Next, we'll add this new target for publishing so that when the remote call happens, we don't get a "Target not found" error:

buildAndDeploy/Build.msbuild

```
<Target Name="Publish">

<Unzip ZipFileName="GetOrganized.zip"
  TargetDirectory="C:\inetpub\GetOrganized" />

<CallTargets Targets="LocalDeploy"/>

</Target>
```

The Publish target first unzips the contents of the file. It then runs the local deploy target using the CallTargets task. This will reuse our work from the LocalDeploy target to publish the site remotely.

Success! Your site can now be automatically deployed both locally and remotely, saving you hours of time having to repeat this process manually. Now that you have a handle on the overall process, check out an open source project called CM.NET.[6] This project aims to provide best-practice build and deployment scripts for MSBuild and NAnt. With the knowledge you've gained in this chapter, going through the build scripts and using them for your next project will save you even more time.

We now have our build and deployment automated. With the basics of build automation in hand, you're now set up nicely to start using

---

6. http://wiki.github.com/bbyars/CM.NET/

a Continuous Integration (CI) server. To get started with CI, consider trying out Cruise Control.NET, an open-source CI server. [7]

That's All, Folks

Having read and worked through the examples in this book, you're well armed to dive into your next project with MVC and TDD. Of course, there is always more to learn, and a good way to do that is to visit some key MVC sites:

- Scott Guthrie's blog (corporate vice president at Microsoft of the .NET Platform and one of the original authors of ASP.NET): http://weblogs.asp.net/scottgu
- Phil Haack's blog (senior programmer for Microsoft and one of the core developers of ASP.NET MVC): http://haacked.com
- Online user group for monthly tutorials on all things MVC: http://www.c4mvc.net

Just as important as learning more about MVC is going deeper into the related frameworks and libraries that we touched on in the book. Here are some resources and blogs for specific technologies:

- Oren Eini's (aka Ayende Rahien) blog on NHibernate, the Windsor container, and Rhino Mocks: http://www.ayende.com
- John Resig's blog on jQuery: http://ejohn.org/
- Microsoft's MSBuild Team Blog: http://blogs.msdn.com/visualstudio/archive/tags/MSBuild/default.aspx
- Jetbrain's ReSharper and .NET Tool Blog: http://blogs.jetbrains.com/dotnet/
- The ALT .NET Community, a non-Microsoft-based view on all things .NET: http://altdotnet.org/
- My .NET and ASP.NET MVC adventures: http://jonathanmccracken.blogspot.com

Congratulations! You're far along in the journey to becoming a strong MVC developer. With the experience and knowledge you've gained here, you'll be able to tackle the challenges of web application development like never before. As you continue to learn, I encourage you to share your experiences and best practices with the community by blogging or posting in the forums.

---

7. http://ccnet.thoughtworks.com

Appendix A

Bibliography

[All02]   David Allen. *Getting Things Done: The Art of Stress-Free Productivity*. Penguin, New York, 2002.

[Bec00]   Kent Beck. *Extreme Programming Explained: Embrace Change*. Addison-Wesley, Reading, MA, 2000.

[Bec02]   Kent Beck. *Test Driven Development: By Example*. Addison-Wesley, Reading, MA, 2002.

[BK10]   Bear Bibeault and Yehuda Katz. *jQuery in Action*. Manning Publications Co., Greenwich, CT, second edition, 2010.

[Cla04]   Mike Clark. *Pragmatic Project Automation. How to Build, Deploy, and Monitor Java Applications*. The Pragmatic Programmers, LLC, Raleigh, NC, and Dallas, TX, 2004.

[FBB+99]   Martin Fowler, Kent Beck, John Brant, William Opdyke, and Don Roberts. *Refactoring: Improving the Design of Existing Code*. Addison Wesley Longman, Reading, MA, 1999.

[Fow03]   Martin Fowler. *Patterns of Enterprise Application Architecture*. Addison Wesley Longman, Reading, MA, 2003.

[GHJV95]   Erich Gamma, Richard Helm, Ralph Johnson, and John Vlissides. *Design Patterns: Elements of Reusable Object-Oriented Software*. Addison-Wesley, Reading, MA, 1995.

[HT00]   Andrew Hunt and David Thomas. *The Pragmatic Programmer: From Journeyman to Master*. Addison-Wesley, Reading, MA, 2000.

[HT04]   Andrew Hunt and David Thomas. *Pragmatic Unit Testing In C# with NUnit*. The Pragmatic Programmers, LLC, Raleigh, NC, and Dallas, TX, 2004.

[KBKH09]   Pierre Henri Kuaté, Christian Bauer, Gavin King, and Tobin Harris. *NHibernate in Action*. Manning Publications Co., Greenwich, CT, 2009.

[Mas06]   Mike Mason. *Pragmatic Version Control Using Subversion*. The Pragmatic Programmers, LLC, Raleigh, NC, and Dallas, TX, second edition, 2006.

[Tho08]   ThoughtWorks. *ThoughtWorks Anthology*. The Pragmatic Programmers, LLC, Raleigh, NC, and Dallas, TX, 2008.

Index

The Pragmatic Bookshelf

Available in paperback and DRM-free eBooks, our titles are here to help you stay on top of your game. The following are in print as of June 2010; be sure to check our website at pragprog.com for newer titles.

Title	Year	ISBN	Pages
Advanced Rails Recipes: 84 New Ways to Build Stunning Rails Apps	2008	9780978739225	464
Agile Coaching	2009	9781934356432	248
Agile Retrospectives: Making Good Teams Great	2006	9780977616640	200
Agile Web Development with Rails, Third Edition	2009	9781934356166	784
Beginning Mac Programming: Develop with Objective-C and Cocoa	2010	9781934356517	300
Behind Closed Doors: Secrets of Great Management	2005	9780976694021	192
Best of Ruby Quiz	2006	9780976694076	304
Cocoa Programming: A Quick-Start Guide for Developers	2010	9781934356302	450
Core Animation for Mac OS X and the iPhone: Creating Compelling Dynamic User Interfaces	2008	9781934356104	200
Core Data: Apple's API for Persisting Data on Mac OS X	2009	9781934356326	256
Data Crunching: Solve Everyday Problems using Java, Python, and More	2005	9780974514079	208
Debug It! Find, Repair, and Prevent Bugs in Your Code	2009	9781934356289	232
Deploying Rails Applications: A Step-by-Step Guide	2008	9780978739201	280
Design Accessible Web Sites: 36 Keys to Creating Content for All Audiences and Platforms	2007	9781934356029	336
Desktop GIS: Mapping the Planet with Open Source Tools	2008	9781934356067	368
Developing Facebook Platform Applications with Rails	2008	9781934356128	200
Domain-Driven Design Using Naked Objects	2009	9781934356449	375
Enterprise Integration with Ruby	2006	9780976694069	360
Enterprise Recipes with Ruby and Rails	2008	9781934356234	416
Everyday Scripting with Ruby: for Teams, Testers, and You	2007	9780977616619	320
ExpressionEngine 2: A Quick-Start Guide	2010	9781934356524	250
FXRuby: Create Lean and Mean GUIs with Ruby	2008	9781934356074	240
From Java To Ruby: Things Every Manager Should Know	2006	9780976694090	160

Continued on next page

Title	Year	ISBN	Pages
GIS for Web Developers: Adding Where to Your Web Applications	2007	9780974514093	275
Google Maps API, V2: Adding Where to Your Applications	2006	PDF-Only	83
Grails: A Quick-Start Guide	2009	9781934356463	200
Groovy Recipes: Greasing the Wheels of Java	2008	9780978739294	264
Interface Oriented Design	2006	9780976694052	240
Land the Tech Job You Love	2009	9781934356265	280
Language Implementation Patterns: Create Your Own Domain-Specific and General Programming Languages	2009	9781934356456	350
Learn to Program, 2nd Edition	2009	9781934356364	240
Manage It! Your Guide to Modern Pragmatic Project Management	2007	9780978739249	360
Manage Your Project Portfolio: Increase Your Capacity and Finish More Projects	2009	9781934356296	200
Mastering Dojo: JavaScript and Ajax Tools for Great Web Experiences	2008	9781934356111	568
Metaprogramming Ruby: Program Like the Ruby Pros	2010	9781934356470	240
Modular Java: Creating Flexible Applications with OSGi and Spring	2009	9781934356401	260
No Fluff Just Stuff 2006 Anthology	2006	9780977616664	240
No Fluff Just Stuff 2007 Anthology	2007	9780978739287	320
Pomodoro Technique Illustrated: The Easy Way to Do More in Less Time	2009	9781934356500	144
Practical Programming: An Introduction to Computer Science Using Python	2009	9781934356272	350
Practices of an Agile Developer	2006	9780974514086	208
Pragmatic Ajax: A Web 2.0 Primer	2006	9780976694083	296
Pragmatic Project Automation: How to Build, Deploy, and Monitor Java Applications	2004	9780974514031	176
Pragmatic Thinking and Learning: Refactor Your Wetware	2008	9781934356050	288
Pragmatic Unit Testing in C# with NUnit	2007	9780977616671	176
Pragmatic Unit Testing in Java with JUnit	2003	9780974514017	160
Pragmatic Version Control Using Git	2008	9781934356159	200
Pragmatic Version Control using CVS	2003	9780974514000	176
Pragmatic Version Control using Subversion	2006	9780977616657	248
Programming Clojure	2009	9781934356333	304
Programming Cocoa with Ruby: Create Compelling Mac Apps Using RubyCocoa	2009	9781934356197	300
Programming Erlang: Software for a Concurrent World	2007	9781934356005	536

Continued on next page

Title	Year	ISBN	Pages
Programming Groovy: Dynamic Productivity for the Java Developer	2008	9781934356098	320
Programming Ruby: The Pragmatic Programmers' Guide, Second Edition	2004	9780974514055	864
Programming Ruby 1.9: The Pragmatic Programmers' Guide	2009	9781934356081	960
Programming Scala: Tackle Multi-Core Complexity on the Java Virtual Machine	2009	9781934356319	250
Prototype and script.aculo.us: You Never Knew JavaScript Could Do This!	2007	9781934356012	448
Rails Recipes	2006	9780977616602	350
Rails for .NET Developers	2008	9781934356203	300
Rails for Java Developers	2007	9780977616695	336
Rails for PHP Developers	2008	9781934356043	432
Rapid GUI Development with QtRuby	2005	PDF-Only	83
Release It! Design and Deploy Production-Ready Software	2007	9780978739218	368
SQL Antipatterns: Avoiding the Pitfalls of Database Programming	2010	9781934356555	300
Scripted GUI Testing with Ruby	2008	9781934356180	192
Ship It! A Practical Guide to Successful Software Projects	2005	9780974514048	224
Stripes ...and Java Web Development Is Fun Again	2008	9781934356210	375
TextMate: Power Editing for the Mac	2007	9780978739232	208
The Definitive ANTLR Reference: Building Domain-Specific Languages	2007	9780978739256	384
The Passionate Programmer: Creating a Remarkable Career in Software Development	2009	9781934356340	200
ThoughtWorks Anthology	2008	9781934356142	240
Ubuntu Kung Fu: Tips, Tricks, Hints, and Hacks	2008	9781934356227	400
Web Design for Developers: A Programmer's Guide to Design Tools and Techniques	2009	9781934356135	300
iPhone SDK Development	2009	9781934356258	576

Better Practices

Pragmatic Unit Testing

You don't test a bridge by driving a single car over it right down the middle lane on a clear, calm day. Yet many programmers approach testing that same way-one pass right down the middle and they call it "tested." Pragmatic programmers can do better than that! With this book, you will:

• Discover the best hiding places where bugs breed
• Learn how to think of all the things that could go wrong • Test pieces of code without using the whole project • Test effectively with the whole team.

Available in both **C#** and **Java** editions.

Pragmatic Unit Testing in C#, 2nd Ed.
Andy Hunt and Dave Thomas with Matt Hargett
(240 pages) ISBN: 978-0-9776166-7-1. $29.95
http://pragprog.com/titles/utc2

Driving Technical Change

Your co-workers' resistance to new technologies can be baffling. Learn to read users' "patterns of resistance"—and then dismantle their objections. Every developer must master the art of evangelizing. With these techniques and strategies, you'll help your organization adopt your solutions—without selling your soul to organizational politics.

Driving Technical Change: Why People On Your Team Don't Act On Good Ideas, and How to Convince Them They Should
Terrence Ryan
(200 pages) ISBN: 978-1934356-60-9. $32.95
http://pragprog.com/titles/trevan

Better Practices

Debug It!

Debug It! will equip you with the tools, techniques, and approaches to help you tackle any bug with confidence. These secrets of professional debugging illuminate every stage of the bug life cycle, from constructing software that makes debugging easy; through bug detection, reproduction, and diagnosis; to rolling out your eventual fix. Learn better debugging whether you're writing Java or assembly language, targeting servers or embedded micro-controllers, or using agile or traditional approaches.

Debug It! Find, Repair, and Prevent Bugs in Your Code
Paul Butcher
(232 pages) ISBN: 978-1-9343562-8-9. $34.95
http://pragprog.com/titles/pbdp

SQL Antipatterns

If you're programming applications that store data, then chances are you're using SQL, either directly or through a mapping layer. But most of the SQL that gets used is inefficient, hard to maintain, and sometimes just plain wrong. This book shows you all the common mistakes, and then leads you through the best fixes. What's more, it shows you what's *behind* these fixes, so you'll learn a lot about relational databases along the way.

SQL Antipatterns: Avoiding the Pitfalls of Database Programming
Bill Karwin
(300 pages) ISBN: 978-19343565-5-5. $34.95
http://pragprog.com/titles/bksqla

Expand Your Skills

Pomodoro Technique Illustrated

Do you ever look at the clock and wonder where the day went? You spent all this time at work and didn't come close to getting everything done. Tomorrow, try something new. In *Pomodoro Technique Illustrated*, Staffan Nöteberg shows you how to organize your work to accomplish more in less time. There's no need for expensive software or fancy planners. You can get started with nothing more than a piece of paper, a pencil, and a kitchen timer.

Pomodoro Technique Illustrated: The Easy Way to Do More in Less Time
Staffan Nöteberg
(144 pages) ISBN: 9781934356500. $24.95
http://pragprog.com/titles/snfocus

Pragmatic Thinking and Learning

Software development happens in your head. Not in an editor, IDE, or design tool. In this book by Pragmatic Programmer Andy Hunt, you'll learn how our brains are wired, and how to take advantage of your brain's architecture. You'll master new tricks and tips to learn more, faster, and retain more of what you learn.

• Use the Dreyfus Model of Skill Acquisition to become more expert • Leverage the architecture of the brain to strengthen different thinking modes
• Avoid common "known bugs" in your mind
• Learn more deliberately and more effectively
• Manage knowledge more efficiently

Pragmatic Thinking and Learning:
Refactor your Wetware
Andy Hunt
(288 pages) ISBN: 978-1-9343560-5-0. $34.95
http://pragprog.com/titles/ahptl

The Home of Ruby and Rails

Rails for .NET

Rails for .NET Developers introduces the joy of Ruby on Rails development to Microsoft .NET developers. This book demonstrates the essential elements of both the Ruby language and the Rails application framework, geared especially for developers already fluent in the Microsoft .NET platform.

Rails for .NET Developers
Jeff Cohen and Brian Eng
(300 pages) ISBN: 978-1934356-20-3. $34.95
http://pragprog.com/titles/cerailn

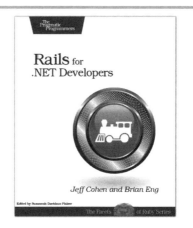

Security on Rails

Security on Rails provides you with the tools and techniques to defend your Rails applications against attackers. With this book, you can conquer the bad guys who are trying to exploit your application. You'll see the very techniques that hackers use, and then journey through this full-fledged guide for writing secure Rails applications.

Security on Rails
Ben Poweski and David Raphael
(304 pages) ISBN: 978-19343564-8-7. $34.95
http://pragprog.com/titles/fr_secure

The Pragmatic Bookshelf

The Pragmatic Bookshelf features books written by developers for developers. The titles continue the well-known Pragmatic Programmer style and continue to garner awards and rave reviews. As development gets more and more difficult, the Pragmatic Programmers will be there with more titles and products to help you stay on top of your game.

Visit Us Online

Home Page for Test-Drive ASP.NET MVC
http://pragprog.com/titles/jmasp
Source code from this book, errata, and other resources. Come give us feedback, too!

Register for Updates
http://pragprog.com/updates
Be notified when updates and new books become available.

Join the Community
http://pragprog.com/community
Read our weblogs, join our online discussions, participate in our mailing list, interact with our wiki, and benefit from the experience of other Pragmatic Programmers.

New and Noteworthy
http://pragprog.com/news
Check out the latest pragmatic developments, new titles and other offerings.

Save on the eBook

Save on the eBook versions of this title. Owning the paper version of this book entitles you to purchase the electronic versions at a terrific discount.

PDFs are great for carrying around on your laptop—they are hyperlinked, have color, and are fully searchable. Most titles are also available for the iPhone and iPod touch, Amazon Kindle, and other popular e-book readers.

Buy now at pragprog.com/coupon.

Contact Us

Online Orders: www.pragprog.com/catalog
Customer Service: support@pragprog.com
Non-English Versions: translations@pragprog.com
Pragmatic Teaching: academic@pragprog.com
Author Proposals: proposals@pragprog.com
Contact us: 1-800-699-PROG (+1 919 847 3884)